Sunset

COMPLETE
Vegetarian
COOK BOOK

By the Editors of Sunset Books and Sunset Magazine

Sunset Publishing Corporation   •   Menlo Park, California

Vegetarian... and Simply Delicious!

Vegetarian cooking, whether you enjoy it every day or just some of the time, offers a harvest of great taste and dining satisfaction. Around the country, more and more cooks are serving up meatless meals with pride. They're a healthy change of pace. And with such a dazzling array of tempting vegetables, fruits, grains, and legumes within easy reach in neighborhood supermarkets, it's a fine time to embrace this style of cooking.

From colorful and creative appetizers to marvelous main courses to desserts that are as wholesome as they are delicious, our recipes show that vegetarian fare can be a feast for the most discerning diner.

For our recipes, we provide a nutritional analysis (see page 6) prepared by Hill Nutrition Associates, Inc., of Florida. We are grateful to Lynne Hill, R.D., for her advice and expertise.

We thank Fran Feldman for editing the manuscript. We also thank Andrea Witlin Co., Fillamento, Forrest Jones, and RH for accessories used in our photographs.

Broccoli-stuffed Pasta Shells (recipe on page 68) and flour-dusted Polenta Cheese Bread (recipe on page 140) make savory supper fare.

Research & Text
Cynthia Scheer

Special Consultant
Patricia Kearney, R.D.
Clinical Dietician
Stanford University
    Hospital
Stanford, California

Coordinating Editor
Linda J. Selden

Design
Susan Sempere

Illustrations
Connie Anderson

Photography
Norman A. Plate: 74; Kevin Sanchez: 31, 63, 79, 90; Darrow M. Watt: 71; Tom Wyatt: 66, 159; Nikolay Zurek: 2, 7, 10, 15, 18, 23, 26, 34, 39, 42, 47, 50, 55, 58, 82, 87, 95, 98, 103, 106, 111, 114, 119, 122, 127, 130, 135, 138, 143, 146, 151, 154.

Photo Styling
Sara Luce Jamison: 74; Susan Massey: 2, 7, 10, 15, 18, 23, 26, 31, 34, 42, 47, 50, 58, 63, 66, 79, 82, 90, 95, 98, 103, 106, 111, 114, 119, 122, 127, 130, 135, 138, 143, 146, 151, 154, 159; Lynne B. Tremble: 39, 55, 87.

Cover
Bountiful vegetarian feast includes hearty Oven Polenta with Red Peppers & Mushrooms (recipe on page 76), Mediterranean Olive Bread (recipe on page 140), a refreshing salad of Avocado Fans with Pistachios (recipe on page 115), and a glass of light red wine. Design by Susan Bryant. Photography by Nikolay Zurek. Photo styling by Susan Massey. Food styling by Cynthia Scheer.

About the Recipes
All of the recipes in this book were tested and developed in the Sunset test kitchens.
Senior Editor (Food and Entertaining), Sunset Magazine: Jerry Anne Di Vecchio

Editorial Director, Sunset Books: Kenneth Winchester

Second printing September 1994

Contents

Special Features

INTRODUCTION

Reasons for going vegetarian abound. One of the most compelling is that the fresh, wholesome foods at the heart of a vegetarian diet—seasonal vegetables and fruits, as well as an all-star cast of pasta, grains, and legumes—are so good-tasting.

And there's never been a better time to enjoy these foods. New varieties of produce from near and far, more whole grain breads, and colorful pastas keep appearing in supermarkets and produce stands. Featuring them affords a rewarding change of pace from the more familiar foods we've been enjoying over the years.

When you follow a vegetarian regime judiciously, it can also offer all the health advantages of a low-cholesterol, high-fiber diet.

The recipes we've chosen for this cook book offer contrasting tastes, colors, and textures derived from cuisines around the world. You'll find recipes for strict vegetarians, also called vegans, who eat no animal-derived foods (meat, poultry, fish, eggs, and dairy products), and recipes for lacto-ovo vegetarians, who do include eggs and dairy products. Recipes that meet the goal set by many nutrition experts of limiting calories from fat to no more than 30 percent of the total are indicated with a special low-fat symbol.

Most of the ingredients for our recipes are readily available in your local supermarket. Occasionally, you may need to stop by an Asian market for a seasoning or a health-food store for a special whole grain flour, legume, or grain.

Getting Enough Protein

If you're new to vegetarian cooking and eating, you may wonder if plant foods provide you with enough protein. The answer is yes, provided that you consume a variety of whole grains, vegetables, and legumes on a daily basis—with enough calories to meet your energy needs.

An essential part of your body's muscles, skin, connective tissue, hair, nails, enzymes, and hormones, protein keeps all your systems in good repair; it's also crucial for growth in children.

Protein from an animal source—milk and eggs are examples—contains essential amino acids (those our bodies can't produce themselves) in the proportions our bodies need. Those proteins are called complete proteins.

Protein from plant sources, with one major exception, has an incomplete amount of one or more essential amino acids (the exception is soybeans, which provide virtually complete protein). The amino acid present in a limited amount is called the limiting amino acid because it limits the usability of the whole protein. For example, if one essential amino acid is 75 percent complete, only 75 percent of the protein can be utilized.

However, if you combine a food that's low in one or two amino acids with a food that's complete in those amino acids, you'll create a high-quality protein combination comparable to animal-source protein. This is called protein complementing. Any animal-source protein will complete an incomplete plant protein. In fact, combining plant sources to make complete protein is part of traditional kitchen wisdom. Just consider bean soup with pasta, tortillas and beans, rice with red beans, tofu and rice, and even such an American favorite as peanut butter on whole wheat bread.

The chart on the facing page shows which foods can be used alone and which need to be combined to create high-quality protein. The foods in the first column, which have virtually no limiting amino acid, can be used as high-quality protein sources by them-selves, or as a boost to any food in one of the other columns. The other columns each contain foods low in an amino acid. To make a complete protein, you combine a food from one of those columns with a different food from one of the others.

Beyond Protein

Balance is the key to meal planning and good overall nutrition, whether you eat meat or not. When you choose from a wide variety of foods every day and eat them in sensible amounts, it's unlikely that you'll get too little protein or too little of any other nutrient.

A balanced, varied diet of vegetarian foods includes grains (breads, cereals, and pasta), legumes (dried beans and peas), vegetables (especially the dark green leafy ones), fruits, dairy products, and eggs. Each of those food groups contributes to a balance of important nutrients: protein, carbohydrates, fats, vitamins, and minerals.

Protein Partnerships

For complete protein, combine a food from column 2, 3, or 4 with a different food from any other column. Foods in column 1 provide complete protein by themselves.

No Limiting Amino Acid	Low in Lysine	Low in Sulfur-carrying Amino Acids	Low in Tryptophan
Dairy Products	**Legumes**	**Legumes**	**Legumes**
Cheese (except cream cheese)	Peanuts	Beans, dried	*Beans, dried
Cottage cheese		(black, red, white, pinto)	(black, red, white, pinto)
Milk (all types, including	**Grains**	Black-eyed peas, dried	Garbanzo beans
powdered)	Barley	Garbanzo beans	Limas
Yogurt	Buckwheat	Lentils	Mung beans
	Bulgur	Limas	*Peanuts
Eggs	Cornmeal	Mung beans	
Whole, and egg whites	Millet	*Peanuts	**Grains**
	Oats		Cornmeal
Legumes	Rice	**Nuts**	
Soybean curd (tofu)	Rye	Hazelnuts	**Nuts**
Soybeans	Wheat		Almonds
Soy flour		**Vegetables**	Brazil nuts
Soy milk	**Nuts & Seeds**	Asparagus	*Walnuts, English
Tempeh	Almonds	Beans, green	
	Brazil nuts	Beet greens	**Vegetables**
Grains	*Cashews	Broccoli	Beet greens
Wheat germ	Coconut	Brussels sprouts	Corn
	Hazelnuts	Mushrooms	Mushrooms
Nuts	Pecans	Parsley	Peas, green
Walnuts, black	Pumpkin seeds	Peas, green	*Swiss chard
	Sunflower seeds	Potatoes	
	Walnuts, English	Swiss chard	
	Vegetables		
	Asparagus		
	Beet greens		
	Corn		
	Kale		
	Mushrooms		
	*Potatoes		
	Sweet potatoes		
	Yams		

*Indicates foods containing more than 90 percent of ideal amount.

Vegans, who eat no meat, dairy products, or eggs, eat an abundance of leafy green vegetables for calcium and combine grains, legumes, and vegetables for protein. And many take vitamin supplements for "insurance."

Nutritious Daily Choices

If you don't eat meat, poultry, or fish, you may be unsure about how many servings of different kinds of food you need, especially when you refer to such conventional nutrition plans as the Food Guide Pyramid.

Grains and legumes should be the foundation of every meal. Here are some general daily guidelines for vegetarians.

Grains: Includes bread, pasta, cereal, and grains. Provides fiber, complex carbohydrates, protein, B-vitamins, zinc, and iron. **6 to 11 servings** (a typical serving is 1 slice bread, 1 ounce ready-to-eat cereal, ½ cup cooked cereal, rice, or pasta).

Legumes: Includes all kinds of beans commonly sold in dried or canned form, such as kidney, navy, lima, black, red, white, and garbanzo beans; black-eyed peas; split peas; lentils; peanuts; soybeans and soybean products. Provides fiber, protein, iron, calcium, zinc, and B-vitamins. **2 or 3 servings** (a typical serving is ½ cup cooked dried beans, peas, or lentils; 2 tablespoons peanut butter; 4 ounces tofu; 1 cup soy milk).

Vegetables: Includes leafy greens, cruciferous vegetables (broccoli-cauliflower family), yellow vegetables, and potatoes. Provides vitamin C, beta-carotene, riboflavin, iron, calcium, and fiber. **3 to 5 servings** (a typical serving is 1 cup raw leafy greens, ½ cup cooked vegetable).

Fruits: Includes apples, bananas, berries, oranges and other citrus fruits, melons, peaches, and pears. Provides fiber, vitamin C, and beta-carotene. **2 to 4 servings** (a typical serving is 1 whole medium-size fruit, such as an apple or orange; 1 cup fruit pieces or berries).

Nuts and seeds: Includes almonds, peanuts, walnuts; sesame, pumpkin, and sunflower seeds. Provides fat, fiber, protein, calcium, and iron. **1 or 2 servings** (a typical serving is 2 tablespoons seeds, ¼ cup nuts).

Dairy products: Includes milk (whole, low-fat, nonfat), yogurt, and cheese. Provides protein, calcium, fat, vitamin B-12, and riboflavin. **2 servings** (a typical serving is 1 cup milk or yogurt, ½ cup ricotta or cottage cheese, 1½ ounces firm cheese).

Eggs: Provides protein, iron, vitamin B-12, fat, and cholesterol. **Up to 4 eggs per week if desired** (a typical serving is 1 large egg).

A Word About Our Nutritional Data

•

For our recipes, we provide a nutritional analysis stating calorie count; percentage of calories from fat; grams of total fat, saturated fat, carbohydrates, and protein; and milligrams of cholesterol and sodium. Generally, the analysis applies to a single serving, based on the number of servings given for each recipe and the amount of each ingredient. If a range is given for the number of servings and/or the amount of an ingredient, the analysis is based on an average of the figures given.

The nutritional analysis does not include optional ingredients or those for which no specific amount is stated. If an ingredient is listed with a substitution, the information was calculated using the first choice.

Black Bean & Fresh Corn Tacos (recipe on page 77) serve up a good measure of high-quality protein, thanks to the combination of essential amino acids that results from pairing beans and corn. Spoon the hot mixture into warm flour tortillas and top with salsa.

Vegetarian Menus

Summer Dinner for Friends

Serve this festive repast for eight to ten in courses—first, the quesadillas (double the recipe to provide seconds for all), then the cold soup, next the salad main dish, and finally the elegant dessert.

Gorgonzola, Walnut & Red Onion Quesadillas (page 21)

Zucchini Vichyssoise (page 29)

Roasted Pepper & Black Bean Salad (page 113)

Cornbread Fuego (page 139) or Corn Muffins

Favorite Lime Cheesecake (page 152)

Iced Tea or Red Wine

Scandinavian Fireside Supper

Cozy is the word for this comforting supper for four. The Finnish rye pastries are a delightful accompaniment to the creamy soup.

Carrot-filled Rye Pastries (page 25)

Barley & Cheese Soup with Parsley Pesto (page 41)

Spicy Red Coleslaw (page 101)

Baked Apples or Hot Spiced Applesauce

Beer or Milk

North African Barbecue

Exotic flavors permeate this grilled feast for four to six. Grill the sweet potatoes or eggplant first and keep warm in a low oven while you grill the skewered vegetables that complement the couscous.

Hummus with Pita Crisps (page 12)

Grilled Sweet Potatoes or Eggplant (page 88)

Couscous Platter with Skewered Vegetables (page 96)

Iced Cucumber Sticks

Hazelnut Crescents (page 149)

Dates, Figs & Grapes

Minted Iced Tea

Make-Ahead Autumn Supper

Everyone loves pasta, especially when it's presented in this hearty form. The menu serves six. You can assemble the main dish ahead and refrigerate it for up to a day; allow an extra 10 to 15 minutes in the oven if you start baking the casserole while it's still cold.

Romaine & Red Leaf Lettuce Salad with Honey Mustard Vinaigrette (page 104)

Broccoli-stuffed Pasta Shells (page 68)

Steamed Carrots

Polenta Cheese Bread (page 140)

Fresh Fruit

Red Wine or Milk

Asian Salad Sampler

Accompany a collection of piquantly flavored, Asian-influenced salads with a couple of help-yourself appetizers. This assortment will serve six buffet style.

Asian Guacamole with Pot Sticker Crisps (page 14)

Onion Tortilla Triangles (page 25)

Cucumber & Green Onion Salad (page 105)

Soy-braised Eggplant Salad (page 109)

Indonesian Brown Rice Salad (page 121)

Rice Crackers

Tangerines

Fortune Cookies

Hot Tea

Mexican Patio Dinner

This lively eat-with-your-fingers menu serves four to six. The appetizer salsa is similar to that served with the soft tacos; if you prepare extra of the first salsa, you'll have enough to use in place of the one called for in the taco recipe.

Cherry Tomato Salsa (page 14)

Cucumber Slices

Tortilla Chips

Black Bean & Fresh Corn Tacos (page 77)

Jicama & Avocado Salad with Orange Vinaigrette (page 100)

Fresh Pineapple Spears Sprinkled with Rum

Margaritas or Mexican Beer

Harvest Dinner

Bright with Mediterranean colors and flavors, this generous evening meal will serve six. In warm weather, serve the soup cold; if it's chilly, hot soup will provide a comforting touch.

Golden Garden Soup (page 29)

Tian Niçoise (page 94)

Grilled Eggplant with Basil Salsa (page 88)

Whole Wheat French Bread

Fresh Apple Cake (page 150)

Beaujolais or Anjou Rosé

Coffee

Indian Summer Brunch or Supper

This colorful brunch for four to six features a cornucopia of late-summer produce. It's just as pleasing as a supper menu; serve the fruit medley for dessert instead of as a starter.

Sliced Nectarines with Blackberries

Red & Yellow Pepper Flat Omelet (page 56)

Green-speckled Brown Rice (page 69)

Toasted Whole Wheat English Muffins

Siena Muffins (page 125)

Hot Tea

Pasta Party

Three Italian-style pastas grace this buffet-style dinner. It will serve 10 to 12 if you prepare all the pasta dishes so that everyone can sample each one; for especially hearty eaters, double the fettuccine recipe.

Hot Artichoke Dip (page 20)

Green & Ripe Olives

Breadsticks

Fettuccine Cambozola (page 60)

Pasta with Roasted Garlic & Peppers (page 61)

Stuffed Manicotti alla Fiorentina (page 62)

Green Salad with Mixed Oil & Vinegar Dressing (page 104)

Garlic Bread

Honeydew Melon with Lime Wedges

Biscotti

Red Wine

Espresso

Three-Course Vegan Special

No dairy products or eggs are used in the tempting dishes featured in this menu for four to six. Just be sure to use margarine—not butter—when you make the first-course soup, the pilaf, and the cookies that are part of the dessert.

Roasted Golden Squash Bisque (page 28)

Curried Garbanzos (page 81)

Steamed Asparagus

Brown Rice Pilaf (page 73)

Crusty Rye Bread

Pineapple Sorbet

Wheat Germ Shortbread (page 149)

Sparkling Cider

Select the tender inner leaves of romaine lettuce—the traditional green or the less familiar red—to present as crisp dippers for Caesar Cream with Parmesan Toast (recipe on page 20).

APPETIZERS

Red Pepper Cheese with Endive Spears

Hummus with Pita Crisps

Spring Asparagus Spread

Chèvre with Golden Fruits

Cherry Tomato Salsa

Asian Guacamole with Pot Sticker Crisps

Ricotta Roquefort Cheesecake

Chinese Bean & Blue Cheese Sauce

Hot Artichoke Dip

Caesar Cream with Parmesan Toast

Gorgonzola, Walnut & Red Onion Quesadillas

Green Pea Mole with Mini Quesadillas

Warm Radicchio Cheese Puddles

Cashew-Cheese Fila Rolls

Mexican Stuffed Mushrooms

Peppered Cheese Crackers

Carrot-filled Rye Pastries

Onion Tortilla Triangles

Red Pepper Cheese with Endive Spears

Preparation time: About 15 minutes

●

This colorful scoop-up-and-eat appetizer is easy to assemble, yet it makes a stylish presentation.

  1 **jar (about 7 oz.) roasted red peppers or pimentos, drained and patted dry**
  3 **packages (about 4 oz. *each*) boursin or other herb-seasoned cheese**
    About 1 pound Belgian endive
  2 **tablespoons finely chopped parsley**

1. Place peppers in a food processor or blender; whirl until smooth. Whirl or stir in cheese. Mound in a shallow bowl or on a plate. (At this point, you may cover and refrigerate for up to 2 days.)

2. Rinse endive; remove any discolored leaves. Cut leaves from cores and arrange, pointed ends out, around cheese.

3. Sprinkle parsley over cheese. Makes 10 servings (about 1¾ cups cheese).

Per serving: 119 calories (71% calories from fat), 4 g protein, 5 g carbohydrates, 10 g total fat,* 34 mg cholesterol, 134 mg sodium

* Data on saturated fat not available

Hummus with Pita Crisps

Preparation time: About 20 minutes

Baking time: 5 to 10 minutes

●

Break off pieces of toasted pita to spread thickly with this Middle Eastern classic made from garbanzo beans and sesame seeds.

    Pita Crisps (recipe follows)
  ¼ **cup sesame seeds**
  1 **can (about 15 oz.) garbanzo beans**
  3 **tablespoons lemon juice**
  3 **tablespoons olive oil**
  1 **or 2 cloves garlic**
    Salt and pepper

1. Prepare Pita Crisps.

2. Toast sesame seeds in a small frying pan over medium-low heat, stirring often, until golden (5 to 7 minutes). Transfer to a food processor or blender.

3. Drain garbanzos, reserving liquid. Add garbanzos, lemon juice, 2 tablespoons of the olive oil, garlic, and 6 tablespoons of the reserved garbanzo liquid to sesame seeds. Whirl, adding more garbanzo liquid if needed, until mixture is smooth and creamy but still thick enough to hold its shape. Season to taste with salt and pepper.

4. Spread on a plate or mound in a bowl. With a spatula, make a swirl on top. Drizzle with remaining 1 tablespoon olive oil. Serve with Pita Crisps. Makes 6 to 8 servings.

Pita Crisps. Split 6 **pita breads** (about 6-inch diameter) into 12 rounds. In a small bowl, mix ¼ cup **olive oil** and 1 clove **garlic,** minced or pressed. Brush insides of pita rounds with oil mixture; sprinkle lightly with **pepper.** Place in a single layer on 2 large baking sheets. Bake in a 400° oven until crisp and golden (5 to 10 minutes). Serve warm or at room temperature.

Per serving: 373 calories (41% calories from fat), 9 g protein, 47 g carbohydrates, 17 g total fat (2 g saturated fat), 0 mg cholesterol, 495 mg sodium

Spring Asparagus Spread

Preparation time: About 25 minutes

Cooking time: 2 to 3 minutes

Serve your favorite crisp crackers or toasted thin slices from a crusty baguette to complement this delicately flavored vegetable pâté.

- 1 **pound asparagus**
- 1 **green onion, thinly sliced**
- 2 **tablespoons water**
- 1 **tablespoon salad oil**
- 1 **small package (about 3 oz.) cream cheese, at room temperature**
- ½ **cup sour cream**
- 1 **to 2 teaspoons lemon juice**
  Salt and pepper

1. **Snap** off and discard tough ends of asparagus; peel stalks if desired. Cut asparagus into small pieces, reserving 3 or 4 whole tips.

2. **Combine** sliced asparagus and whole tips, green onion, water, and oil in a wide frying pan. Cover and cook over medium-high heat, stirring occasionally, until asparagus is bright green and just tender when pierced (2 to 3 minutes). Remove from heat and let stand, uncovered, until cool (about 10 minutes). Set whole asparagus tips aside.

3. **Transfer** asparagus mixture to a food processor or blender; add cream cheese and whirl until smooth. Blend in sour cream; add lemon juice to taste. Season to taste with salt and pepper.

4. **Spread** mixture in a serving bowl. Garnish with reserved asparagus tips. If made ahead, cover and refrigerate for up to a day. Makes 6 to 8 servings (about 1½ cups).

Per serving: 103 calories (81% calories from fat), 3 g protein, 3 g carbohydrates, 10 g total fat (5 g saturated fat), 21 mg cholesterol, 46 mg sodium

Chèvre with Golden Fruits

Preparation time: About 5 minutes

Baking time: About 10 minutes

Look for a soft, creamy goat cheese that you can swirl into an attractive mound for this easy appetizer. The cheese is delicious spread on juicy apple or pear slices.

- 2 **tablespoons hazelnuts**
- 8 **to 10 ounces soft goat cheese (chèvre)**
- 3 **small Golden Delicious apples or firm-ripe Bosc or Comice pears (about 1½ lbs. *total*)**

1. **Spread** hazelnuts in a shallow baking pan and toast in a 350° oven until pale golden beneath skins (about 10 minutes). Let cool slightly; then use your fingers to rub off skins. Chop nuts coarsely.

2. **Mound** cheese on a board or platter. Sprinkle with hazelnuts.

3. **Place** apples alongside for spreading (provide an apple wedge cutter or a knife to slice fruit as needed). Makes 8 to 10 servings.

Per serving: 127 calories (49% calories from fat), 6 g protein, 11 g carbohydrates, 7 g total fat (4 g saturated fat), 13 mg cholesterol, 104 mg sodium

Cherry Tomato Salsa

Pictured on facing page

Preparation time: About 20 minutes

•

Mounded on crisp cucumber slices, this fresh salsa sparkles with color, especially when made with both red and yellow cherry tomatoes.

 1 **clove garlic, minced or pressed**

 ⅓ **cup packed cilantro**

 2 **fresh jalapeño chiles, seeded and finely chopped**

 2 **cups red or yellow cherry tomatoes or a combination (about 12 oz. *total*), halved**

 2 **tablespoons *each* thinly sliced green onion and lime juice**

    Salt and pepper

    About 3 cups cucumber slices

    Tortilla chips (optional)

1. Combine garlic, cilantro, chiles, and tomatoes in a food processor or on a large chopping board; whirl or cut with a knife until coarsely chopped.

2. Transfer to a bowl and stir in onion and lime juice. Season to taste with salt and pepper.

3. Serve with cucumber slices and, if desired, tortilla chips. Makes 6 servings (about 2 cups).

Per serving: 22 calories (9% calories from fat), 1 g protein, 5 g carbohydrates, 0.3 g total fat (0 g saturated fat), 0 mg cholesterol, 8 mg sodium

Asian Guacamole with Pot Sticker Crisps

Pictured on page 23

Preparation time: About 15 minutes

Baking time: 4 to 8 minutes

•

Guacamole with black sesame seeds gets a kick from pickled ginger and wasabi (powdered green horseradish). Look for the ingredients in an Asian market or in the Asian foods section of a large supermarket. Spoon the chunky mixture on oven-crisped pot sticker rounds.

    Pot Sticker Crisps (recipe follows)

 1 **tablespoon black or white (regular) sesame seeds**

 1 **large firm-ripe avocado (about 12 oz.)**

 1 **tablespoon shredded pickled ginger**

 3 **tablespoons seasoned rice vinegar, or 3 tablespoons cider vinegar plus 1 teaspoon sugar**

 ½ **teaspoon wasabi powder or prepared horseradish**

1. Prepare Pot Sticker Crisps.

2. Toast sesame seeds in a small frying pan over medium-high heat, stirring often, until seeds begin to pop (3 to 4 minutes). Remove from pan and set aside.

3. Pit and peel avocado; dice into a bowl. Add ginger, vinegar, wasabi, and ½ teaspoon of the sesame seeds; mix gently.

4. Transfer to a serving bowl and sprinkle with remaining sesame seeds. Serve with Pot Sticker Crisps. Makes 4 to 6 servings.

Pot Sticker Crisps. Dip 12 round **pot sticker wrappers,** one at a time, in water, shaking off excess. Place in a single layer on a large greased baking sheet. Bake in a 450° oven until browned and crisp (4 to 8 minutes, depending on thickness of wrappers). Let cool on racks. If made ahead, package airtight and store at room temperature for up to 2 days.

Per serving: 194 calories (40% calories from fat), 6 g protein, 25 g carbohydrates, 9 g total fat (1 g saturated fat), 0 mg cholesterol, 220 mg sodium

Red and yellow cherry tomatoes, cilantro, and jalapeño chiles enliven Cherry Tomato Salsa (recipe on facing page). Scoop up the chunky salsa with corn chips or spoon it onto crisp cucumber slices.

Wholesome Snacks

Easy to make and good-tasting, these nutritious snacks feature grains, legumes, sunflower and sesame seeds, coconut, dried fruits, and honey. Spices enliven the mix. They're perfect when you feel the need for something to munch at home or on the trail.

Whole Grain Crisps with Cumin Salt

Preparation time: *1¼ to 2 hours (including standing time)*
Cooking time: *About 10 minutes*

1 cup whole grain oats, rye, triticale, or wheat, or long-grain brown rice

Cumin Salt (recipe follows)

3 tablespoons salad oil

1. **Sort** through grain, discarding any debris. In a 2- to 3-quart pan, bring grain and 1 quart water to a boil over high heat. Cover, remove from heat, and let stand until grain is tender enough to chew but not soft (about 1 hour for grain, 15 to 20 minutes for rice). Drain.

2. **Line** a shallow 10- by 15-inch baking pan with several layers of paper towels. Spread grain in pan and let dry for about an hour, blotting occasionally with more paper towels. Meanwhile, prepare Cumin Salt.

3. **Heat** oil in a wide frying pan over medium-high heat. Stir in grain and Cumin Salt. Cook, stirring, until grain smells toasted and becomes crisp and dry to bite (about 5 minutes).

4. **Spread** grain on paper towels, blotting excess oil. If made ahead, package airtight and store at room temperature for up to 2 weeks. Makes about 1½ cups.

Cumin Salt. In a small bowl, mix ½ teaspoon **coarse salt,** ¼ teaspoon *each* **ground cumin** and **celery salt,** and ⅛ teaspoon *each* **ground red pepper** (cayenne) and **garlic powder.**

Per ¼ cup: 162 calories (47% calories from fat), 4 g protein, 17 g carbohydrates, 9 g total fat (1 g saturated fat), 0 mg cholesterol, 182 mg sodium

Legume Crisps with Red Spices

Preparation time: *About 15 minutes*
Cooking time: *15 to 20 minutes*

1 cup dry garbanzo beans, dry brown or red (decorticated) lentils, or dry green or yellow split peas

Red Spices Salt (recipe follows)

3 tablespoons salad oil

1. **Sort** through legume, discarding any debris. In a 2- to 3-quart pan, bring legume (except red lentils) and 1 quart water to a boil over high heat. Cover, remove from heat, and let stand until legume is just tender enough to chew (about 15 minutes for garbanzos or brown lentils, about 10 minutes for split peas). To prepare red lentils, place in a medium-size bowl and pour in 1 quart hottest tap water to cover; let stand just until tender to bite (about 10 minutes).

2. **Drain** legume and spread on paper towels; blot dry with more paper towels. Meanwhile, prepare Red Spices Salt.

3. **Heat** oil in a wide frying pan over medium-high heat. Stir in legume and Red Spices Salt. Cook, stirring, until legume smells toasted and becomes crisp and dry to bite (about 5 minutes).

4. **Spread** on paper towels, blotting excess oil. If made ahead, package airtight and store at room temperature for up to 2 weeks. Makes about 1 cup.

Red Spices Salt. In a small bowl, mix ¾ teaspoon **coarse salt,** ½ teaspoon *each* **chili powder** and **paprika,** and ⅛ teaspoon **ground red pepper** (cayenne).

Per ¼ cup: 274 calories (43% calories from fat), 10 g protein, 31 g carbohydrates, 13 g total fat (2 g saturated fat), 0 mg cholesterol, 291 mg sodium

Peanut Butter & Oats Granola Snack

Preparation time: *About 35 minutes*
Baking time: *About 45 minutes*

2 cups quick-cooking rolled oats

½ cup *each* nonfat dry milk, shredded unsweetened coconut, shelled raw sunflower seeds, regular wheat germ, roasted unsalted peanuts, sesame seeds, raisins, and chopped dried apricots

⅔ cup *each* crunchy peanut butter and firmly packed brown sugar

½ cup salad oil

¼ cup honey

1. **Mix** oats, dry milk, coconut, sunflower seeds, wheat germ, peanuts, sesame seeds, raisins, and apricots in a shallow 12- by 15-inch baking pan. Set aside.

2. **Combine** peanut butter, brown sugar, oil, and honey in a 1- to 2-quart pan. Cook over medium-high heat, stirring, until mixture comes to a boil.

3. **Pour** peanut butter mixture over oat mixture; stir with a fork to blend.

4. **Bake** in a 300° oven, stirring every 10 minutes, until lightly browned (about 45 minutes). Remove from oven and press down firmly with a wide spatula so mixture will hold together; let cool.

5. **Break** granola into bite-size chunks. If made ahead, package airtight and store at room temperature for up to a week. Makes about 6 cups.

Per ¼ cup: 233 calories (52% calories from fat), 6 g protein, 23 g carbohydrates, 14 g total fat (3 g saturated fat), 0.3 mg cholesterol, 47 mg sodium

Chocolate Sun Butter

Follow directions for **Sun Butter Spread** (at left), but whirl sunflower seeds with 1 tablespoon **salad oil**. Omit salt; stir in ½ cup **powdered sugar**, ¼ cup **unsweetened cocoa**, and ½ teaspoon **vanilla**.

Spread on **banana slices**, toasted whole wheat English muffins, or plain cookies, such as shortbread. Makes about 1¼ cups.

Per tablespoon: 103 calories (65% calories from fat), 3 g protein, 6 g carbohydrates, 8 g total fat (1 g saturated fat), 0 mg cholesterol, 1 mg sodium

Baked Candied Popcorn

Preparation time: About 10 minutes
Cooking time: 8 to 10 minutes
Baking time: 8 to 15 minutes

| ¼ cup salad oil |
| 1 cup unpopped popcorn |
| 1½ cups salted or unsalted dry roasted peanuts |
| ½ cup butter or margarine |
| ½ cup light or dark molasses |
| ½ cup honey |

1. **Pour** oil into a 5- to 6-quart pan. Add popcorn. Cover and place over medium-high heat. When kernels start to pop, shake pan very often until popping almost stops; remove from heat.

2. **Transfer** popcorn to a large bowl; discard any unpopped kernels. Stir in peanuts.

3. **Melt** butter in same pan over low heat. Add molasses and honey. Increase heat to high and cook, stirring, until bubbles begin to form. Immediately pour mixture over popcorn mixture. Stir to coat popcorn and peanuts evenly.

4. **Spread** popcorn mixture in 2 shallow 10- by 15-inch baking pans. Bake in a 350° oven, stirring often, until coating is slightly darker (8 to 15 minutes; if margarine is used, time will be longer); if using one oven, switch position of baking pans halfway through baking.

5. **Let** cool completely in pans on racks. If made ahead, package airtight and let stand at room temperature for up to 3 days. Makes about 6 quarts.

Per cup: 177 calories (53% calories from fat), 3 g protein, 18 g carbohydrates, 11 g total fat (3 g saturated fat), 10 mg cholesterol, 115 mg sodium

Sun Butter Spread

Preparation time: 15 to 20 minutes

| 2 cups unsalted raw sunflower seeds or purchased salted roasted sunflower seeds |
| 1 to 3 teaspoons salad oil (optional) |
| Salt (optional) |
| Whole grain bread or crackers, celery sticks, or apple or banana slices |

1. **Spread** raw sunflower seeds, if used, in an even layer in a shallow 10- by 15-inch baking pan. Bake in a 350° oven, stirring occasionally, until most of the seeds are golden brown (15 to 20 minutes). Let cool. (Do not bake roasted seeds.)

2. **Transfer** seeds to a food processor; whirl until smooth (5 to 7 minutes). Or whirl at high speed in a blender; if necessary, add oil, a little at a time, to help form a smooth butter. If desired, season to taste with salt.

3. **Serve** with bread. Makes about 1 cup.

Per tablespoon: 103 calories (73% calories from fat), 4 g protein, 3 g carbohydrates, 9 g total fat (1 g saturated fat), 0 mg cholesterol, 1 mg sodium

Seasoned Nori Popcorn

Preparation time: About 10 minutes

| 3 tablespoons Oriental sesame oil |
| 2 tablespoons soy sauce |
| ½ teaspoon chili oil |
| ¼ cup salad oil |
| ½ cup unpopped popcorn |
| 3 tablespoons finely snipped seasoned nori (seaweed) |

1. **Mix** sesame oil, soy sauce, and chili oil in a small bowl; set aside.

2. **Pour** salad oil into a 5- to 6-quart pan. Add popcorn. Cover and place over medium-high heat. When kernels start to pop, shake pan very often until popping almost stops; remove from heat. Or, omit salad oil and pop corn in a hot air popper, following manufacturer's directions.

3. **Transfer** popcorn to a large bowl; discard any unpopped kernels. Pour sesame oil mixture over popcorn and mix well. Sprinkle with nori and mix again. Serve warm. Makes about 3 quarts.

Per cup: 105 calories (71% calories from fat), 1 g protein, 6 g carbohydrates, 9 g total fat (1 g saturated fat), 0 mg cholesterol, 174 mg sodium

For a distinctive appetizer to accompany dry sherry, spread creamy Ricotta Roquefort Cheesecake (recipe on facing page) on crunchy radishes or on your favorite crackers.

Ricotta Roquefort Cheesecake

Pictured on facing page

Preparation time: About 25 minutes

Baking time: 35 to 45 minutes

Chilling time: At least 2 hours

●

Savory cheesecake lightened with ricotta makes a zesty spread for crisp rye or whole wheat crackers and crunchy radishes.

> 4 cups part-skim or whole-milk ricotta cheese
> 1 cup (about 6 oz.) packed Roquefort cheese
> 1 teaspoon freshly ground pepper
> Salt
> 6 large egg whites
> ¼ cup freshly grated Parmesan cheese
> 36 to 48 radishes
> Chopped parsley
> Crisp rye or whole wheat crackers

1. Combine ricotta, Roquefort, and pepper in a food processor or bowl; whirl or mix until blended. Season to taste with salt. Beat in egg whites.

2. Spread mixture in a 10-inch spring-form pan. Sprinkle evenly with Parmesan cheese.

3. Bake in a 325° oven until cheesecake is firm in center when pan is gently shaken (35 to 45 minutes). Let cool; cover and refrigerate for at least 2 hours or up to a day. Meanwhile, trim and discard root ends of radishes; rinse well and drain. Pinch off and discard all but 1 or 2 pretty leaves from each radish. Wrap radishes in a damp towel, place in a plastic bag, and refrigerate for at least 30 minutes or up to a day.

4. Remove pan rim and set cake on a platter. Slice a few radishes. Surround cake with whole radishes. Garnish with radish slices and parsley. Serve with crackers. Makes 16 to 18 servings.

Per serving: 131 calories (56% calories from fat), 11 g protein, 4 g carbohydrates, 8 g total fat (5 g saturated fat), 28 mg cholesterol, 302 mg sodium

Chinese Bean & Blue Cheese Sauce

Preparation time: About 20 minutes

●

Pungent fermented salted black beans, a popular Chinese seasoning, are a good match for equally nippy blue cheese. Spoon the sauce onto slices of hot or cool cooked potato.

> 1 tablespoon fermented salted black beans
> 1 clove garlic, minced or pressed
> 1 tablespoon salad oil
> 2 tablespoons rice vinegar
> 1 medium-size pear-shaped (Roma-type) tomato, finely diced
> ¼ cup coarsely crumbled blue-veined cheese
> 2 tablespoons finely chopped green onion
> 5 cooked thin-skinned potatoes (*each* about 3 inches long)

1. Rinse and sort through beans, discarding any debris; drain.

2. Combine beans and garlic in a bowl; mash coarsely with a fork. Mix in oil and vinegar; stir in tomato, cheese, and onion. (At this point, you may cover and let stand at room temperature for up to 2 hours.)

3. Slice potatoes crosswise about ⅜ inch thick. Spoon about 1 teaspoon of the bean mixture onto each slice. Arrange on a platter. Makes about 24 appetizers.

Per appetizer: 26 calories (36% calories from fat), 0.7 g protein, 3 g carbohydrates, 1 g total fat (0.3 g saturated fat), 1 mg cholesterol, 40 mg sodium

Hot Artichoke Dip

Preparation time: About 10 minutes

Baking time: 30 to 45 minutes

●

Scoop up this creamy baked artichoke dip with toasted French bread slices or artichoke leaves.

- **1 cup (about 5 oz.) grated Parmesan cheese**
- **1 large package (about 8 oz.) Neufchâtel cheese, at room temperature**
- **1 cup light sour cream or reduced-calorie mayonnaise**
- **⅛ teaspoon dry dill weed**
- **1 large can (about 13¾ oz.) artichoke hearts, drained and chopped**
- **Toasted baguette slices**
- **Whole cooked artichokes (optional)**

1. **Set** aside 1 tablespoon of the Parmesan cheese.

2. **Combine** remaining Parmesan cheese, Neufchâtel cheese, sour cream, and dill weed in large bowl of an electric mixer; beat until well blended and creamy. Stir in chopped artichoke hearts.

3. **Transfer** mixture to an attractive shallow 3- to 4-cup baking dish; sprinkle with reserved 1 tablespoon Parmesan cheese. (At this point, you may cover and refrigerate for up to a day.)

4. **Bake,** uncovered, in a 325° oven until top is lightly browned and mixture is hot in center (30 to 45 minutes). Serve hot with baguette slices and, if desired, whole artichokes. Makes 16 to 18 servings (about 3 cups).

Per serving: 97 calories (66% calories from fat), 6 g protein, 3 g carbohydrates, 7 g total fat (4 g saturated fat), 21 mg cholesterol, 195 mg sodium

Caesar Cream with Parmesan Toast

Pictured on page 10

Preparation time: About 20 minutes

Baking time: About 15 minutes

●

The vibrant flavors of Caesar salad are captured in this smooth, pale green dip, good with crisp romaine leaves and crusty croutons.

- **Parmesan Toast (recipe follows)**
- **½ cup freshly grated Parmesan cheese**
- **1 clove garlic**
- **½ cup lightly packed parsley**
- **2 to 3 tablespoons lemon juice**
- **1 cup light or regular sour cream**
- **Parsley sprig**
- **1 to 2 quarts small inner green or red romaine lettuce leaves or a combination, rinsed and crisped**

1. **Prepare** Parmesan Toast.

2. **Combine** cheese, garlic, the ½ cup parsley, and 2 tablespoons of the lemon juice in a blender or food processor; whirl until smooth, adding 3 to 4 tablespoons of the sour cream if necessary to form a purée.

3. **Transfer** to a bowl and stir in remaining sour cream. Add additional lemon juice to taste, if desired. If made ahead, cover and refrigerate for up to a day.

4. **Place** dip on a serving tray; garnish with parsley sprig. Arrange lettuce and Parmesan Toast alongside. Makes 8 to 10 servings (about 1¼ cups).

Parmesan Toast. Slice half an 8-ounce **baguette** about ⅜ inch thick. Arrange bread on a large baking sheet. Bake in a 350° oven, turning slices once or twice, until lightly toasted (about 10 minutes). Remove from oven and brush with **olive oil** (about 1 tablespoon *total*); sprinkle lightly with freshly grated **Parmesan cheese** (about 2 tablespoons *total*). Return to oven and bake until golden brown (3 to 5 more minutes). Serve warm or at room temperature. If made ahead, package airtight and let stand at room temperature for up to a day.

Per serving: 134 calories (50% calories from fat), 6 g protein, 11 g carbohydrates, 8 g total fat (3 g saturated fat), 15 mg cholesterol, 205 mg sodium

Gorgonzola, Walnut & Red Onion Quesadillas

Preparation time: About 20 minutes

Baking and cooking time: About 35 minutes

●

Filled with wine-drenched sautéed onions, toasted nuts, and melted cheese, these tempting tortilla triangles are browned on a griddle or in a nonstick frying pan.

> **Caramelized Red Onions (recipe follows)**
> ⅓ cup coarsely chopped walnuts
> ¾ cup (about 6 oz.) crumbled Gorgonzola or other blue-veined cheese
> 4 flour tortillas (about 7-inch diameter), at room temperature

1. **Prepare** Caramelized Red Onions.

2. **Spread** walnuts in a shallow pan and toast in a 350° oven until golden brown (about 8 minutes).

3. **Layer** a fourth of the cheese, a fourth of the onions, and a fourth of the nuts on half of one of the tortillas; repeat with remaining tortillas. Gently fold each in half to make a turnover.

4. **Cook** quesadillas, 2 at a time, on a greased or well-seasoned griddle or in a wide nonstick frying pan over medium heat until lightly browned (about 5 minutes); turn carefully and cook until other sides are lightly browned (about 3 more minutes). Keep warm while cooking remaining quesadillas. Cut each into 3 wedges and serve hot. Makes 12 appetizers.

Caramelized Red Onions. Spray a wide nonstick frying pan with **vegetable oil cooking spray.** Add 1 medium-size **red onion,** thinly sliced; 1 tablespoon **brown sugar;** and ½ cup **dry red wine.** Cook over medium-low heat, stirring often, until onion is very soft and most of the liquid has evaporated (about 15 minutes).

Per appetizer: 132 calories (50% calories from fat), 5 g protein, 12 g carbohydrates, 8 g total fat (3 g saturated fat), 11 mg cholesterol, 285 mg sodium

Green Pea Mole with Mini Quesadillas

Preparation time: About 30 minutes

Baking time: About 12 minutes

●

Though it looks like guacamole, this dip is made not with avocados but with sweet green peas.

> 1 large package (about 16 oz.) frozen peas, thawed and drained
> 1 small onion, chopped
> 1 tablespoon lemon juice
> ½ to 1 small fresh jalapeño or other hot green chile, seeded and chopped
> ½ teaspoon ground cumin
> 1 jar (about 7 oz.) roasted red peppers, drained
> 8 flour tortillas (about 7-inch diameter), at room temperature
> 2 cups (about 8 oz.) shredded jack cheese
> ¼ to ½ cup sour cream

1. **Combine** peas, onion, lemon juice, chile, and cumin in a blender or food processor; whirl until coarsely puréed. Set aside.

2. **Cut** roasted peppers into ¼-inch-wide strips. Chop 2 or 3 of the strips and reserve for garnish.

3. **Cut** tortillas into quarters; top with roasted pepper strips and cheese. Working with one quarter at a time, dot corners of curved edge with water; press moistened corners together to seal. Place quesadillas slightly apart on 2 large baking sheets and brush tops lightly with water. Bake in a 350° oven until crisp (about 12 minutes).

4. **Mound** pea purée on a serving platter; arrange quesadillas alongside. Spoon dollops of sour cream over purée; sprinkle with reserved peppers. Makes 4 to 6 servings.

Per serving: 531 calories (41% calories from fat), 23 g protein, 57 g carbohydrates, 24 g total fat (2 g saturated fat), 47 mg cholesterol, 769 mg sodium

Warm Radicchio Cheese Puddles

Preparation time: About 15 minutes

Baking time: 4 to 6 minutes

●

Baked leaves of slightly bitter-tasting, red-and-white radicchio cradle warm teleme cheese to make an eye-catching first course. Serve it with knives and forks.

2 teaspoons *each* **extra-virgin olive oil and lemon juice**

6 **large radicchio leaves (about 4 oz. *total*), rinsed and patted dry**

3 **ounces teleme or jack cheese, sliced ¼ inch thick**

Freshly ground pepper

Lemon wedges and chive spears

1. **Mix** oil and lemon juice in a small bowl. Brush mixture all over radicchio leaves. Set leaves, cupped side up, in a 9- by 13-inch baking dish.

2. **Place** cheese in radicchio cups and season to taste with pepper. Bake in a 350° oven just until cheese is melted (4 to 6 minutes).

3. **Garnish** each serving with a lemon wedge and 3 or 4 chives. Serve hot or warm. Makes 6 servings.

Per serving: 56 calories (72% calories from fat), 3 g protein, 1 g carbohydrates, 5 g total fat (0.2 g saturated fat), 3 mg cholesterol, 77 mg sodium

Cashew-Cheese Fila Rolls

Pictured on facing page

Preparation time: About 30 minutes

Baking time: About 15 minutes

●

Flaky fila dough encloses melted jarlsberg cheese and luscious cashews in these tempting appetizer pastries. They can be assembled ahead, refrigerated, and then baked just before serving.

½ **cup chopped roasted salted cashews**

1 **cup (about 4 oz.) shredded jarlsberg cheese**

8 **sheets fila dough (about 5⅓ oz. *total*), *each* about 12 by 17 inches**

About ¼ cup melted butter or margarine

1. **Mix** cashews and cheese in a small bowl; set aside.

2. **Lay** a sheet of fila out flat and brush lightly with melted butter, keeping remaining dough covered with plastic wrap. Leaving a ½-inch margin on long edges, spoon an eighth of the nut mixture in an even band along a 12-inch side, 1 inch from that edge.

3. **Fold** 1-inch margin over mixture and roll just until nut mixture is enclosed. Fold ½-inch margins over filling and continue to roll fila into a cylinder. Brush underside of fila edge with butter to seal.

4. **Set** roll, seam side down, in a shallow 10- by 15-inch baking pan. Repeat with remaining fila, filling 2 pans. (At this point, you may cover airtight with plastic wrap and refrigerate for up to a day.)

5. **Bake** rolls in a 425° oven until golden brown (about 15 minutes); if using one oven, switch position of pans halfway through baking. With a wide spatula, ease rolls out of pan. Cut each roll into 3 equal lengths. Serve hot; or let cool on racks and serve at room temperature. Makes 24 appetizers.

Per appetizer: 69 calories (57% calories from fat), 2 g protein, 5 g carbohydrates, 4 g total fat (1 g saturated fat), 8 mg cholesterol, 86 mg sodium

Pair Asian Guacamole with Pot Sticker Crisps (recipe on page 14), redolent with pickled ginger and wasabi powder, and flaky Cashew-Cheese Fila Rolls (recipe on facing page) for a sophisticated appetizer offering.

23

Mexican Stuffed Mushrooms

Preparation time: About 30 minutes

Baking time: 15 to 20 minutes

●

Mounded high with a piquant chile-accented filling, these hot morsels make a snappy party appetizer with beer or fruit drinks.

- 12 **large mushrooms (*each* about 2½-inch diameter)**
- ⅓ **cup sliced green onions**
- 1 **clove garlic, minced or pressed**
- ¾ **teaspoon *each* ground cumin and chili powder**
  About 6 tablespoons water
- 1 **can (about 8 oz.) tomato sauce**
- 1 **can (about 4 oz.) diced green chiles**
- 4 **ounces jalapeño jack cheese, shredded**
- 2 **cups unseasoned stuffing mix**
- 2 **teaspoons salad oil**

1. Twist off and finely chop mushroom stems; set mushroom caps aside.

2. Combine chopped stems, green onions, garlic, cumin, chili powder, and ¼ cup of the water in a wide frying pan. Cook over medium heat, stirring often, until vegetables begin to brown. Add about 2 tablespoons more water and scrape browned bits free; continue to cook, stirring often, until liquid has evaporated.

3. Stir in tomato sauce, chiles, and half the cheese. Remove from heat and gently stir in stuffing mix.

4. Rub mushrooms with oil. Arrange, cup sides up, in a 9- by 13-inch baking pan. Mound stuffing mixture into mushrooms; sprinkle with remaining cheese. Bake in a 400° oven until cheese is lightly browned (15 to 20 minutes). Makes 12 appetizers.

Per appetizer: 99 calories (37% calories from fat), 5 g protein, 12 g carbohydrates, 4 g total fat (2 g saturated fat), 10 mg cholesterol, 365 mg sodium

Peppered Cheese Crackers

Preparation time: About 35 minutes

Baking time: 6 to 8 minutes

●

These snappy cheese cracker strips accompany an apéritif with style; they're also delicious with soup.

- 2 **tablespoons butter or margarine, at room temperature**
- 1 **large egg**
- ½ **teaspoon paprika**
- ⅛ **teaspoon ground black pepper**
- 1/16 **to ⅛ teaspoon ground red pepper (cayenne)**
- 2 **cups (about 8 oz.) finely shredded extra-sharp Cheddar cheese**
- 1 **cup unbleached all-purpose flour**
  Cracked pepper

1. Beat butter until creamy in medium-size bowl of an electric mixer. Add egg, paprika, and black pepper; season to taste with ground red pepper. Beat until blended.

2. Beat in cheese, a third at a time, until combined. Stir in flour until thoroughly blended. Press dough into a flattened ball. (At this point, you may enclose in plastic wrap and refrigerate for up to 3 days.)

3. Divide dough in half. Evenly roll each half between sheets of wax paper into a 7- by 14-inch rectangle. Using a pastry wheel or knife, cut dough into ½- by 7-inch strips.

4. Place strips slightly apart on large baking sheets. Sprinkle with cracked pepper, lightly pressing pepper into dough. Bake in a 400° oven until deep golden (6 to 8 minutes). Serve hot; or let cool on racks and serve at room temperature. If made ahead, package airtight and store at room temperature for up to a week. Makes 54 crackers.

Per cracker: 31 calories (57% calories from fat), 1 g protein, 2 g carbohydrates, 2 g total fat (1 g saturated fat), 9 mg cholesterol, 32 mg sodium

Carrot-filled Rye Pastries

Preparation and chilling time: About 2 hours

Baking time: About 35 minutes

•

Shaped like little boats, these savory rye pastries come from Finland, where they're called *piirakka*. For make-ahead convenience, you can bake the pastries, refrigerate them, and reheat the next day.

  Carrot Filling (recipe follows)
 1 cup rye flour
 ⅓ cup unbleached all-purpose flour
 ¼ teaspoon salt
 6 tablespoons butter or margarine,
    melted and cooled
 1 large egg
 ⅓ cup sour cream
    Egg Butter (recipe follows)

1. Prepare Carrot Filling.

2. Stir together rye flour, all-purpose flour, and salt in a medium-size bowl. Add butter, egg, and sour cream; stir with a fork until well mixed. With lightly floured hands, shape dough into a ball. On a lightly floured board, knead until smooth (2 to 3 minutes). Divide dough into 24 equal pieces, rolling each into a ball. Cover with plastic wrap.

3. Place a ball of dough on a floured board and roll into a circle about 4½ inches in diameter. Spread with 2 tablespoons of the Carrot Filling to within about ½ inch of edge. Bring up opposite edges of circle, pinching at ends to form a boat (leave filling exposed in center). Repeat for remaining dough. Place pastries slightly apart on greased baking sheets.

4. Bake in a 350° oven until well browned (about 35 minutes). Meanwhile, prepare Egg Butter.

5. Serve pastries hot. If made ahead, let cool on racks; cover and refrigerate for up to a day. To reheat, place pastries on a baking sheet and bake, uncovered, in a 350° oven until hot (8 to 10 minutes). Serve with Egg Butter to spread on pastries. Makes 24 pastries.

Carrot Filling. Melt ½ cup (¼ lb.) **butter** or margarine in a wide frying pan over medium heat. Add 6 cups

shredded **carrots** (about 12 medium-size); 1 large **onion,** finely chopped; and 2 tablespoons **sugar.** Cook, stirring often, until carrots are soft and begin to brown (about 15 minutes). Season to taste with **salt.** Refrigerate until cold (about 2 hours).

Egg Butter. In a medium-size bowl, mash 3 **hard-cooked eggs** with a fork (or force through a wire strainer). Stir in 10 tablespoons (¼ lb. plus 2 tablespoons) **butter** or margarine at room temperature. Serve at room temperature. If made ahead, cover and refrigerate for up to a day.

Per pastry: 161 calories (72% calories from fat), 2 g protein, 9 g carbohydrates, 13 g total fat (8 g saturated fat), 68 mg cholesterol, 162 mg sodium

Onion Tortilla Triangles

Preparation time: About 15 minutes

Baking time: About 15 minutes

•

Here's an easy version of a favorite Chinese snack. To make these crisp, puffy wedges, you start with flour tortillas.

 1 large egg
 1 teaspoon soy sauce
 8 flour tortillas (about 7-inch diameter)
 ½ cup thinly sliced green onions
 ¼ cup butter or margarine, melted

1. Beat egg and soy sauce in a small bowl until blended. Spread about 1½ tablespoons of the egg mixture over one side of each of 4 of the tortillas; sprinkle evenly with onions. Cover each prepared tortilla with another tortilla, pressing edges together.

2. Place tortilla stacks on 2 large baking sheets. Brush both sides generously with butter.

3. Bake in a 400° oven until golden brown (about 15 minutes). Cut each stack into quarters and serve hot. Makes 16 appetizers.

Per appetizer: 106 calories (43% calories from fat), 2 g protein, 13 g carbohydrates, 5 g total fat (2 g saturated fat), 21 mg cholesterol, 183 mg sodium

Brimming with vegetables—leeks, carrots, potatoes, and green beans—and laced with spaghetti, Pistou Soup with Split Peas (recipe on page 37) gets its reddish hue from a tomato-base pistou seasoning mixture.

SOUPS

Roasted Golden Squash Bisque

Golden Tomato-Papaya Gazpacho with Basil

Golden Garden Soup

Zucchini Vichyssoise

Red Onion Borscht

Hot Ginger Pear Soup

Spiced Sweet Potato Bisque

Cream of Cauliflower Soup

Curry Soup with Wilted Spinach

Corn Chowder with Cheese

Leek Soup with Brie

Fresh Tomato Soup

Pistou Soup with Split Peas

Wholesome Lentil Soup

Winter Minestrone

Vinegar Bean Soup

Jalapeño Vegetable Chowder

Peanut Butter Vegetable Soup

Barley & Cheese Soup with Parsley Pesto

Robust Greens Soup

Roasted Golden Squash Bisque

Pictured on page 138

Preparation time: About 20 minutes

Baking time: 1¼ to 1½ hours

Cooking time: About 5 minutes

Purée oven-roasted butternut squash, onions, and apples for this golden soup, a tempting autumn offering.

> **About 2½ pounds butternut, banana, or other yellow-fleshed winter squash**
>
> 2 **tablespoons butter or margarine**
>
> 2 **tablespoons extra-virgin olive oil or salad oil**
>
> 2 **medium-size Newtown Pippin or other tart apples (about 1 lb. *total*), halved and cored**
>
> 2 **small onions (about 12 oz. *total*), unpeeled, halved**
>
> ½ **cup hazelnuts**
>
> 3 **cups homemade (page 33) or canned vegetable broth**
>
> 1 **cup apple juice or cider**

1. **Cut** squash, if whole, in half lengthwise; scoop out and discard seeds and string.

2. **Heat** butter and oil in a shallow 10- by 15-inch baking pan in a 400° oven (about 3 minutes).

3. **Place** squash, apple, and onion halves, cut sides down, in pan. Bake until squash is very tender when pierced (1¼ to 1½ hours). Meanwhile, spread hazelnuts in a shallow baking pan. Bake in same oven until pale golden beneath skins (about 10 minutes). Let cool slightly; then use your fingers to rub off skins. Chop nuts coarsely and set aside.

4. **Let** squash stand until cool enough to handle; scoop flesh from shell. Remove peels from apples and skins from onions.

5. **Transfer** squash, apples, and onions to a food processor or blender; whirl, adding about 1 cup of the broth, until smooth.

6. **Combine** squash mixture, remaining broth, and apple juice in a 3- to 4-quart pan. Cook over medium-high heat, stirring often, until steaming hot. Garnish each serving with chopped nuts. Makes 6 servings.

Per serving: 299 calories (43% calories from fat), 4 g protein, 42 g carbohydrates, 16 g total fat (4 g saturated fat), 10 mg cholesterol, 555 mg sodium

Golden Tomato-Papaya Gazpacho with Basil

Preparation time: About 25 minutes

Chilling time: At least 1 hour

Take advantage of summer-fresh golden tomatoes to make this distinctive cold soup for an outdoor party or picnic.

> 2 **pounds yellow regular or cherry tomatoes**
>
> 1 **large ripe papaya (about 1¼ lbs.), peeled, seeded, and diced**
>
> 1 **cup diced cucumber**
>
> ¼ **cup finely chopped white onion**
>
> 2 **tablespoons white wine vinegar**
>
> 2 **cups canned vegetable broth**
>
> 2 **tablespoons minced fresh basil**
>
> ⅛ **teaspoon liquid hot pepper seasoning**
> **Salt**
> **Basil sprigs**

1. **Dice** tomatoes and place in a large bowl.

2. **Stir** in papaya, cucumber, onion, vinegar, broth, minced basil, and hot pepper seasoning. Season to taste with salt. Cover and refrigerate for at least 1 hour or up to a day.

3. **Garnish** each serving with basil sprigs. Makes 10 to 12 servings.

Per serving: 39 calories (8% calories from fat), 1 g protein, 9 g carbohydrates, 0.4 g total fat (0 g saturated fat), 0 mg cholesterol, 197 mg sodium

Golden Garden Soup

Preparation time: About 25 minutes

Cooking time: About 30 minutes

Chilling time (optional): At least 2 hours

This rich-tasting soup is thickened with vegetables puréed with their cooking broth; buttermilk adds tang. Enjoy this soup hot or cold with toasted onion bagels and strands of string cheese.

> 2 tablespoons salad oil
>
> 1 large onion, chopped
>
> 2 medium-size pear-shaped (Roma-type) tomatoes, chopped
>
> 1½ pounds yellow crookneck squash (about 5 medium-size), chopped
>
> 3 cups canned vegetable broth
>
> 1 cup buttermilk
>
> ¼ cup loosely packed fresh basil, minced
>
> Basil sprigs

1. Heat oil in a 4- to 5-quart pan over medium heat. Add onion and cook, stirring often, until lightly browned (8 to 10 minutes). Add tomatoes and cook, stirring often, until tomatoes are soft (about 5 more minutes).

2. Add squash and broth. Increase heat to high and bring to a boil; reduce heat, cover, and boil gently until squash is very tender when pierced (about 15 minutes).

3. Transfer squash mixture, a third or half at a time, to a food processor or blender; whirl, adding some of the buttermilk to each batch, until smooth.

4. Pour into a bowl, stir in minced basil, and refrigerate, covered, for at least 2 hours or up to a day to serve cold. To serve hot, return to pan, stir in minced basil, and cook, stirring occasionally, until steaming hot (do not boil).

5. Garnish each serving with basil sprigs. Makes 4 to 6 servings.

Per serving: 128 calories (46% calories from fat), 4 g protein, 15 g carbohydrates, 7 g total fat (1 g saturated fat), 2 mg cholesterol, 664 mg sodium

Zucchini Vichyssoise

Preparation time: About 15 minutes

Cooking time: About 20 minutes

Chilling time: At least 2 hours

Serve frosty mugs of this creamy green soup with Chili-Cornmeal Stretch Breadsticks (page 142).

> 3 tablespoons salad oil
>
> 1 large onion, chopped
>
> 2 pounds zucchini (about 6 medium-large)
>
> 3 cups canned vegetable broth
>
> 2 tablespoons chopped fresh basil or 1½ teaspoons dry basil
>
> ¼ teaspoon *each* ground nutmeg and ground white pepper
>
> 1 cup milk or half-and-half
>
> Basil sprigs (optional)

1. Heat oil in a 3- to 4-quart pan over medium heat. Add onion and cook, stirring often, until soft but not browned (5 to 7 minutes). Meanwhile, slice zucchini about ¼ inch thick.

2. Add zucchini, broth, chopped basil, nutmeg, and pepper to pan. Bring to a boil; reduce heat, cover, and simmer until zucchini is tender when pierced (about 10 minutes).

3. Transfer zucchini mixture, a third or half at a time, to a food processor or blender; whirl until smooth. Pour into a large bowl and stir in milk.

4. Cover and refrigerate for at least 2 hours or up to a day. Garnish each serving with basil sprigs. Makes 6 main-dish or 10 to 12 first-course servings.

Per main-dish serving: 129 calories (59% calories from fat), 3 g protein, 11 g carbohydrates, 9 g total fat (2 g saturated fat), 6 mg cholesterol, 532 mg sodium

Red Onion Borscht

Pictured on facing page

Preparation time: About 15 minutes

Cooking time: 40 to 45 minutes

●

Slow cooking brings out the natural sweetness of red onions; shredded beets intensify their vivid color. Together, they make a flavorful soup low in both fat and calories.

- 1½ tablespoons salad oil
- 4 large red onions (2½ to 3 lbs. *total*), thinly sliced
- ½ cup red wine vinegar
- 2 medium-size beets (8 to 10 oz. *total*), peeled and shredded
- 2½ tablespoons unbleached all-purpose flour
- 6 cups homemade (page 33) or canned vegetable broth
- ⅓ cup port
  Salt and pepper
  Light sour cream (optional)

1. Heat oil in a 5- to 6-quart pan over medium-low heat. Add onions, vinegar, and beets. Cook, stirring often, until onions are very soft but not browned (25 to 30 minutes).

2. Add flour and cook, stirring, until bubbly. Remove pan from heat and gradually stir in broth. (At this point, you may cover and refrigerate for up to 2 days.)

3. Return soup to medium heat and bring to a boil, stirring occasionally; reduce heat and simmer for 10 minutes.

4. Stir in port. Season to taste with salt and pepper. Garnish each serving with sour cream, if desired. Makes 8 servings.

Per serving: 134 calories (26% calories from fat), 2 g protein, 22 g carbohydrates, 4 g total fat (0.4 g saturated fat), 0 mg cholesterol, 781 mg sodium

Hot Ginger Pear Soup

Preparation time: About 25 minutes

Cooking time: About 45 minutes

●

This distinctive fruit soup makes a refreshing lunch with grilled Cheddar cheese sandwiches on whole grain bread and a pot of steaming spiced herb tea.

- 3 pounds firm-ripe Bartlett pears
- 3 tablespoons sugar
- 1 cinnamon stick (2 to 3 inches long)
- 3 whole cloves
- 2 slices fresh ginger (*each* about ⅛ inch thick and 1 inch in diameter)
- 3 to 4 cups water
- 1 vanilla bean (6 to 7 inches long), split lengthwise, or 1 teaspoon vanilla
  Mint sprigs

1. Peel, halve, and core pears; place in a 3- to 4-quart pan. Add sugar, cinnamon stick, cloves, ginger, and 3 cups of the water; if using vanilla bean, add now. Bring mixture to a boil over high heat; reduce heat, cover, and simmer for 30 minutes.

2. Lift pears and ginger from cooking liquid, using a slotted spoon, and transfer to a food processor or blender; reserve liquid. Whirl pear mixture until smooth; set aside.

3. Boil reserved cooking liquid over high heat until reduced to 1½ cups (about 10 minutes); remove from heat. Discard cinnamon stick and cloves. Lift out vanilla bean, pat dry, and reserve for other uses.

4. Stir pear purée into reduced liquid; if using vanilla, stir in now. If necessary, add water to make 6 cups. Cook over medium heat, stirring, until steaming hot. Garnish each serving with mint. Makes 4 servings.

Per serving: 226 calories (5% calories from fat), 1 g protein, 57 g carbohydrates, 1 g total fat (0 g saturated fat), 0 mg cholesterol, 0.4 mg sodium

Beets contribute vivid color, slow-cooked onions lend sweetness to low-fat Red Onion Borscht (recipe on facing page), an impressive first course or, when accompanied by whole grain bread and fresh fruit, a main-dish offering.

Spiced Sweet Potato Bisque

Preparation time: About 20 minutes

Cooking time: About 30 minutes

●

For a cooling touch, spoon dollops of yogurt over each serving of this aromatic first-course soup.

2 tablespoons butter or margarine

1 large onion, chopped

1 clove garlic, minced or pressed

2 teaspoons ground coriander

1 teaspoon curry powder

½ teaspoon ground cumin

1 pound sweet potatoes or yams, peeled and cut into 1-inch cubes

1 quart homemade (facing page) or canned vegetable broth

Plain yogurt

1. Melt butter in a 3- to 4-quart pan over medium heat. Add onion and garlic. Cook, stirring often, until onion is soft but not browned (5 to 7 minutes).

2. Stir in coriander, curry powder, and cumin; cook, stirring, for about 30 seconds. Add potatoes and broth. Increase heat to high and bring to a boil; reduce heat, cover, and boil gently until potatoes are tender when pierced (about 20 minutes).

3. Transfer potato mixture, half at a time, to a food processor or blender; whirl until smooth.

4. Return to pan and cook over medium-low heat, stirring, until steaming hot. Garnish each serving with a dollop of yogurt. Makes 4 to 6 servings.

Per serving: 142 calories (36% calories from fat), 2 g protein, 22 g carbohydrates, 6 g total fat (3 g saturated fat), 12 mg cholesterol, 868 mg sodium

Cream of Cauliflower Soup

Preparation time: About 15 minutes

Cooking time: About 20 minutes

●

Cauliflower is cooked in broth with carrots and onion, and the mixture is then puréed to make this golden-hued first-course soup.

2 tablespoons butter or margarine

1 large onion, chopped

3½ cups homemade vegetable broth (facing page) or 2 cans (about 14½ oz. *each*) vegetable broth

2 medium-size carrots

1 medium-size cauliflower (1¼ to 1½ lbs.)

1 cup half-and-half or milk

⅛ teaspoon ground nutmeg

Salt and ground white pepper

1 tablespoon dry sherry (optional)

1 tablespoon chopped parsley

1. Melt butter in a 3- to 4-quart pan over medium heat. Add onion and cook, stirring often, until soft but not browned (5 to 7 minutes).

2. Stir in broth; increase heat to high and bring to a boil. Meanwhile, slice carrots ¼ inch thick and separate cauliflower into small flowerets.

3. Add carrots and cauliflower to boiling broth. Reduce heat, cover, and boil gently until vegetables are tender when pierced (about 7 minutes).

4. Transfer vegetable mixture, a third or half at a time, to a food processor or blender; whirl until smooth.

5. Return to pan and stir in half-and-half and nutmeg. Cook over medium heat, stirring occasionally, until steaming hot. Season to taste with salt and pepper; stir in sherry, if desired. Garnish each serving with parsley. Makes 6 servings.

Per serving: 134 calories (60% calories from fat), 3 g protein, 11 g carbohydrates, 9 g total fat (5 g saturated fat), 25 mg cholesterol, 685 mg sodium

Homemade Vegetable Broth

Flavorful broth is where rich-tasting homemade soup begins. Vegetables available the year around imbue Root Vegetable Broth with a distinctly earthy taste. Somewhat more subtle is Mushroom, Leek & Tomato Broth, with its rosy-red color and slight spicy taste.

If you're in a hurry, substitute canned vegetable broth for homemade. Or rely on convenient instant vegetable stock base (labeled as vegetable-flavored instant bouillon or vegetarian-style instant bouillon); for each cup of vegetable broth called for in a recipe, substitute 1 cube or 1 teaspoon granules per cup of boiling water.

Because both canned broths and prepared vegetable stock bases are inclined to be salty, be sure to taste the soup you're making before adding any salt.

Root Vegetable Broth

Preparation time: About 20 minutes
Cooking time: About 2 hours

2 tablespoons butter or margarine
3 large carrots, coarsely chopped
1 large turnip, coarsely chopped
2 large stalks celery, thinly sliced (include any leaves)
2 large onions, chopped
3 quarts water
1 teaspoon salt
6 large parsley sprigs
½ bay leaf
1 teaspoon dry thyme
2 cloves garlic, crushed
¼ teaspoon whole black peppercorns

1. Melt butter in a 5½- to 6-quart pan over medium heat. Add carrots, turnip, celery, and onions. Cook, stirring occasionally, until vegetables are golden (about 15 minutes).

2. Stir in water, salt, parsley, bay leaf, thyme, garlic, and peppercorns. Increase heat to medium-high and bring mixture to a boil; reduce heat, cover, and simmer until broth is richly flavored (1½ to 2 hours).

3. Strain broth, pressing down on the solids to remove as much liquid as possible. Discard vegetables and seasonings. If made ahead, let cool; cover and refrigerate for up to 3 days or freeze for longer storage. Makes about 2½ quarts.

Per cup: 30 calories (67% calories from fat), 0.3 g protein, 2 g carbohydrates, 2 g total fat (1 g saturated fat), 6 mg cholesterol, 251 mg sodium

Low-Fat

Mushroom, Leek & Tomato Broth

Preparation time: About 20 minutes
Cooking time: About 2 hours

2 large leeks
1 large onion, coarsely chopped
3 cloves garlic, minced or pressed
2 cups coarsely chopped parsley
8 ounces mushrooms, coarsely chopped
1 large can (about 28 oz.) crushed tomatoes
1 teaspoon *each* salt and dry thyme
1 bay leaf
½ teaspoon whole black peppercorns
¼ teaspoon whole cloves
2½ quarts water

1. Cut off and discard root ends of leeks. Trim tops, leaving about 3 inches of green leaves. Discard coarse outer leaves. Split leeks in half lengthwise and rinse well. Thinly slice.

2. Combine leeks, onion, garlic, parsley, mushrooms, tomatoes and their liquid, salt, thyme, bay leaf, peppercorns, cloves, and water in a 5½- to 6-quart pan. Bring to a boil over medium-high heat; reduce heat, cover, and simmer until broth is richly flavored (about 2 hours).

3. Strain broth, pressing down on the solids to remove as much liquid as possible. Discard vegetables and seasonings. If made ahead, let cool; cover and refrigerate for up to 3 days or freeze for longer storage. Makes about 2½ quarts.

Per cup: 30 calories (8% calories from fat), 1 g protein, 6 g carbohydrates, 0.3 g total fat (0 g saturated fat), 0 mg cholesterol, 355 mg sodium

Curry Soup with Wilted Spinach (recipe on facing page) makes a substantial meal when you spoon cooked brown rice into the bowl with the spinach. Toasted pita bread triangles help tame the soup's spicy bite.

Curry Soup with Wilted Spinach

Pictured on facing page

Preparation time: About 30 minutes

Cooking time: About 25 minutes

●

The classic curry flavor of this fragrant soup comes from small amounts of many seasonings. For a heartier soup, spoon in cooked brown rice.

> 3 tablespoons butter or margarine
> 1 small onion, finely chopped
> 2 large cloves garlic, minced or pressed
> 1 teaspoon finely chopped fresh ginger
> 1 medium-size tomato, chopped
> ½ teaspoon *each* cumin seeds, ground coriander, and ground turmeric
> ⅛ teaspoon *each* ground red pepper (cayenne) and fennel seeds
> 1 quart homemade (page 33) or canned vegetable broth
> 1 pound spinach, coarse stems removed
> 2 teaspoons lemon juice
> 1½ teaspoons chopped cilantro
> Salted roasted peanuts
> Chopped fresh red chile (optional)

1. Melt butter in a 3- to 4-quart pan over medium-high heat. Add onion, garlic, and ginger. Cook, stirring often, until onion is lightly browned (5 to 7 minutes).

2. Stir in tomato, cumin, coriander, turmeric, ground red pepper, and fennel. Cook, stirring occasionally, until tomato is soft (about 8 minutes). Transfer to a food processor or blender; whirl until smooth. Return to pan and blend in broth.

3. Bring to a boil over high heat and continue to boil until reduced to 3 cups. Meanwhile, rinse spinach well; place (with moisture clinging to leaves) in a 4- to 5-quart pan. Cook over medium-high heat, stirring often, until wilted (4 to 5 minutes). Transfer spinach to a colander and press with back of a spoon to extract as much liquid as possible.

4. Spoon spinach into soup bowls. Stir lemon juice and cilantro into hot broth. Ladle broth into bowls. Garnish with peanuts and, if desired, chile. Makes 4 servings.

Per serving: 133 calories (64% calories from fat), 3 g protein, 10 g carbohydrates, 10 g total fat (5 g saturated fat), 23 mg cholesterol, 1,170 mg sodium

Corn Chowder with Cheese

Preparation time: About 25 minutes

Cooking time: About 30 minutes

●

A shower of shredded Cheddar cheese lends a golden glow to this creamy, herb-scented soup chunky with potatoes and corn. Alongside, offer Soft Sesame Biscuits (page 133).

> 3 tablespoons butter or margarine
> 2 large onions, finely chopped
> 1 clove garlic, minced or pressed
> ½ teaspoon dry thyme
> 1 bay leaf
> 1 quart homemade (page 33) or canned vegetable broth
> 1 pound thin-skinned potatoes
> 3 cups (about 1 lb.) frozen corn kernels, thawed
> 2 cups milk
> ½ cup whipping cream
> Salt and ground white pepper
> 1½ cups (about 6 oz.) shredded sharp Cheddar cheese

1. Melt butter in a 5- to 6-quart pan over medium heat. Add onions and garlic. Cook, stirring occasionally, until onions are soft but not browned (8 to 10 minutes).

2. Stir in thyme, bay leaf, and broth. Increase heat to high and bring to a boil. Meanwhile, cut potatoes into ½-inch cubes.

3. Add potatoes to boiling broth; reduce heat, cover, and boil gently until potatoes are tender when pierced (10 to 15 minutes).

4. Stir in corn, milk, and cream. Cook over low heat, stirring, until steaming hot (do not boil).

5. Remove and discard bay leaf. Season to taste with salt and pepper. Serve with cheese to add to taste. Makes 4 to 6 servings.

Per serving: 525 calories (51% calories from fat), 18 g protein, 49 g carbohydrates, 31 g total fat (18 g saturated fat), 95 mg cholesterol, 1,159 mg sodium

Leek Soup with Brie

Preparation time: About 25 minutes

Baking time: 30 to 35 minutes

Cooking time: About 20 minutes

Sliced Brie melted over croutons afloat in ramekins of leek and mushroom soup adds rich flavor and creaminess. Serve the soup as a first course or as a light supper.

Toasted French Bread (recipe follows)
6 **to 9 large leeks**
2 **tablespoons butter or margarine**
8 **ounces mushrooms, thinly sliced**
1 **clove garlic, minced or pressed**
½ **teaspoon dry tarragon**
¼ **teaspoon ground white pepper**
2½ **tablespoons unbleached all-purpose flour**
1 **quart homemade (page 33) or canned vegetable broth**
⅓ **cup whipping cream**
6 **ounces Brie cheese**

1. **Prepare** Toasted French Bread.

2. **Cut** off and discard root ends of leeks. Trim tops, leaving about 3 inches of green leaves. Discard coarse outer leaves. Split leeks in half lengthwise and rinse well. Thinly slice (you should have about 2 quarts).

3. **Melt** butter in a 4- to 5-quart pan over medium heat. Add leeks, mushrooms, garlic, tarragon, and pepper. Cook, stirring occasionally, until vegetables are very soft and most of the liquid has evaporated (about 15 minutes).

4. **Add** flour and cook, stirring, until bubbly. Remove from heat and gradually stir in broth and cream. Return to heat and bring to a boil, stirring constantly.

5. **Ladle** soup into 6 heatproof 1½- to 2-cup soup bowls. Top each serving with a piece of Toasted French Bread, buttered side up.

6. **Slice** Brie ½ inch thick; place a cheese slice on each toast slice. Bake in a 425° oven until bubbly (about 10 minutes). Then broil about 6 inches below heat until lightly browned (1 to 2 minutes). Makes 6 servings.

Toasted French Bread. Cut 6 slices (*each* about ½ inch thick) from a loaf of **French bread.** Arrange slices in a single layer on a baking sheet. Bake in a 325° oven until dry (20 to 25 minutes). Spread one side with **butter** or margarine, using ½ teaspoon for each slice. (At this point, you may wrap in foil and let stand at room temperature for up to a day.)

Per serving: 357 calories (48% calories from fat), 11 g protein, 37 g carbohydrates, 20 g total fat (6 g saturated fat), 59 mg cholesterol, 1,048 mg sodium

Fresh Tomato Soup

Preparation time: About 30 minutes

Cooking time: About 40 minutes

For a lunch or supper reminiscent of favorite foods of childhood, serve basil-laced tomato soup with grilled jack cheese sandwiches.

2 **tablespoons butter or margarine**
1 **large onion, chopped**
1 **large carrot, chopped**
5 **large tomatoes (about 2 lbs. *total*), seeded and quartered**
¼ **cup firmly packed fresh basil**
¾ **teaspoon sugar**
½ **teaspoon ground white pepper**
3 **cups homemade (page 33) or canned vegetable broth**

1. **Melt** butter in a 3- to 4-quart pan over medium-low heat. Add onion and carrot; cook, stirring often, until carrot is very tender (about 20 minutes).

2. **Add** tomatoes, basil, sugar, and pepper. Reduce heat, cover, and simmer until tomatoes are very soft (about 15 minutes). Transfer to a food processor or blender; whirl until smooth.

3. **Return** tomato mixture to pan and stir in broth. Cook over high heat, stirring, until steaming hot (3 to 5 minutes). Makes 4 servings.

Per serving: 143 calories (43% calories from fat), 3 g protein, 20 g carbohydrates, 7 g total fat (4 g saturated fat), 16 mg cholesterol, 847 mg sodium

Pistou Soup with Split Peas

Pictured on page 26

Preparation time: About 35 minutes

Cooking time: About 1½ hours

Here's a wintry version of a sturdy whole-meal soup from the south of France.

- **1 pound large leeks**
- **2 tablespoons olive oil**
- **1 cup chopped carrots**
- **⅛ to ¼ teaspoon ground red pepper (cayenne)**
- **2 medium-size thin-skinned potatoes (about 12 oz. *total*), peeled and diced**
- **⅔ cup green split peas, rinsed and drained**
- **1½ quarts homemade (page 33) or canned vegetable broth**
- **1½ quarts water**
- **Pistou (recipe follows)**
- **1 cup frozen cut green beans**
- **⅔ cup 2-inch pieces dry spaghetti**
- **Grated Parmesan cheese (optional)**

1. Cut off and discard root ends of leeks. Trim tops, leaving about 3 inches of green leaves. Discard coarse outer leaves. Split leeks in half lengthwise and rinse well. Thinly slice.

2. Heat oil in a 6- to 8-quart pan over medium heat. Stir in leeks, carrots, and ground red pepper. Cook, stirring often, until leeks are soft but not browned (6 to 8 minutes).

3. Stir in potatoes, split peas, broth, and water. Bring to a boil; reduce heat, cover, and simmer until peas are tender to bite (about 1 hour). Meanwhile, prepare Pistou.

4. Stir beans, spaghetti, and Pistou into soup. Increase heat to medium-high and boil gently, uncovered, until spaghetti is just tender to bite (8 to 10 minutes). Serve with cheese to add to taste, if desired. Makes 6 to 8 servings.

Pistou. In a medium-size bowl, combine 4 cloves **garlic,** minced or pressed; 1 can (about 6 oz.) **tomato paste;** ¾ cup grated **Parmesan cheese;** ¼ cup minced **parsley;** 1½ tablespoons **dry basil;** and ¼ cup **olive oil.** Stir well.

Per serving: 359 calories (39% calories from fat), 13 g protein, 44 g carbohydrates, 16 g total fat (3 g saturated fat), 7 mg cholesterol, 1,241 mg sodium

Wholesome Lentil Soup

Preparation time: About 30 minutes

Cooking time: About 1¼ hours

Lentils simmer with herbs and an abundance of vegetables to make this thick and satisfying soup.

- **2 large onions, finely chopped**
- **6 cups homemade (page 33) or canned vegetable broth**
- **1 package (about 12 oz.) or 2 cups lentils, rinsed and drained**
- **1 quart water**
- **2 pounds carrots, thinly sliced**
- **2 cups sliced celery**
- **1 large can (about 28 oz.) pear-shaped (Roma-type) tomatoes**
- **2 teaspoons *each* dry basil and dry thyme**
- **3 bay leaves**
- **1 teaspoon *each* fennel seeds and pepper**
- **Salt**

1. Combine onions and ½ cup of the broth in an 8- to 10-quart pan. Bring to a boil over high heat and continue to boil until onions begin to brown and liquid has evaporated (6 to 8 minutes).

2. Add remaining broth, stirring to scrape browned bits free. Add lentils, water, carrots, celery, tomatoes and their liquid, basil, thyme, bay leaves, fennel, and pepper. Bring to a boil; reduce heat, cover, and boil gently until lentils are soft to bite (about 1 hour).

3. Remove and discard bay leaves. Season to taste with salt. Makes 10 to 12 servings.

Per serving: 184 calories (6% calories from fat), 11 g protein, 35 g carbohydrates, 1 g total fat (0.1 g saturated fat), 0 mg cholesterol, 722 mg sodium

Winter Minestrone

Pictured on facing page

Preparation time: About 45 minutes

Cooking time: About 1¼ hours

●

This robust soup should satisfy even the most ravenous winter appetite. Pass around a bowl of shredded jack cheese to sprinkle atop each serving.

3	**tablespoons olive oil**
1	**large onion, finely chopped**
1	**large stalk celery, finely chopped**
2	**large cloves garlic, minced or pressed**
1	**teaspoon dry basil**
½	**teaspoon** *each* **dry rosemary, dry oregano, and dry thyme**
¼	**cup pearl barley, rinsed and drained**
2	**medium-size thin-skinned potatoes (about 12 oz.** *total***), diced**
2	**large carrots, diced**
2	**quarts homemade (page 33) or canned vegetable broth**
1	**large turnip, peeled and diced**
1	**can (about 15 oz.) red kidney beans or white kidney beans (cannellini)**
⅔	**cup small dry shell or elbow macaroni**
¼	**cup tomato paste**
2	**cups finely shredded green cabbage**
	Salt and pepper
1½	**cups (about 6 oz.) shredded jack cheese**

1. Heat oil in a 5- to 6-quart pan over medium heat. Add onion, celery, garlic, basil, rosemary, oregano, and thyme. Cook, stirring often, until onion is soft (8 to 10 minutes).

2. Add barley, potatoes, carrots, and broth. Increase heat to high and bring to a boil; reduce heat, cover, and boil gently for 20 minutes.

3. Add turnip; cover and continue to cook for 20 more minutes.

4. Stir in beans and their liquid, macaroni, and tomato paste. Increase heat to high and bring to a boil; reduce heat, cover, and boil gently until macaroni is tender to bite (12 to 15 minutes).

5. Add cabbage and cook, uncovered, until cabbage is tender-crisp (about 5 more minutes). Season to taste with salt and pepper. Serve with cheese to add to taste. Makes 6 to 8 servings.

Per serving: 362 calories (37% calories from fat), 14 g protein, 45 g carbohydrates, 15 g total fat (0.9 g saturated fat), 21 mg cholesterol, 1,615 mg sodium

Low-Fat

Vinegar Bean Soup

Preparation time: About 20 minutes

Cooking time: About 20 minutes

●

Made with canned butter beans, this hearty sweet-and-sour soup makes a quick main dish to serve with bran muffins or whole grain bread.

1	**tablespoon olive oil or salad oil**
3	**large onions, finely chopped**
2	**bay leaves**
4	**cans (about 15 oz.** *each***) butter beans or lima beans**
3½	**cups homemade vegetable broth (page 33) or 2 cans (about 14½ oz.** *each***) vegetable broth**
½	**cup firmly packed brown sugar**
6	**tablespoons cider vinegar**
2	**tablespoons dry mustard**
1	**teaspoon grated lemon peel**
¼	**cup finely chopped parsley**

1. Heat oil in a 5- to 6-quart pan over medium-high heat. Add onions and bay leaves. Cook, stirring often, until onions are soft (about 10 minutes). Meanwhile, place 2 cans of the beans and their liquid in a food processor or blender; whirl until smooth.

2. Add bean purée, remaining beans and their liquid, broth, brown sugar, vinegar, mustard, and lemon peel to onion mixture. Increase heat to high and cook, stirring often, until mixture begins to simmer.

3. Remove and discard bay leaves. Garnish each serving with parsley. Makes 6 to 8 servings.

Per serving: 317 calories (11% calories from fat), 13 g protein, 61 g carbohydrates, 4 g total fat (0.5 g saturated fat), 0 mg cholesterol, 1,138 mg sodium

What could be more satisfying on a chilly day than a bowlful of sturdy Winter Minestrone (recipe on facing page), offered with jack cheese and pieces of Garlic Cheese Bread (recipe on page 141), a simple version of Italian focaccia.

Jalapeño Vegetable Chowder

Preparation time: About 35 minutes

Cooking time: About 35 minutes

●

This creamy vegetable soup gets its bite from jalapeño chiles (use the smaller quantity if you prefer a less fiery flavor). Accompany cheese-topped bowlfuls with warm corn or flour tortillas.

  2 tablespoons salad oil
  1 large onion, finely chopped
  2 cloves garlic, minced or pressed
  ½ teaspoon *each* ground cumin and dry oregano
  ⅓ to ½ cup stemmed, seeded, and finely chopped fresh or canned jalapeño chiles
  1 large red bell pepper, seeded and finely chopped
  2 tablespoons unbleached all-purpose flour
  1 quart homemade (page 33) or canned vegetable broth
  1 large sweet potato (8 to 10 oz.), peeled and cut into ½-inch cubes
  2 large ears corn
  ½ cup whipping cream
     Salt and pepper
     Cilantro sprigs
  1 cup (about 4 oz.) shredded Cheddar or jalapeño jack cheese

1. Heat oil in a 5- to 6-quart pan over medium heat. Add onion, garlic, cumin, oregano, chiles, and bell pepper. Cook, stirring often, until onion is soft but not browned (8 to 10 minutes).

2. Add flour and cook, stirring, until bubbly. Remove from heat and gradually stir in broth.

3. Return to high heat and bring to a boil. Add sweet potato; reduce heat, cover, and boil gently until potato is tender when pierced (10 to 15 minutes). Meanwhile, remove and discard corn husks and silk; cut corn kernels from cobs.

4. Add corn and cream to soup. Increase heat to high and cook, stirring occasionally, until soup comes to a boil. Season to taste with salt and pepper. Garnish each serving

with cilantro. Serve with cheese to add to taste. Makes 4 to 6 servings.

Per serving: 341 calories (56% calories from fat), 9 g protein, 29 g carbohydrates, 22 g total fat (10 g saturated fat), 50 mg cholesterol, 974 mg sodium

Peanut Butter Vegetable Soup

Preparation time: About 25 minutes

Cooking time: About 30 minutes

●

To complement servings of this hearty soup, bring on a basket of corn muffins and a pitcher of warm honey.

  1 tablespoon salad oil
  1 large onion, finely chopped
  2 large carrots, thinly sliced
  1 large stalk celery, finely chopped
  3 cloves garlic, minced or pressed
  1 cup crunchy peanut butter
  ⅛ to ¼ teaspoon ground red pepper (cayenne)
  2 quarts homemade (page 33) or canned vegetable broth
  2 large thin-skinned potatoes (about 1 lb. *total*), cut into ½-inch cubes
  3 tablespoons red wine vinegar
     Salt and pepper
     Chopped parsley

1. Heat oil in a 5- to 6-quart pan over medium heat. Add onion, carrots, celery, and garlic. Cook, stirring often, until onion is soft but not browned (5 to 7 minutes).

2. Remove from heat and add peanut butter, stirring until blended. Season to taste with ground red pepper and gradually stir in broth.

3. Add potatoes and return soup to high heat. Bring to a boil; reduce heat, cover, and boil gently until potatoes and carrots are very tender when pierced (about 20 minutes).

4. Stir in vinegar. Season to taste with salt and pepper. Garnish each serving with parsley. Makes 6 servings.

Per serving: 393 calories (55% calories from fat), 13 g protein, 34 g carbohydrates, 25 g total fat (4 g saturated fat), 0 mg cholesterol, 1,585 mg sodium

Barley & Cheese Soup with Parsley Pesto

Preparation time: About 20 minutes

Cooking time: About 1¼ hours

●

A dollop of bright pesto on each serving of this thick, creamy soup adds sparkling flavor.

- ½ cup pearl barley, rinsed and drained
- 3 cups water
- Parsley Pesto (recipe follows)
- 1 tablespoon butter or margarine
- 1 small onion, finely chopped
- ⅛ teaspoon ground mace or nutmeg
- 1 jar (about 2 oz.) diced pimentos, drained
- 2 cups milk
- 2 cups (about 8 oz.) shredded Havarti or jack cheese
- Salt and ground white pepper

1. Combine barley and water in a 2- to 3-quart pan. Bring to a boil over high heat, stirring occasionally; reduce heat, cover, and simmer until barley is very tender to bite (about 1 hour). Meanwhile, prepare Parsley Pesto.

2. Melt butter in a 3- to 4-quart pan over medium heat. Add onion and cook, stirring often, until soft but not browned (5 to 7 minutes).

3. Reduce heat to low and stir in mace, pimentos, and milk. Drain barley and add to milk mixture.

4. Stir in cheese, about ½ cup at a time; continue to cook, stirring constantly, until cheese is melted and blended and soup is steaming hot. Season to taste with salt and pepper. Serve with Parsley Pesto to add to taste. Makes 4 servings.

Parsley Pesto. In a food processor or blender, combine 1 cup lightly packed **parsley;** 1 clove **garlic;** 1 tablespoon **pine nuts,** if desired; ¼ cup grated **Parmesan cheese;** ½ cup **plain nonfat yogurt;** and 1 tablespoon **olive oil.** Whirl until smooth. Transfer to a small serving bowl. If made ahead, cover and refrigerate for up to a day; bring to room temperature before serving. Makes about ¾ cup.

Per serving: 463 calories (52% calories from fat), 25 g protein, 32 g carbohydrates, 27 g total fat (15 g saturated fat), 87 mg cholesterol, 642 mg sodium

Robust Greens Soup

Preparation time: About 25 minutes

Cooking time: 15 to 20 minutes

●

Serve this wholesome chard and spinach soup with crunchy whole grain bread croutons and Parmesan cheese.

- 2 tablespoons olive oil or salad oil
- 2 large onions, finely chopped
- 2 cloves garlic, minced or pressed
- 1 tablespoon dry basil
- 1 teaspoon dry rosemary
- 1 large bunch spinach (about 12 oz.), coarse stems removed
- 1 large bunch Swiss chard (about 1 lb.), coarse stems removed
- 1 quart homemade (page 33) or canned vegetable broth
- 1 can (about 14 oz.) diced pear-shaped (Roma-type) tomatoes
- Salt and pepper
- Croutons and grated Parmesan cheese (optional)

1. Heat oil in a 5- to 6-quart pan over medium heat. Add onions, garlic, basil, and rosemary. Cook, stirring often, until onions are soft but not browned (8 to 10 minutes). Meanwhile, rinse spinach and chard, drain, and chop coarsely; set aside.

2. Add broth to pan. Increase heat to high, cover, and bring to a boil. Add greens; reduce heat and boil gently, uncovered, until greens are wilted (about 3 minutes).

3. Stir in tomatoes and their liquid. Cook just until heated through (about 2 more minutes). Season to taste with salt and pepper. Serve with croutons and cheese to add to taste, if desired. Makes 6 servings.

Per serving: 114 calories (41% calories from fat), 4 g protein, 15 g carbohydrates, 6 g total fat (1 g saturated fat), 0 mg cholesterol, 966 mg sodium

An inviting brunch brings together refreshing Minted Goat Cheese Tart with Hazelnuts (recipe on page 45), fresh fruit, and orange-accented Cranberry Cornmeal Scones (recipe on page 132). For a beverage, offer white wine or sparkling apple juice.

EGGS & CHEESE

Spinach-Mushroom Pie

Finnish Oven Pancake

Minted Goat Cheese Tart with Hazelnuts

Summertime Frittata

Spinach Enchiladas

Tomato & Egg Supper

Chard, Feta & Fila Pie

Onion Crêpes with Pistachio Sauce

Avocado Salad Tart

Green Corn Quiche

Gruyère & Mushroom Tarts

Scrambled Eggs & Bulgur

Spiced Bell Pepper Soufflés

Lean Spinach-Marjoram Soufflé

Mushroom-Cheese Crêpes

Chiles Rellenos Casserole

Red & Yellow Pepper Flat Omelet

Joe's Swiss Chard Special

Zuchizza Casserole

Lightened-up Chiles Rellenos

Spinach-Mushroom Pie

Preparation time: About 45 minutes

Cooking and baking time: About 1 hour

●

Supper under a crust is an old-fashioned concept that's now enjoying a revival. This main-dish pie makes a hearty dinner with a salad of sliced tomatoes.

Cream Cheese Pastry (recipe follows)
1½ tablespoons salad oil
1 large onion, finely chopped
8 ounces mushrooms, thinly sliced
3 cloves garlic, minced or pressed
1 teaspoon dry tarragon
2 packages (about 10 oz. *each*) frozen chopped spinach, thawed and squeezed dry
1 cup part-skim ricotta cheese
1 cup soft bread crumbs
2 large eggs
½ cup grated Parmesan cheese
½ teaspoon salt
⅓ cup finely chopped parsley

1. Prepare Cream Cheese Pastry.

2. Heat oil in a wide frying pan over medium heat. Add onion, mushrooms, garlic, and tarragon. Cook, stirring often, until liquid has evaporated and onion is golden brown (12 to 15 minutes). Remove pan from heat.

3. Crumble spinach into mixture in pan; add ricotta, bread crumbs, eggs, Parmesan, salt, and parsley. Mix well. Spoon into a 9-inch pie pan.

4. Roll pastry on a lightly floured board into a 10-inch circle. Using a cookie cutter, cut 1 or 2 pieces from center of pastry; set aside. Lay pastry over filling. Fold edge under and flute firmly against rim. Arrange cutouts decoratively on top of pastry. Brush pastry and cutouts with slightly beaten egg white (reserved from pastry).

5. Bake on lowest rack of a 400° oven until pastry is well browned and filling is hot in center (40 to 45 minutes). Makes 6 to 8 servings.

Cream Cheese Pastry. In a food processor or bowl, combine 1¼ cups **unbleached all-purpose flour;** ½ cup **butter** or margarine, diced; and ⅓ cup (about 3 oz.) **Neufchâtel cheese.** Whirl or rub with your fingers until coarse crumbs form. Add 1 large **egg yolk** (reserve white for brushing pastry); whirl or stir with a fork until dough clings together. Pat into a flat, smooth round. (At this point, you may cover and refrigerate for up to 2 days.)

Per serving: 419 calories (56% calories from fat), 17 g protein, 30 g carbohydrates, 26 g total fat (14 g saturated fat), 151 mg cholesterol, 612 mg sodium

Finnish Oven Pancake

Preparation time: About 15 minutes

Baking time: About 25 minutes

●

For a summertime brunch, offer juicy slices of fresh peaches, a sprinkling of powdered sugar, and a dollop of sour cream to top squares of this dramatic puffy pancake.

5 large eggs
1 tablespoon granulated sugar
½ teaspoon salt
2½ cups milk
1 cup small-curd cottage cheese
1 cup unbleached all-purpose flour
1 teaspoon baking powder
½ cup butter or margarine, diced
2 to 3 cups sliced peaches or nectarines (optional)
Powdered sugar or warm honey (optional)
About 1 cup sour cream (optional)

1. Place a 9- by 13-inch baking pan in oven while it preheats to 425°. Meanwhile, combine eggs, granulated sugar, and salt in large bowl of an electric mixer; beat until thick and tripled in volume. Add milk, cottage cheese, flour, and baking powder; beat well.

2. Add butter to hot pan in oven; when butter is melted, swirl to coat bottom. Pour in egg batter and bake until well browned and puffed high around sides (about 25 minutes).

3. Cut pancake into squares and lift out with a wide spatula. Serve hot with fruit, powdered sugar, and sour cream, if desired, to add to taste. Makes 6 to 8 servings.

Per serving: 326 calories (58% calories from fat), 13 g protein, 21 g carbohydrates, 21 g total fat (12 g saturated fat), 204 mg cholesterol, 561 mg sodium

Minted Goat Cheese Tart with Hazelnuts

Pictured on page 42

Preparation time: About 40 minutes

Baking time: About 1 hour

●

Fresh mint enlivens the toasted nut and cheese filling of this unusual quiche.

      Tart Pastry (recipe follows)
  ½ **cup hazelnuts**
  4 **large eggs**
  1 **cup milk**
  ½ **cup whipping cream**
  ¼ **teaspoon salt**
  ⅛ **teaspoon ground white pepper**
  6 **ounces soft goat cheese (chèvre), crumbled**
  ¼ **cup slivered fresh mint**

1. Prepare Tart Pastry. While it chills, spread hazelnuts in a shallow baking pan and toast in a 350° oven until pale golden beneath skins (about 10 minutes). Let cool slightly; then use your fingers to rub off skins. Chop nuts coarsely.

2. Beat eggs in a large bowl until frothy. Add milk, cream, salt, and pepper; beat well.

3. Distribute cheese over bottom of partially baked pastry; sprinkle with nuts and mint. Pour in egg mixture.

4. Bake in a 450° oven for 15 minutes. Reduce heat to 325° and continue to bake until crust is golden brown and filling is almost set when a knife is inserted (20 to 25 more minutes). Let stand briefly; then remove pan sides and cut into wedges. Makes 6 servings.

Tart Pastry. In a food processor or bowl, combine 1 cup **unbleached all-purpose flour,** ⅓ cup **whole wheat flour,** ¼ teaspoon **salt,** and ½ cup firm **butter** or margarine, diced. Whirl with on-off bursts or rub with your fingers until coarse crumbs form. Add 1 large **egg;** whirl or stir with a fork until dough clings together. Pat into a flat, smooth round. Enclose in plastic wrap and refrigerate for about 30 minutes.

On a floured surface, roll pastry into a 12-inch circle. Ease into an 8½- to 9-inch spring-form pan, trimming top edge, if necessary, to make a 2-inch-deep pastry shell. Line with aluminum foil and fill to a depth of about 1 inch with pie weights or dried beans. Bake in a 450° oven for 10 minutes. Remove from oven and carefully lift out foil and weights. Set aside.

Per serving: 540 calories (68% calories from fat), 18 g protein, 26 g carbohydrates, 42 g total fat (22 g saturated fat), 269 mg cholesterol, 562 mg sodium

Summertime Frittata

Preparation time: About 15 minutes

Cooking time: About 20 minutes

●

Served straight from the frying pan, this savory egg dish makes a quick-cooking supper for two.

  8 **ounces thin-skinned potatoes, unpeeled, diced**
  2 **teaspoons salad oil**
  8 **ounces mushrooms, thinly sliced**
  ½ **cup water**
  4 **green onions, thinly sliced**
  4 **large eggs**
  ⅓ **cup shredded Cheddar cheese**
      Salt and pepper

1. Combine potatoes, oil, mushrooms, and ¼ cup of the water in a 10- to 12-inch frying pan with an ovenproof handle. Cover and cook over medium-high heat, stirring occasionally, until potatoes are tender when pierced (about 12 minutes).

2. Uncover and continue cooking until liquid has evaporated. Meanwhile, set aside 2 tablespoons of the onions. Combine remaining onions, eggs, cheese, and remaining ¼ cup water in a medium-size bowl; beat until blended.

3. Pour egg mixture over vegetables. Reduce heat to low and cook until eggs begin to set at edge of pan (about 4 minutes).

4. Transfer pan to oven and broil about 6 inches below heat until eggs feel set when lightly touched (2 to 3 minutes). Sprinkle with reserved onions. Season to taste with salt and pepper. Makes 2 servings.

Per serving: 394 calories (48% calories from fat), 22 g protein, 29 g carbohydrates, 22 g total fat (8 g saturated fat), 445 mg cholesterol, 260 mg sodium

Spinach Enchiladas

Preparation time: About 30 minutes

Cooking and baking time: About 40 minutes

●

Tangy feta cheese flavors both filling and sauce in this variation of a traditional Mexican dish.

- 4 **tablespoons butter or margarine**
- 2 **tablespoons raisins**
- 2 **medium-size onions, finely chopped**
- 3 **packages (about 10 oz. *each*) frozen chopped spinach, thawed and squeezed dry**
- 1½ **cups (about 8 oz.) crumbled feta cheese**
- 2 **tablespoons unbleached all-purpose flour**
- 1 **teaspoon *each* ground nutmeg and pepper**
- 3 **cups canned vegetable broth**
- 2 **to 3 tablespoons salad oil**
- 8 **corn tortillas (about 7-inch diameter)**
- 1 **can (about 10 oz.) red enchilada sauce**

1. **Melt** 1 tablespoon of the butter in a wide frying pan over medium heat. Add raisins and cook, stirring, until puffed (about 1 minute). Remove raisins from pan and set aside. To same pan, add 1 tablespoon more butter and onions. Cook over medium-high heat, stirring, until onions are soft (about 5 minutes).

2. **Transfer** onions to a large bowl and stir in spinach. Spoon out and reserve 1¼ cups of the spinach mixture. To spinach mixture in bowl, add raisins and ¾ cup of the cheese; mix lightly.

3. **Melt** remaining 2 tablespoons butter in pan over medium heat. Add flour, nutmeg, and pepper. Cook, stirring, until well blended. Remove from heat and smoothly blend in 1½ cups of the broth. Bring to a boil over high heat, stirring. Remove from heat. Add ½ cup of the thickened broth to spinach-raisin mixture. Set aside.

4. **Combine** remaining thickened broth, reserved 1¼ cups spinach mixture, remaining 1½ cups broth, and ½ cup more of the cheese in a food processor or blender; whirl until smooth. Set sauce aside.

5. **Heat** 2 tablespoons of the oil in a medium-size nonstick frying pan over medium-high heat. Add tortillas, one at a time, and cook, turning once, just until softened (2 to 3 seconds on each side); add more oil if needed. Drain tortillas on paper towels.

6. **Spoon** about ⅓ cup of the spinach-raisin mixture down center of each tortilla; roll to enclose. Arrange tortillas in a single layer, seam sides down, in a shallow 3-quart casserole. (At this point, you may cover and refrigerate tortillas and spinach sauce for up to 4 hours.)

7. **Pour** spinach sauce evenly over tortillas. Bake, uncovered, in a 350° oven until heated through (20 to 30 minutes). Meanwhile, heat enchilada sauce in a 1-quart pan over low heat, stirring occasionally.

8. **Sprinkle** enchiladas with remaining ¼ cup cheese. Drizzle with enchilada sauce. Serve remaining sauce to add to taste. Makes 4 servings.

Per serving: 570 calories (55% calories from fat), 18 g protein, 49 g carbohydrates, 36 g total fat (17 g saturated fat), 82 mg cholesterol, 2,410 mg sodium

Tomato & Egg Supper

Pictured on facing page

Preparation time: About 10 minutes

Cooking time: About 15 minutes

●

Slipped among sautéed Roma tomatoes, eggs cook gently in garlic-seasoned olive oil to make a speedy main dish.

- 3 **tablespoons olive oil**
- 6 **pear-shaped (Roma-type) tomatoes, halved lengthwise**
- 4 **large cloves garlic, chopped**
- 8 **large eggs**
- 3 **tablespoons chopped parsley**
  Salt and pepper

1. **Heat** oil in a wide frying pan over medium heat. Add tomatoes, cut sides down, and garlic. Cook, turning once, until tomatoes are browned (about 10 minutes).

2. **Reduce** heat to low. Break eggs into pan, placing them around tomatoes. Cover and cook just until egg whites are firm (1½ to 2 minutes).

3. **Sprinkle** with parsley and serve from pan. Season to taste with salt and pepper. Makes 4 servings.

Per serving: 272 calories (67% calories from fat), 14 g protein, 9 g carbohydrates, 21 g total fat (5 g saturated fat), 425 mg cholesterol, 139 mg sodium

Enjoy the intense flavor of pear-shaped Roma tomatoes in season by preparing quick-cooking Tomato and Egg Supper (recipe on facing page). Simple accompaniments include a mixed lettuce salad and crusty French bread.

Chard, Feta & Fila Pie

Preparation time: About 35 minutes

Cooking and baking time: About 1 hour

●

Serve this fila-topped vegetable and cheese casserole with a tomato and cucumber salad and crisp breadsticks.

2 pounds Swiss chard, coarse stems removed
5 tablespoons butter or margarine
1 large onion, thinly sliced
4 large eggs
1½ teaspoons *each* dry basil and dry oregano
¼ teaspoon pepper
2 cups (about 12 oz.) crumbled feta cheese
4 sheets fila dough (*each* about 12 by 17 inches)

1. **Rinse** chard well. Fill a 5- to 6-quart pan three-quarters full of water and bring to a boil over high heat. Push about a third of the chard into water; cook until stems are limp (about 3 minutes). Lift out with a slotted spoon and drain. Repeat with remaining chard. Let cool; then chop coarsely. Meanwhile, melt 2 tablespoons of the butter in a wide frying pan over medium heat. Add onion and cook, stirring occasionally, until soft (about 10 minutes).

2. **Beat** eggs in a large bowl just until blended. Stir in chard, onion, basil, oregano, pepper, and cheese. Spread mixture in a shallow 2-quart casserole or baking pan.

3. **Stack** sheets of fila and fold once so width fits or is slightly larger than narrow dimension of casserole. Set casserole on fila; cut around casserole so fila will fit, discarding trimmings.

4. **Melt** remaining 3 tablespoons butter. Lay a sheet of fila on chard mixture; brush with butter. Repeat with remaining fila and butter. With a sharp knife, cut through fila in a diamond-shaped pattern. (At this point, you may cover and refrigerate for up to a day.)

5. **Bake,** uncovered, in a 375° oven until fila is well browned (40 to 45 minutes). Cut through markings to serve. Makes 6 servings.

Per serving: 361 calories (62% calories from fat), 16 g protein, 19 g carbohydrates, 25 g total fat (15 g saturated fat), 218 mg cholesterol, 1,120 mg sodium

Onion Crêpes with Pistachio Sauce

Preparation time: About 45 minutes

Cooking and baking time: About 40 minutes

●

Finely ground pistachios contribute rich flavor to the sauce for these spicy onion-filled cheese crêpes.

12 Basic Crêpes or Sesame Crêpes (facing page)
3 tablespoons butter or margarine
4 large onions, thinly sliced
1 tablespoon minced fresh ginger
½ teaspoon *each* ground cumin and ground coriander
⅛ teaspoon ground turmeric
¼ cup golden raisins
2 cups (about 8 oz.) shredded jack cheese
¾ cup shelled roasted salted or unsalted pistachios (about 1½ cups nuts in shells)
½ cup whipping cream
About ⅓ cup canned vegetable broth

1. **Prepare** Basic Crêpes.

2. **Melt** butter in a 12- to 14-inch frying pan over medium heat. Add onions and ginger. Cook, stirring often, until onions are very soft and light golden (about 15 minutes). Add cumin, coriander, turmeric, and raisins. Reduce heat to low and cook, stirring, for 1 more minute. Remove from heat and let stand for 5 minutes; stir in cheese.

3. **Spoon** a generous ¼ cup of the onion mixture over half of each crêpe; fold into quarters. Arrange crêpes in a single layer in 2 greased shallow baking pans. (At this point, you may cover and refrigerate for up to a day.)

4. **Bake** crêpes, uncovered, in a 400° oven until heated through (about 10 minutes). Meanwhile, whirl ½ cup of the pistachios in a blender or food processor until finely ground. Transfer to a small pan. Add cream and ⅓ cup of the broth. Cook over high heat, stirring, until heated through. Stir in additional broth, 1 tablespoon at a time, if necessary, to make a pourable sauce. Coarsely chop remaining ¼ cup pistachios.

5. **Arrange** crêpes on warm plates. Spoon sauce over crêpes and sprinkle with chopped nuts. Makes 4 servings.

Per serving: 770 calories (64% calories from fat), 27 g protein, 44 g carbohydrates, 56 g total fat (15 g saturated fat), 225 mg cholesterol, 783 mg sodium

Versatile Crêpes

Tender crêpes make fine wrappers for sweet or savory fillings. Though crêpes seem so delicate as to virtually melt in your mouth, the eggs in the batter actually lend enough strength to make baked crêpes quite sturdy.

For added convenience, you can make a batch of crêpes ahead and store them in the freezer as the starting point for a variety of entrées.

For the basic batter use unbleached all-purpose flour or, for a more vigorous, slightly nutty flavor, whole wheat flour. Crêpes gain extra protein and a slight crunch when you add sesame seeds to the batter.

For a real departure from the ordinary, make bright spinach-flecked crêpes—they're delightful simply with melted butter or a dollop of sour cream or plain yogurt, or rolled around a favorite filling, such as sautéed sliced mushrooms.

Basic Crêpes

Preparation time: About 10 minutes
Standing time: 1 hour
Cooking time: 20 to 25 minutes

| 1 cup milk |
| 3 large eggs |
| ¾ cup unbleached all-purpose flour |
| ⅛ teaspoon salt |
| About 1½ tablespoons salad oil |

1. Combine milk, eggs, flour, salt, and 1 tablespoon of the oil in a food processor or blender; whirl until smooth. (Or use a wire whisk, egg beater, or electric mixer.) Cover batter and refrigerate for an hour.

2. Heat a 6- to 7-inch crêpe pan or other flat-bottomed frying pan over medium heat. Add about ¼ teaspoon of the remaining oil and swirl to coat surface. When pan is sizzling hot (test with a few drops of water), pour in about 2 tablespoons of the batter all at once, tilting pan so batter flows quickly over bottom. Cook until surface looks dry and edge is lightly browned. With a spatula, turn crêpe; cook other side until lightly browned.

3. Repeat with remaining batter, adding oil as needed to prevent sticking. Stack crêpes. If made ahead, place wax paper between crêpes, wrap airtight, and refrigerate for up to 3 days; freeze for longer storage. Bring to room temperature before separating. Makes 16 to 18 crêpes.

Per crêpe: 53 calories (45% calories from fat), 2 g protein, 5 g carbohydrates, 3 g total fat (1 g saturated fat), 40 mg cholesterol , 35 mg sodium

Whole Wheat Crêpes

Prepare **Basic Crêpes** (at left), but substitute ¾ cup **whole wheat flour** (not stone ground) for unbleached flour.

Per crêpe: 50 calories (46% calories from fat), 2 g protein, 5 g carbohydrates, 3 g total fat (1 g saturated fat), 40 mg cholesterol , 35 mg sodium

Sesame Crêpes

Prepare **Basic Crêpes** (at left), but use only ⅔ cup unbleached all-purpose flour and add ¼ cup **sesame seeds.**

Per crêpe: 63 calories (52% calories from fat), 2 g protein, 5 g carbohydrates, 4 g total fat (1 g saturated fat), 40 mg cholesterol , 35 mg sodium

Spinach Crêpes

Preparation time: About 20 minutes
Cooking time: 20 to 25 minutes

| 8 ounces spinach, coarse stems removed |
| 3 large eggs |
| 1 tablespoon salad oil |
| 1 cup unbleached all-purpose flour |
| 1½ cups milk |
| About 2 tablespoons butter or margarine |

1. Rinse spinach well and chop coarsely. Transfer to a food processor or blender. Add eggs and oil; whirl until smooth. Add flour and whirl until blended. Pour in milk and whirl until mixture is well combined, scraping down sides of container as needed.

2. Make crêpes as directed for Basic Crêpes (at left), using butter in place of oil in pan and allowing about 3 tablespoons of the batter for each crêpe.

3. Stack crêpes and store, if desired, as directed for Basic Crêpes. Makes about 16 crêpes.

Per crêpe: 79 calories (47% calories from fat), 3 g protein, 7 g carbohydrates, 4 g total fat (2 g saturated fat), 47 mg cholesterol , 46 mg sodium

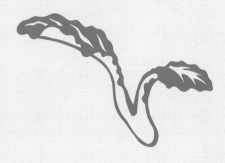

50

Here's a unique way to combine familiar ingredients: spread a salsalike chile filling in rich pastry,
top with cheese, and garnish with avocado, sour cream, and, if desired, sunflower seeds.
The result? Warm-cool Avocado Salad Tart (recipe on facing page).

Avocado Salad Tart

Pictured on facing page

Preparation time: About 25 minutes

Cooking and baking time: About 1¼ hours

●

Though it may seem unconventional, this warm-cool salad pie is delicious as a light lunch or supper.

Press-in Tart Shell (recipe follows)
1 tablespoon salad oil
1 medium-size onion, finely chopped
3 medium-size tomatoes, chopped
1 large can (about 7 oz.) diced green chiles
½ teaspoon ground cumin
1 cup (about 4 oz.) shredded smoked Gouda cheese
1 medium-size avocado
⅓ cup sour cream or plain yogurt
Cilantro sprigs
Salted sunflower seeds (optional)

1. **Prepare** Press-in Tart Shell.

2. **Heat** oil in a wide nonstick frying pan over medium-high heat. Add onion and cook, stirring often, until lightly browned (about 5 minutes). Add tomatoes, chiles, and cumin. Cook, stirring often, until sauce thickens (12 to 15 minutes).

3. **Spoon** sauce into tart shell, spreading evenly. Sprinkle with cheese. Bake in a 400° oven until cheese is melted (about 8 minutes). Meanwhile, halve, pit, and peel avocado. Cut each half lengthwise into 8 slices.

4. **Arrange** avocado slices over hot tart. Mound sour cream in center; garnish with cilantro. Serve with sunflower seeds, if desired, to add to taste. Makes 4 to 6 servings.

Press-in Tart Shell. In a food processor or bowl, combine 1½ cups **unbleached all-purpose flour** and ½ cup **butter** or margarine, diced. Whirl with on-off bursts or rub with your fingers until coarse crumbs form. Add 1 large **egg;** whirl or stir with a fork until dough clings together. Pat into a ball.

Press dough evenly over bottom and about 1 inch up sides of a 9-inch tart pan with a removable bottom, spring-form pan, or quiche dish. Bake in a 325° oven until golden (about 45 minutes). If made ahead, cover and let stand at room temperature for up to a day.

Per serving: 548 calories (62% calories from fat), 13 g protein, 40 g carbohydrates, 38 g total fat (19 g saturated fat), 125 mg cholesterol, 648 mg sodium

Green Corn Quiche

Preparation time: About 25 minutes

Baking time: 50 to 55 minutes

●

Green chiles contribute verdant color to this creamy pie.

1 cup dehydrated masa flour (corn tortilla flour)
½ cup whole wheat flour
1 teaspoon sugar
1 can (about 17 oz.) cream-style corn
4 large eggs
1 can (about 12 oz.) evaporated milk
1 tablespoon liquid hot pepper seasoning
1 teaspoon chili powder
2 cans (about 4 oz. *each*) diced green chiles
1 can (about 2¼ oz.) sliced ripe olives, drained
½ cup *each* shredded jack cheese and sharp Cheddar cheese
1 cup thinly sliced green onions
Prepared salsa

1. **Combine** masa flour, whole wheat flour, sugar, and corn in a large bowl; mix well. Spread mixture evenly over bottom and pat about 1½ inches up sides of a greased 10-inch spring-form pan.

2. **Bake** in a 425° oven for 10 minutes. Meanwhile, combine eggs and milk in a large bowl; beat until blended. Stir in hot pepper seasoning, chili powder, chiles, olives, jack and Cheddar cheeses, and ½ cup of the onions.

3. **Remove** crust from oven; reduce oven temperature to 375°. Pour egg mixture into crust and bake until filling is set when pan is gently shaken (40 to 45 minutes). Let stand for 10 minutes; remove pan sides. Sprinkle quiche with remaining onions and cut into wedges. Serve with salsa to add to taste. Makes 6 to 8 servings.

Per serving: 357 calories (35% calories from fat), 16 g protein, 44 g carbohydrates, 14 g total fat (5 g saturated fat), 153 mg cholesterol, 726 mg sodium

Gruyère & Mushroom Tarts

Preparation time: About 1 hour

Chilling and rising time: 1½ to 2 hours

Cooking and baking time: About 30 minutes

●

For convenience, you can start these open-face main-dish cheese tarts two days ahead.

    Rich Yeast Pastry (recipe follows)
- **12** ounces medium-size to large mushrooms
- **2** tablespoons butter or margarine
- **½** cup finely chopped onion
- **2** tablespoons chopped parsley
- **2** cups (about 8 oz.) firmly packed shredded Gruyère or Swiss cheese
    Salt and pepper

1. Prepare Rich Yeast Pastry. While it chills, twist off mushroom stems, chop finely, and set aside. Cut caps in half.

2. Heat butter in a wide frying pan over medium-high heat. Add mushroom caps; cook, stirring often, until liquid has evaporated and mushrooms are browned (8 to 10 minutes). Lift out and set aside.

3. Add chopped mushrooms and onion to pan. Cook, stirring often, until onion begins to brown (about 8 minutes). Stir in 1 tablespoon of the parsley.

4. Divide pastry into quarters. Keeping unrolled pastry cold, shape each portion into a flattened ball and roll on a lightly floured board into a 7- to 8-inch circle. Transfer to 2 large greased baking sheets. Turn up a ½-inch rim around edge of pastry; flute or crimp.

5. Sprinkle each pastry shell with cheese and top with mushroom caps and onion mixture. Season to taste with salt and pepper. Cover pans lightly with plastic wrap. (At this point, you may refrigerate for up to a day.)

6. Let tarts rise in a warm place until rims are nearly doubled in size (30 minutes to 1 hour). Bake in a 450° oven until pastry is well browned on bottom (5 to 7 minutes); if using one oven, switch position of baking sheets halfway through baking. Sprinkle with remaining parsley. Makes 4 servings.

Rich Yeast Pastry. In a small pan, warm ½ cup **milk** to 110° over low heat. Remove from heat. Sprinkle 1 package **active dry yeast** over milk and let stand until softened (about 5 minutes). Meanwhile, mix 2 cups **unbleached all-purpose flour** and 2 teaspoons **sugar** in a large bowl. Add ½ cup **butter** or margarine, diced; rub with your fingers until coarse crumbs form. Add yeast mixture and 1 large **egg yolk.** Stir until moistened. Pat into a ball. Place in a greased bowl, cover, and refrigerate until easy to handle (at least 1 hour or up to a day).

Per serving: 800 calories (57% calories from fat), 28 g protein, 58 g carbohydrates, 51 g total fat (30 g saturated fat), 200 mg cholesterol, 517 mg sodium

Scrambled Eggs & Bulgur

Preparation time: About 20 minutes

Cooking time: About 10 minutes

●

This colorful scrambled egg dish makes a filling lunch.

- **2** cups canned vegetable broth
- **1** cup bulgur (cracked wheat)
- **1** tablespoon butter or margarine
- **1** medium-size onion, thinly sliced
- **1** medium-size red or green bell pepper (about 6 oz.), seeded and thinly sliced
- **4** large eggs
- **¼** cup water
    Grated Parmesan cheese

1. Bring broth to a boil in a 1- to 1½-quart pan over high heat. Stir in bulgur. Cover tightly, remove from heat, and let stand until broth is absorbed (5 to 10 minutes). Meanwhile, melt 1 teaspoon of the butter in a wide nonstick frying pan over medium-high heat. Add onion and bell pepper. Cook, stirring often, until onion is lightly browned (6 to 8 minutes). While onion cooks, combine eggs and water in a small bowl; beat until blended.

2. Add remaining 2 teaspoons butter to frying pan; reduce heat to medium-low. Pour in egg mixture and cook, gently lifting edges to let uncooked egg flow underneath, until softly set.

3. Spoon bulgur onto plates and add scrambled eggs. Serve with cheese to add to taste. Makes 4 servings.

Per serving: 248 calories (32% calories from fat), 11 g protein, 33 g carbohydrates, 9 g total fat (3 g saturated fat), 220 mg cholesterol, 606 mg sodium

Spiced Bell Pepper Soufflés

Preparation time: About 30 minutes

Cooking and baking time: About 1 hour

●

Choose squarish peppers that will stand upright as containers for these airy individual soufflés.

    4 **large red, yellow, or green bell peppers (6 to 8 oz. *each*)**

    3 **tablespoons butter or margarine**

    3 **tablespoons minced, seeded fresh jalapeño chiles**

    2 **teaspoons dry oregano**

   ¼ **cup polenta or cornmeal**

    1 **cup milk**

   ¾ **cup shredded jack or Cheddar cheese**

    3 **large eggs, separated**

    1 **large egg white (about 2 tablespoons)**

1. Trim a thin sliver from base of peppers, if necessary, so they sit solidly (do not pierce interior). Cut off tops about ½ inch below bottom of stems; remove seeds. Set peppers upright in a 9-inch-square baking pan; set aside. Trim and discard stems from tops; finely chop tops.

2. Melt butter in a 2- to 3-quart pan over medium-high heat. Add chiles, oregano, and chopped tops. Cook, stirring often, until vegetables are soft (8 to 10 minutes). Add polenta and cook, stirring, for 1 more minute. Remove from heat and gradually stir in milk. Return to heat and bring mixture to a boil, stirring constantly; reduce heat and simmer, stirring often, for 5 minutes.

3. Remove from heat. Add cheese and stir until melted. Stir in egg yolks, one at a time. (At this point, you may cover and refrigerate sauce, egg whites, and peppers for up to a day; to continue, stir sauce over low heat until mixture simmers.)

4. Place egg whites in large bowl of an electric mixer. Beat until they hold firm, moist peaks. Stir about a fourth of the whites into cheese sauce; then gently fold sauce into remaining whites. Pile soufflé mixture into peppers. Bake in a 375° oven until soufflés are puffed and well browned (35 to 40 minutes). Serve immediately. Makes 4 servings.

Per serving: 333 calories (56% calories from fat), 15 g protein, 22 g carbohydrates, 21 g total fat (8 g saturated fat), 210 mg cholesterol, 297 mg sodium

Lean Spinach-Marjoram Soufflé

Preparation time: About 30 minutes

Cooking and baking time: About 30 minutes

●

Fat—but not flavor—has been pared from this Parmesan-flecked spinach soufflé; it uses fewer egg yolks than is customary, and the sauce base is made with nonfat milk and cornstarch.

      Vegetable oil cooking spray

    1 **cup nonfat milk**

 1½ **tablespoons cornstarch**

    1 **tablespoon *each* dry marjoram and instant minced onion**

   ½ **teaspoon pepper**

   ⅛ **teaspoon ground nutmeg**

   ¾ **cup frozen chopped spinach, thawed and squeezed dry**

    2 **large eggs, separated**

   ¼ **cup shredded Parmesan cheese**

    4 **large egg whites (about ½ cup)**

   ¼ **teaspoon cream of tartar**

1. Coat interior of a 1½- to 1¾-quart soufflé or other deep, straight-sided baking dish with cooking spray. Set aside.

2. Stir milk gradually into cornstarch in a 2- to 3-quart pan. Add marjoram, onion, pepper, and nutmeg. Cook over high heat, stirring, until mixture comes to a boil.

3. Transfer to a food processor or blender. Add spinach, egg yolks, and 2 tablespoons of the cheese; whirl until smooth.

4. Combine egg whites and cream of tartar in large bowl of an electric mixer. Beat until whites hold soft peaks. Gently fold spinach mixture into egg whites. Transfer to prepared baking dish and sprinkle with remaining 2 tablespoons cheese. With tip of a knife, draw a circle on soufflé 1 inch from edge.

5. Bake in a 375° oven until soufflé is richly browned and center jiggles only slightly when gently shaken (about 25 minutes). Serve immediately. Makes 4 servings.

Per serving: 128 calories (33% calories from fat), 12 g protein, 9 g carbohydrates, 5 g total fat (2 g saturated fat), 111 mg cholesterol, 242 mg sodium

Mushroom-Cheese Crêpes

Pictured on facing page

Preparation time: About 1 hour

Cooking and baking time: 50 to 55 minutes

•

Here's a classic filling for whole wheat crêpes.

    Béchamel Sauce (recipe follows)
12 Whole Wheat Crêpes (page 49)
 3 tablespoons butter or margarine
 1 pound mushrooms, thinly sliced
 1 shallot or green onion, finely chopped
 1 small clove garlic, minced or pressed
 ¼ teaspoon dry tarragon
 1 tablespoon dry sherry
 ½ cup whipping cream
1½ cups (about 6 oz.) shredded Gruyère or Swiss cheese
    Tomato wedges, parsley sprigs, and chopped parsley (optional)

1. **Prepare** Béchamel Sauce and Whole Wheat Crêpes.

2. **Melt** butter in a wide frying pan over medium-high heat. Add mushrooms, shallot, and garlic. Cook, stirring often, until mushrooms are lightly browned and liquid has evaporated (8 to 10 minutes). Lift out about ¼ cup of the mushrooms; set aside for garnish.

3. **Sprinkle** tarragon over mixture in pan. Remove from heat and stir in sherry and half the Béchamel Sauce.

4. **Spoon** filling down center of each crêpe; roll to enclose. Arrange in a single layer, seam sides down, in a lightly greased shallow 3-quart casserole. (At this point, you may cover and refrigerate crêpes, reserved mushrooms, and sauce for up to a day.)

5. **Add** cream to remaining sauce and cook over medium heat, stirring, until heated through. Pour over crêpes; sprinkle with cheese. Bake in a 425° oven until lightly browned and bubbly (12 to 18 minutes).

6. **Spoon** reserved mushrooms over crêpes. Garnish, if desired, with tomato wedges, parsley sprigs, and chopped parsley. Makes 4 servings.

Béchamel Sauce. Melt ¼ cup **butter** or margarine in a 1½- to 2-quart pan over medium heat. Stir in ¼ cup **unbleached all-purpose flour,** ¼ teaspoon **salt,** and a dash of **ground red pepper** (cayenne). Cook, stirring, until bubbly. Remove from heat and slowly pour in 2 cups **milk,** stirring until blended. Cook, stirring, until sauce bubbles and thickens.

In a medium-size bowl, beat 3 **egg yolks.** Slowly stir in some of the hot sauce; then add egg mixture to sauce and cook over medium heat, stirring, just until sauce thickens (do not boil).

Per serving: 776 calories (68% calories from fat), 30 g protein, 33 g carbohydrates, 59 g total fat (32 g saturated fat), 429 mg cholesterol, 668 mg sodium

Chiles Rellenos Casserole

Preparation time: About 45 minutes

Baking time: 30 to 35 minutes

•

A puffy egg batter topped with cheese bakes over fresh tomatoes, diced green chiles, cheese, and onion.

 5 large pear-shaped (Roma-type) tomatoes
 2 large cans (about 7 oz. *each*) diced green chiles, drained
 4 cups (about 1 lb.) shredded sharp Cheddar cheese
 4 green onions, thinly sliced
2½ cups milk
 9 large eggs
 1 cup unbleached all-purpose flour
 3 cups (about 12 oz.) shredded jack cheese

1. **Cut** each tomato in half crosswise; squeeze out and discard seeds and juice. Chop tomatoes. Spread half each of the chiles, Cheddar cheese, onions, and tomatoes in even layers in a shallow 3-quart casserole. Repeat layers.

2. **Combine** milk, eggs, and flour in a food processor or blender; whirl until smooth. Pour over casserole. Sprinkle with jack cheese.

3. **Bake** in a 350° oven until center jiggles only slightly when gently shaken (30 to 35 minutes). Let stand for 5 to 10 minutes; cut into squares. Makes 12 to 16 servings.

Per serving: 345 calories (60% calories from fat), 21 g protein, 14 g carbohydrates, 23 g total fat (9 g saturated fat), 198 mg cholesterol, 571 mg sodium

*Delectable Mushroom-Cheese Crêpes (recipe on facing page) are made with Whole Wheat Crêpes,
but the filling is equally good with Sesame Crêpes or Spinach Crêpes (recipes on page 49).
Tangy White Bean Salad (recipe on page 117) rounds out the menu.*

55

Red & Yellow Pepper Flat Omelet

Pictured on page 122

Preparation time: About 25 minutes

Cooking time: 20 to 25 minutes

This omelet is served flat rather than folded, the better to display its colorful topping of sautéed vegetables. Offer it with a warm loaf of crusty bread and glasses of crisp Sauvignon Blanc.

> 3 **tablespoons butter or margarine**
> 1 **small onion, finely chopped**
> ½ **cup chopped yellow or green bell pepper**
> 1 **medium-size red bell pepper, seeded and thinly sliced**
> 8 **ounces mushrooms, thinly sliced**
> ¼ **teaspoon dry thyme**
> 10 **large eggs**
> ¼ **cup water**
> ½ **cup fresh basil leaves (optional)**
> **Salt and pepper**

1. Melt 2 tablespoons of the butter in a wide nonstick frying pan over medium-high heat. Add onion, yellow and red bell peppers, mushrooms, and thyme. Cook, stirring often, until juices have evaporated and vegetables begin to brown (12 to 15 minutes). Meanwhile, combine eggs and water in a large bowl; beat until blended.

2. Transfer vegetables to a bowl and keep warm.

3. Melt remaining 1 tablespoon butter in pan. Pour in egg mixture. Cook, gently lifting edges with a wide spatula to let uncooked egg flow underneath, until set but still moist on top (7 to 10 minutes).

4. Sprinkle with basil, if desired. Spoon vegetable mixture onto omelet. Season to taste with salt and pepper. Makes 4 to 6 servings.

Per serving: 231 calories (66% calories from fat), 14 g protein, 6 g carbohydrates, 17 g total fat (7 g saturated fat), 444 mg cholesterol, 199 mg sodium

Joe's Swiss Chard Special

Preparation time: About 25 minutes

Cooking time: About 15 minutes

This updated version of a favorite scrambled egg dish substitutes mushrooms for ground beef and Swiss chard for spinach. It's a speedy brunch or supper entrée.

> 1½ **tablespoons olive oil**
> 1 **large onion, finely chopped**
> 1 **clove garlic, minced or pressed**
> 8 **ounces mushrooms, thinly sliced**
> 6 **large eggs**
> 2 **tablespoons water**
> ¼ **teaspoon dry oregano**
> ⅛ **teaspoon ground nutmeg**
> 4 **cups shredded Swiss chard (coarse stems removed)**
> **Salt and pepper**
> 4 **small Swiss chard leaves, rinsed and patted dry (optional)**
> **Grated Parmesan cheese**

1. Heat oil in a wide frying pan over medium-high heat. Add onion, garlic, and mushrooms. Cook, stirring often, until mushrooms are lightly browned (6 to 8 minutes). Meanwhile, combine eggs, water, oregano, and nutmeg in a large bowl; beat until blended. Set aside.

2. Add shredded chard to onion mixture and continue to cook, stirring often, until chard is limp and bright green (about 3 minutes). Reduce heat to medium-low.

3. Pour in egg mixture. Using a wide spatula, gently stir until eggs are softly set (2 to 3 minutes). Season to taste with salt and pepper.

4. Place a chard leaf, if desired, on each plate. Top with egg mixture. Serve with cheese to add to taste. Makes 4 servings.

Per serving: 194 calories (59% calories from fat), 12 g protein, 9 g carbohydrates, 13 g total fat (3 g saturated fat), 319 mg cholesterol, 175 mg sodium

Zuchizza Casserole

Preparation time: About 30 minutes

Standing time: About 15 minutes

Cooking and baking time: About 35 minutes

●

The "crust" of this pizza-flavored main dish is shredded zucchini baked in an herbed custard.

- 3½ cups (about 1 lb.) shredded zucchini
- 1 teaspoon salt
- 3 large eggs, beaten
- ⅓ cup unbleached all-purpose flour
- 1 teaspoon Italian herb seasoning, or ¼ teaspoon *each* dry basil, dry marjoram, dry oregano, and dry thyme
- 3 cups (about 12 oz.) shredded mozzarella cheese
- 3 tablespoons butter or margarine
- 8 ounces mushrooms, thinly sliced
- 1 can (about 14 oz.) pizza sauce
- ½ cup sliced ripe olives
- 1 cup chopped green bell pepper

1. Mix zucchini and salt in a large bowl; let stand for 15 minutes. Drain, squeezing out as much liquid as possible. Return zucchini to bowl and add eggs, flour, herb seasoning, and ½ cup of the cheese; mix lightly until well combined.

2. Spread mixture in a greased shallow 3-quart casserole. Bake in a 350° oven until center feels set when touched (about 15 minutes). Meanwhile, melt butter in a wide frying pan over medium heat. Add mushrooms and cook, stirring often, until browned (about 10 minutes).

3. Spoon half the pizza sauce over zucchini mixture. Cover with mushrooms and half the olives. Sprinkle with bell pepper and half the remaining cheese. Top with remaining olives, sauce, and cheese.

4. Bake in a 350° oven until bubbly (about 20 minutes). Makes 6 servings.

Per serving: 347 calories (60% calories from fat), 18 g protein, 17 g carbohydrates, 23 g total fat (12 g saturated fat), 166 mg cholesterol, 866 mg sodium

Lightened-up Chiles Rellenos

Preparation time: About 1 hour

Cooking and baking time: 25 to 30 minutes

●

Tofu in the filling, reduced-fat cheeses, and egg whites in place of most of the whole eggs reduce the fat content of this flavorful Mexican-style casserole.

- About 1 pound soft tofu, rinsed
- 2 cans (about 7 oz. *each*) whole green chiles
- 1½ cups (about 6 oz.) shredded reduced-fat or regular jack cheese
- 6 large egg whites (about ¾ cup)
- 2 large eggs
- ⅔ cup nonfat or low-fat milk
- 1 cup unbleached all-purpose flour
- 1 teaspoon baking powder
- 1¼ cups (about 5 oz.) shredded reduced-fat or regular Cheddar cheese
- 1 can (about 15 oz.) marinara sauce
- Sliced ripe olives

1. Mash tofu coarsely. Drain in a colander for at least 10 minutes. Meanwhile, cut a slit down side of each chile.

2. Mix tofu and jack cheese in a bowl. Fill chiles with tofu mixture and arrange in a single layer in a lightly greased shallow 2½- to 3-quart casserole.

3. Combine egg whites and whole eggs in large bowl of an electric mixer. Beat until thick and foamy. Add milk, flour, and baking powder; beat until smooth. Fold in half the Cheddar cheese. Pour egg mixture over chiles; sprinkle with remaining cheese.

4. Bake in a 375° oven until top is golden brown (25 to 30 minutes). Meanwhile, place marinara sauce in a 1- to 1½-quart pan and cook over low heat, stirring occasionally, until heated through.

5. Garnish casserole with olives. Serve with sauce to add to taste. Makes 8 servings.

Per serving: 291 calories (37% calories from fat), 21 g protein, 24 g carbohydrates, 12 g total fat (5 g saturated fat), 81 mg cholesterol, 1,022 mg sodium

58

Colorful vegetables mingle with gossamer angel hair pasta in tempting Paradise Pasta with Pine Nuts (recipe on page 61). Alongside, offer thin and crunchy Chili-Cornmeal Breadsticks (recipe on page 142).

PASTA, GRAINS & LEGUMES

Fettuccine Cambozola

Linguine with Fresh Tomato Sauce

Paradise Pasta with Pine Nuts

Pasta with Roasted Garlic & Peppers

Farfalle with Fresh Tomatoes & Basil

Stuffed Manicotti alla Fiorentina

Black Bean Lasagne

Green Pasta with Spinach Pesto

Linguine with Lentils

Artichoke Pesto Pasta

Wolf Creek Macaroni & Cheese

Broccoli-stuffed Pasta Shells

Rice-stuffed Zucchini

Green-speckled Brown Rice

Split Pea Dal, Brown Rice & Broccoli

Barley, Carrot & Onion Pilaf

Wild Mushroom Polenta Boards

Mexican Polenta

Lentil & Golden Squash Pot Pie

Hominy, Cheese & Chile Casserole

Oven Polenta with Red Peppers & Mushrooms

Minted Wild Rice Pilaf with Feta & Olives

Bulgur Mexicana

Black Bean & Fresh Corn Tacos

Pinto Bean Cakes with Salsa

Tabbouleh Burritos

Black Bean Chilaquiles

Four Quarters Bean & Barley Stew

Curried Garbanzos

Tofu Indonesian-style

Fettuccine Cambozola

Preparation time: About 10 minutes

Cooking time: About 10 minutes

●

Creamy blue-veined cheese forms a distinctive sauce as it melts over pasta strands. Accompany this speedy dish with breadsticks and a crisp green salad with marinated artichoke hearts.

- 1 **package (about 8 ounces) fresh fettuccine**
- 1 **package (about 10 oz.) frozen peas**
- 1 **cup (about 6 oz.) diced cambozola or Gorgonzola cheese**
  Freshly ground pepper

1. Bring 3 quarts water to a boil in a 5- to 6-quart pan. Add pasta and cook just until tender to bite (3 to 4 minutes); or cook according to package directions. Stir in peas. Drain well.

2. Return pasta and peas to pan over low heat. Add cheese and 2 tablespoons hot water. Mix lightly until pasta is well coated with melted cheese (2 to 3 minutes).

3. Season to taste with pepper. Makes 2 to 4 servings.

Per serving: 492 calories (33% calories from fat), 27 g protein, 56 g carbohydrates, 18 g total fat (11 g saturated fat), 131 mg cholesterol, 918 mg sodium

Linguine with Fresh Tomato Sauce

Low-Fat

Preparation time: About 30 minutes

Cooking time: About 30 minutes

●

The sauce for this pasta dish, which can be served either hot or at room temperature, showcases such summer produce as flavor-packed Roma-type tomatoes, golden bell peppers, and fresh basil.

- 2 **cloves garlic, minced or pressed**
- 3 **pounds pear-shaped (Roma-type) tomatoes, coarsely chopped**
- 2 **large yellow bell peppers (about 1 lb. *total*), seeded and finely chopped**
- 1 **cup lightly packed slivered fresh basil or ¼ cup dry basil**
- 12 **ounces dry or fresh linguine**
  Salt and pepper
  Basil sprigs (optional)
  Grated Parmesan cheese

1. Combine garlic, two-thirds each of the tomatoes and bell peppers, and half the slivered basil in a 3- to 4-quart pan. Cook over medium heat, stirring often, until tomatoes begin to fall apart (about 20 minutes). If serving hot, keep warm. If serving at room temperature, let stand for up to 6 hours.

2. Bring 3 quarts water to a boil in a 5- to 6-quart pan. Add pasta and cook just until tender to bite (about 8 minutes); or cook according to package directions. Drain well. If serving hot, place pasta in a warm wide bowl. If serving at room temperature, immerse in cold water until cool; drain well and place in a bowl.

3. Stir remaining tomatoes, peppers, and slivered basil into tomato sauce.

4. Spoon hot sauce over hot pasta or cool sauce over cool pasta; mix lightly. Season to taste with salt and pepper. Garnish with basil sprigs, if desired. Serve with cheese to add to taste. Makes 4 to 6 servings.

Per serving: 341 calories (6% calories from fat), 12 g protein, 71 g carbohydrates, 2 g total fat (0.3 g saturated fat), 0 mg cholesterol, 32 mg sodium

Paradise Pasta with Pine Nuts

Pictured on page 58

Preparation time: About 25 minutes

Cooking time: About 30 minutes

●

A medley of fresh vegetables goes into the sauce for this angel hair pasta dish with toasted pine nuts.

⅓   **cup pine nuts**

1   **tablespoon salad oil**

1   **pound mushrooms, thinly sliced**

1   **medium-size onion, finely chopped**

4   **cloves garlic, minced or pressed**

1   **teaspoon *each* dry basil and dry oregano**

4   **cups broccoli flowerets**

1   **small red bell pepper, seeded and thinly sliced**

1½   **cups canned vegetable broth**

8   **ounces dry angel hair pasta**

½   **cup grated Parmesan cheese**
     Salt and pepper

1. Toast pine nuts in a wide frying pan over medium heat, stirring often, until golden (6 to 8 minutes). Remove from pan and set aside.

2. Heat oil in same pan over high heat. Add mushrooms, onion, garlic, basil, and oregano. Cover and cook, stirring often, until liquid has accumulated (3 to 5 minutes). Uncover and continue to cook, stirring often, until vegetables are lightly browned (about 8 more minutes).

3. Add broccoli, bell pepper, and broth to onion mixture. Bring to a boil; cover and cook until broccoli is just tender when pierced (about 5 minutes). Meanwhile, bring 2½ quarts water to a boil in a 4- to 5-quart pan. Add pasta and cook just until tender to bite (about 3 minutes); or cook according to package directions. Drain well and place in a warm wide bowl.

4. Spoon vegetable sauce over pasta. Sprinkle with pine nuts and cheese. Season to taste with salt and pepper. Makes 4 servings.

Per serving: 441 calories (28% calories from fat), 22 g protein, 62 g carbohydrates, 15 g total fat (3 g saturated fat), 8 mg cholesterol, 607 mg sodium

Pasta with Roasted Garlic & Peppers

Preparation time: About 20 minutes

Baking and cooking time: About 1¼ hours

●

Roast bell peppers, onions, and a whole head of garlic to make the luscious sauce for this ample pasta dish.

1   **large head garlic, unpeeled**

2   **medium-size onions, sliced**

2   **large red or yellow bell peppers (about 1¼ lbs. *total*), seeded and sliced**

2   **tablespoons olive oil**

¼   **cup balsamic or red wine vinegar**

1   **tablespoon Dijon mustard**

1   **teaspoon dry oregano**

⅛   **teaspoon fennel seeds, coarsely crushed**

1   **pound dry penne or other tubular pasta**

¼   **cup coarsely chopped Italian parsley**
     Grated Parmesan cheese (optional)

1. Place whole garlic, onions, and bell peppers in a 9- by 13-inch baking pan; drizzle with oil. Bake in a 425° oven, stirring several times, until vegetables are soft and edges are dark brown (about 1 hour). Keep warm.

2. Remove garlic and cut in half crosswise; squeeze cloves into a medium-size bowl. Stir in vinegar, mustard, oregano, and fennel. Set aside.

3. Bring 4 quarts water to a boil in a 6- to 8-quart pan. Add pasta and cook just until tender to bite (8 to 10 minutes); or cook according to package directions. Drain well and place in a warm wide bowl.

4. Add parsley, onion mixture, and garlic mixture to pasta; mix well. Serve with cheese to add to taste, if desired. Makes 6 servings.

Per serving: 383 calories (14% calories from fat), 12 g protein, 70 g carbohydrates, 6 g total fat (1 g saturated fat), 0 mg cholesterol, 86 mg sodium

Farfalle with Fresh Tomatoes & Basil

Pictured on facing page

Preparation time: About 10 minutes

Cooking time: About 10 minutes

●

Typical of the simple goodness of Italian food, this dish can be assembled in minutes, but it's full of lasting flavor. Use farfalle (butterflies), also known as bow-tie pasta, or another whimsical shape.

- 12 ounces farfalle or other dry pasta
- 1 tablespoon olive oil
- 2 cloves garlic, minced or pressed
- 1 pound pear-shaped (Roma-type) tomatoes, coarsely chopped
- 1 cup firmly packed fresh basil, torn into pieces
     Coarsely ground pepper
     Grated Parmesan cheese

1. Bring 4 quarts water to a boil in a 6- to 8-quart pan. Add pasta and cook just until tender to bite (7 to 9 minutes); or cook according to package directions. Meanwhile, heat oil in a wide frying pan over medium heat. Add garlic and cook, stirring, for 1 minute. Add tomatoes and cook, stirring, just until tomatoes begin to soften (about 3 more minutes). Remove from heat.

2. Drain pasta and place in a warm wide bowl or on a deep platter. Add tomato mixture and basil; mix well.

3. Season to taste with pepper. Serve with cheese to add to taste. Makes 4 servings.

Per serving: 384 calories (12% calories from fat), 13 g protein, 72 g carbohydrates, 5 g total fat (1 g saturated fat), 0 mg cholesterol, 18 mg sodium

Stuffed Manicotti alla Fiorentina

Preparation time: About 45 minutes

Cooking and baking time: About 1¼ hours

●

In this rendition of the Italian specialty, pasta shells are stuffed with a spinach, ricotta, and feta filling and then baked in a convenient prepared pasta sauce.

- 2 tablespoons olive oil
- 1 large onion, finely chopped
- 1 medium-size red bell pepper (about 6 oz.), seeded and finely chopped
- 8 ounces spinach, coarse stems removed
- ¾ cup lightly packed crumbled feta cheese
- 1 cup ricotta cheese
     Freshly ground pepper
- 1 jar (about 30 oz.) Italian-style pasta sauce
- 1 package (about 8 oz.) large dry manicotti
- 1 large tomato (8 to 10 oz.), seeded and chopped
- 3 tablespoons grated Parmesan cheese

1. Heat oil in a wide frying pan over medium heat. Add onion and bell pepper. Cook, stirring often, until vegetables are soft but not browned (about 10 minutes). Let cool. Meanwhile, chop spinach finely.

2. Combine spinach, feta, ricotta, and onion mixture in a large bowl; mix well. Season to taste with pepper.

3. Spoon half the pasta sauce into a shallow 3-quart casserole. Divide spinach mixture into as many portions as there are manicotti. One at a time, rinse manicotti with cold water, shake off excess, and push spinach mixture into center of pasta tube with your fingers. Arrange in a single layer in sauce; spoon remaining sauce over pasta.

4. Cover and bake in a 400° oven for 45 minutes; uncover and continue to bake until pasta is tender when pierced (10 to 15 more minutes). Let stand for about 5 minutes.

5. Sprinkle with tomato and Parmesan. Makes 6 servings.

Per serving: 434 calories (40% calories from fat), 17 g protein, 51 g carbohydrates, 20 g total fat (8 g saturated fat), 38 mg cholesterol, 1,190 mg sodium

*Low in fat and quick to assemble, this summertime menu features Farfalle with Fresh Tomatoes &
Basil (recipe on facing page), a selection of fresh fruit, and tall glasses of cool lemonade.*

Cooking Legumes

Low in cost, high in nutrition, and rich in good, earthy flavors, legumes are one of the best food bargains going. To begin with, they pack in a powerhouse of protein — a navy bean, for example, is a full 20 percent protein. Legumes also contain plenty of iron, calcium, potassium, and B vitamins. They're high in fiber, low in sodium, and devoid of cholesterol.

Ideal a food as they may sound, legumes do have a few minor drawbacks. Some people find them hard to digest at first, though adequate soaking and cooking usually help solve that problem. The long soaking-cooking time is another drawback, but you can always speed things up by using the quick-soaking method described at right. Lentils and split peas are the fastest of all legumes to prepare and require no soaking at all.

SOAKING LEGUMES

Before soaking, rinse and sort through legumes, discarding any debris.

• **Quick soaking:** For each pound dry legumes, bring 2 quarts **water** to a boil. Add washed and sorted **legumes** and boil for 2 minutes. Remove from heat, cover, and let stand for 1 hour. Drain and rinse, discarding water.

• **Overnight soaking:** For each pound dry legumes, dissolve 2 teaspoons **salt** in 1½ quarts **water.** Add washed and sorted **legumes;** soak until next day. Drain and rinse, discarding water.

COOKING LEGUMES

Cooking times given on packaged legumes will vary and may differ from the times listed here. Always test for doneness after the minimum suggested cooking time; legumes should be tender to bite.

For each pound dry legumes (weight before soaking), dissolve 2 teaspoons **salt** in 1½ quarts **water;** bring to a boil. Add soaked **legumes** and boil gently, partially covered, until tender (individual cooking times are listed in chart below). Add more water, if needed, to keep legumes submerged. Drain cooked legumes; if desired, season to taste with **salt.** Each pound dry legumes makes 6 to 7 cups cooked legumes.

A GUIDE TO LEGUMES

NAME	DESCRIPTION	SOAKING	COOKING TIME
Black beans	Robust flavor; popular in Caribbean, Central American and South American cooking.	Yes	1–1½ hours
Black-eyed peas	Smooth texture, pealike flavor; good mixed with other vegetables.	Yes	About 1 hour
Garbanzo beans (chick-peas, ceci beans)	Firm texture, nutlike flavor; popular in Middle Eastern and African cooking. Good in minestrone, salads.	Yes	2–2½ hours
Great Northern beans (white beans)	Mild flavor; good in soups or combined with other vegetables.	Yes	1–1½ hours
Kidney beans	Firm texture, hearty flavor. Hold shape well in chilis, casseroles.	Yes	1–1½ hours
Lentils	Mild flavor blends well with many foods and spices. Popular in Middle Eastern, Indian, and European cooking.	No	25–30 minutes
Lima, baby	Mild flavor; use like other white beans in soups, casseroles.	Yes	¾–1¼ hours
Pink, pinto & red beans	Hearty flavor; good in soups, casseroles, barbecue-style beans. Popular in Mexican cooking.	Yes	1¼–1½ hours
Soybeans	Strong flavor; ancient crop of Asia.	Yes*	3–3½ hours
Split peas, green & yellow	Earthy flavor; good in soups, side dishes.	No	35–45 minutes
White beans, small (navy beans)	Mild flavor. Hold shape well; classic for baked beans.	Yes	About 1 hour

* Soak soybeans overnight in the refrigerator.

Black Bean Lasagne

Preparation time: About 45 minutes

Cooking and baking time: About 2 hours

●

Because it serves a crowd and can be made up to a day ahead, lasagne is ideal for a party or for the family. Black beans are featured in this unusual version of a longtime favorite.

- 3 pounds pear-shaped (Roma-type) tomatoes, halved lengthwise
- 1 tablespoon olive oil or salad oil
- 2 cloves garlic, minced or pressed
- ½ cup firmly packed cilantro
- 10 dry lasagne noodles (about 5 oz. *total*)
- 4 cups cooked black beans (facing page) or 2 cans black beans (about 15 oz. *each*), drained and rinsed
- ¼ cup canned vegetable broth
- 1 teaspoon ground cumin
- ½ teaspoon chili powder
- 2 cups part-skim ricotta cheese
- ½ teaspoon salt
- 3 cups (about 12 oz.) shredded jack cheese

1. Arrange tomatoes, cut sides up, in a shallow 10- by 15-inch baking pan. Sprinkle with oil and garlic. Bake in a 425° oven until well browned (about 1¼ hours). Set aside until cool enough to handle.

2. Remove tomato skins. Place tomatoes in a colander and press lightly to drain liquid. Combine with cilantro in a food processor or blender; whirl until smooth. Set aside.

3. Bring 3 quarts water to a boil in a 5- to 6-quart pan. Add lasagne and cook just until tender to bite (about 8 minutes); or cook according to package directions. Drain; immediately immerse in cold water. Set aside.

4. Combine beans, broth, cumin, and chili powder in a large bowl. Using a potato masher or back of a large spoon, coarsely mash beans. In another bowl, mix ricotta, salt, and 2½ cups of the jack cheese.

5. Drain lasagne and pat dry. Arrange 5 of the noodles, overlapping slightly, in a lightly greased shallow 3-quart casserole. Layer with half each of the beans, cheese mixture, and tomato sauce. Repeat, using remaining lasagne, beans, cheese mixture, and sauce. Sprinkle with remaining jack cheese. (At this point, you may cover and refrigerate for up to a day.)

6. Bake, uncovered, in a 375° oven until top is browned and casserole is bubbly (about 40 minutes; 45 to 50 minutes if cold). Let stand for 10 minutes before serving. Makes 8 servings.

Per serving: 479 calories (38% calories from fat), 29 g protein, 46 g carbohydrates, 21 g total fat (3 g saturated fat), 56 mg cholesterol, 522 mg sodium

Green Pasta with Spinach Pesto

Preparation time: About 25 minutes

Cooking time: About 10 minutes

●

Here's a pasta entrée with a rousing contrast of crunchy and smooth, hot and cold—steaming green noodles enhanced by raw vegetables.

- 10 ounces spinach, coarse stems removed
  Spinach Pesto (recipe follows)
- 10 ounces dry spinach noodles
- ½ cup finely chopped red onion
- 1 cup radishes, thinly sliced
  Salt and pepper
  Grated Parmesan cheese

1. Shred spinach thinly. Lightly pack enough spinach into a cup measure to make 1 cup. Prepare Spinach Pesto, using the 1 cup spinach; set remaining spinach aside.

2. Bring 3 quarts water to a boil in a 5- to 6-quart pan. Add noodles and cook just until tender to bite (8 to 10 minutes); or cook according to package directions. Drain well and place in a wide bowl.

3. Pour Spinach Pesto over noodles. Sprinkle with onion, radishes, and remaining shredded spinach. Mix lightly. Season to taste with salt and pepper. Serve with cheese to add to taste. Makes 4 servings.

Spinach Pesto. In a food processor or blender, combine 1 clove **garlic**, the 1 cup **spinach**, ¼ cup **pine nuts**, 1 cup (about 5 oz.) grated **Romano cheese**, 1 cup **plain yogurt**, and ¼ cup **olive oil** or salad oil. Whirl until smooth.

Per serving: 635 calories (44% calories from fat), 29 g protein, 61 g carbohydrates, 32 g total fat (4 g saturated fat), 108 mg cholesterol, 566 mg sodium

Toss steaming-hot pasta with a tempting sauce of Swiss chard, lentils, and Neufchâtel cheese
to create hearty Linguine with Lentils (recipe on facing page), served with basil-scented tomato slices
and whole grain bread.

Linguine with Lentils

Pictured on facing page

Preparation time: About 15 minutes

Cooking time: About 55 minutes

For a satisfying main dish, try combining pasta, chard, and lentils, along with creamy Neufchâtel cheese.

3 cups homemade (page 33) or canned vegetable broth
1 cup lentils, rinsed and drained
1 teaspoon cumin seeds
1 pound Swiss chard, coarse stems removed
2 tablespoons olive oil
1 large onion, chopped
2 cloves garlic, minced or pressed
½ teaspoon crushed red pepper flakes
12 ounces dry linguine
6 ounces Neufchâtel cheese, diced
   Salt and pepper

1. **Bring** 2 cups of the broth to a boil in a 5- to 6-quart pan over high heat. Add lentils and cumin. Reduce heat, cover, and simmer until lentils are tender to bite (about 30 minutes). Drain, if necessary; transfer to a bowl. Set aside.

2. **Cut** chard stems and leaves crosswise into ¼-inch strips, keeping stems and leaves separate.

3. **Combine** chard stems, oil, onion, garlic, and red pepper flakes in pan. Cook over medium heat, stirring often, until onion is lightly browned (about 15 minutes). Add chard leaves; cook, stirring, until limp (about 3 minutes). Add lentils and remaining 1 cup broth; cook just until hot (about 3 more minutes). Set aside and keep warm.

4. **Bring** 3 quarts water to a boil in another 5- to 6-quart pan. Add pasta and cook just until tender to bite (about 7 minutes); or cook according to package directions. Drain well and place in a warm wide bowl.

5. **Add** lentil mixture and cheese to pasta; mix lightly. Season to taste with salt and pepper. Makes 6 servings.

Per serving: 470 calories (25% calories from fat), 21 g protein, 69 g carbohydrates, 13 g total fat (5 g saturated fat), 22 mg cholesterol, 777 mg sodium

Artichoke Pesto Pasta

Preparation time: About 15 minutes

Cooking time: 15 to 20 minutes

Creamy artichoke pesto and toasted pine nuts distinguish this fettuccine dish.

½ cup pine nuts
1 can (about 10 oz.) artichoke hearts in water, drained, or 1½ cups cooked artichoke hearts
½ cup grated Parmesan cheese
1 small package (about 3 oz.) cream cheese
¼ cup finely chopped onion
1 tablespoon Dijon mustard
1 clove garlic, minced or pressed
⅛ teaspoon ground nutmeg
   About 1 cup canned vegetable broth
12 ounces dry fettuccine
¼ cup finely chopped parsley
¼ teaspoon crushed red pepper flakes

1. **Toast** pine nuts in a medium-size frying pan over medium heat, stirring often, until golden (about 8 minutes). Remove from pan and set aside.

2. **Combine** artichokes, Parmesan, cream cheese, onion, mustard, garlic, and nutmeg in a food processor or blender. Add ½ cup of the broth (if using fresh artichokes, increase broth to ¾ cup). Whirl until smooth. Set aside.

3. **Bring** 4 quarts water to a boil in a 6- to 8-quart pan. Add fettuccine and cook just until tender to bite (about 8 minutes); or cook according to package directions. Drain well.

4. **Return** pasta to pan over medium heat; at once add ¼ cup more broth. Using 2 forks, lift and turn pasta lightly until broth is hot (about 30 seconds). Place in a warm wide bowl.

5. **Pour** artichoke mixture over pasta. Sprinkle with pine nuts, parsley, and red pepper flakes. Mix lightly. Makes 6 to 8 servings.

Per serving: 333 calories (36% calories from fat), 14 g protein, 41 g carbohydrates, 14 g total fat (36 g saturated fat), 64 mg cholesterol, 382 mg sodium

Wolf Creek Macaroni & Cheese

Preparation time: About 30 minutes

Cooking time: About 15 minutes

●

Macaroni and cheese with vegetables? Why not? This quick and easy adaptation from Oregon bathes vegetables and tender macaroni in a smooth cheese sauce.

1 tablespoon butter or margarine

1 medium-size onion, finely chopped

¼ cup unbleached all-purpose flour

1 cup *each* milk and canned vegetable broth

3 cups (about 12 oz.) shredded sharp Cheddar cheese

1 tablespoon Dijon mustard

3 large carrots (about 12 oz. *total*), thinly sliced

4 cups broccoli flowerets

2 cups cauliflowerets

1½ cups dry elbow macaroni

Salt and pepper

Paprika

1. Melt butter in a 2- to 3-quart pan over medium-high heat. Add onion and cook, stirring often, until soft but not browned (about 5 minutes). Stir in flour; remove from heat and smoothly blend in milk and broth.

2. Return to high heat and cook, stirring, until mixture comes to a boil. Reduce heat to low, add cheese and mustard, and cook, stirring, until cheese is melted. Keep sauce warm.

3. Bring 3 quarts water to a boil in a 6- to 8-quart pan over high heat. Add carrots, broccoli, cauliflower, and macaroni. Cook until vegetables are just tender when pierced and macaroni is just tender to bite (about 7 minutes). Drain well.

4. Pour pasta mixture into a warm wide bowl; lightly mix in cheese sauce. Season to taste with salt and pepper. Dust with paprika. Makes 8 to 10 servings.

Per serving: 305 calories (45% calories from fat), 16 g protein, 27 g carbohydrates, 15 g total fat (9 g saturated fat), 47 mg cholesterol, 455 mg sodium

Broccoli-stuffed Pasta Shells

Pictured on page 2

Preparation time: About 45 minutes

Cooking and baking time: About 2 hours

●

For make-ahead convenience, prepare the rich tomato sauce and oversize pasta shells the day before you want to serve them.

Tomato-Mushroom Sauce (recipe follows)

2 tablespoons olive oil

1 medium-size onion, finely chopped

1 clove garlic, minced or pressed

½ teaspoon dry oregano

1 package (about 10 oz.) frozen chopped broccoli, thawed and drained

2 large eggs

2 cups part-skim ricotta cheese

2 tablespoons chopped parsley

½ teaspoon salt

⅛ teaspoon ground nutmeg

¾ cup grated Parmesan cheese

30 to 36 jumbo-size seashell-shaped pasta (about 10 oz. *total*)

1. Prepare Tomato-Mushroom Sauce. Meanwhile, heat oil in a medium-size frying pan over medium heat. Add onion, garlic, and oregano. Cook, stirring often, until onion is soft but not browned (about 5 minutes). Remove from heat and stir in broccoli.

2. Blend eggs, ricotta, parsley, salt, nutmeg, and ½ cup of the Parmesan in a large bowl. Stir in broccoli mixture. Set aside.

3. Cook pasta according to package directions until almost tender (8 to 10 minutes; shells may break if overcooked). Drain, rinse with cold water, and drain again.

4. Spoon half the Tomato-Mushroom Sauce into a shallow 3-quart casserole. Fill shells with ricotta mixture. Arrange in a single layer, cheese sides up, in sauce. Drizzle with remaining sauce and sprinkle with remaining ¼ cup Parmesan. (At this point, you may cover and refrigerate for up to a day.)

5. Cover tightly with foil and bake in a 350° oven until shells are tender to bite and filling is heated through (about 45 minutes; about 1 hour if cold). Makes 6 servings.

Tomato-Mushroom Sauce. Place ⅓ cup Italian or domestic **dried mushrooms** in a small bowl; pour in 1 cup boiling **water.** Let stand for about 30 minutes. Meanwhile, heat 2 tablespoons **olive oil** in a 2-quart pan over medium heat. Add 1 medium-size **onion,** finely chopped; 1 clove **garlic,** minced or pressed; ⅛ teaspoon **crushed red pepper flakes;** and 1 teaspoon **Italian herb seasoning** or ¼ teaspoon *each* dry basil, dry marjoram, dry oregano, and dry thyme. Cook, stirring often, until onion is soft but not browned (5 to 7 minutes).

Mix in 1 can (about 14½ oz.) **pear-shaped (Roma-type) tomatoes** (cut up) and their liquid and 1 large can (about 15 oz.) **tomato sauce.** Drain mushrooms, reserving ⅓ cup of the soaking liquid. Chop mushrooms and add to sauce with the ⅓ cup liquid. Bring to a boil; reduce heat, cover, and simmer for 45 minutes.

Per serving: 503 calories (38% calories from fat), 25 g protein, 54 g carbohydrates, 21 g total fat (8 g saturated fat), 104 mg cholesterol, 1,052 mg sodium

Rice-stuffed Zucchini

Preparation time: About 25 minutes

Cooking and baking time: About 35 minutes

●

Zucchini shells cradle a savory blend of chopped zucchini, brown rice, green onions, and Swiss cheese.

 4 **medium-size zucchini** (*each* **4 to 5 inches long**)
 1 **tablespoon butter or margarine**
 6 **green onions, finely chopped**
 1 **cup cooked brown rice (page 73)**
 ½ **cup shredded Swiss cheese**
 1 **large egg**
 ¼ **cup seasoned dry bread crumbs**

1. Trim and discard ends of zucchini; cut each in half lengthwise. With a small knife or spoon, scoop out centers, leaving a shell ¼ inch thick. Finely chop centers.

2. Melt 2 teaspoons of the butter in a medium-size frying pan over medium-high heat. Add chopped zucchini and onions. Cook, stirring often, until zucchini is lightly browned (8 to 10 minutes).

3. Transfer zucchini mixture to a bowl. Add rice and cheese; mix lightly. Stir in egg. Mound filling in zucchini

shells. Arrange in a single layer in a shallow 2½- to 3-quart casserole. Cover tightly with foil.

4. Bake in a 400° oven until shells are tender when pierced (about 20 minutes). Meanwhile, rinse and dry frying pan. Melt remaining butter in pan over medium heat; mix in bread crumbs. Sprinkle crumb mixture over baked zucchini.

5. Broil 4 to 6 inches below heat until crumbs are browned (1 to 2 minutes). Makes 4 servings.

Per serving: 212 calories (37% calories from fat), 10 g protein, 24 g carbohydrates, 9 g total fat (5 g saturated fat), 74 mg cholesterol, 322 mg sodium

Green-speckled Brown Rice

Preparation time: About 15 minutes

Cooking time: About 55 minutes

●

Creamy like a risotto, brown rice generously flecked with parsley goes well with grilled vegetables and a leafy salad.

 2 **tablespoons butter or margarine**
 1 **medium-size onion, finely chopped**
 1 **small green bell pepper, seeded and chopped**
 2 **cloves garlic, minced or pressed**
 ¾ **cup short-grain brown rice**
 1 **can (about 14½ oz.) vegetable broth**
 1 **small package (about 3 oz.) cream cheese, cut into ½-inch cubes**
 ¾ **cup chopped parsley**

1. Melt butter in a 2-quart pan over medium-high heat. Add onion, bell pepper, and garlic. Cook, stirring occasionally, until onion is soft but not browned (5 to 7 minutes). Add rice and continue to cook, stirring often, for 2 more minutes.

2. Pour in broth, stirring to free any particles clinging to pan. Bring to a boil; reduce heat, cover, and simmer until rice is tender to bite and liquid is absorbed (40 to 45 minutes).

3. Stir in cheese and parsley. Cover and let stand for about 2 minutes before serving. Makes 4 servings.

Per serving: 281 calories (47% calories from fat), 5 g protein, 33 g carbohydrates, 15 g total fat (8 g saturated fat), 39 mg cholesterol, 588 mg sodium

Split Pea Dal, Brown Rice & Broccoli

Pictured on facing page

Preparation time: About 45 minutes

Cooking time: About 2¼ hours

Indian flavors permeate this hearty vegetable stew. Serve it as you would a curry, with such condiments as yogurt, lime, chiles, and cilantro.

> About 5½ cups homemade (page 33) or canned vegetable broth
> 2 large onions, finely chopped
> 2 large carrots (about 8 oz. *total*), diced
> 2 tablespoons minced fresh ginger
> 2 large cloves garlic, minced or pressed
> 1 cup yellow split peas, rinsed and drained
> 2 teaspoons *each* ground turmeric and chili powder
> 1 large can (about 28 oz.) crushed tomatoes
> 1 pound banana or Hubbard squash, peeled and cut into ¾-inch cubes
> Salt
> About 6 cups hot cooked brown rice (page 73)
> 3 cups hot cooked broccoli flowerets
> ½ cup cilantro
> About 1 cup plain nonfat yogurt
> Lime wedges
> Crushed red pepper flakes

1. Pour 1 cup of the broth into a 6- to 8-quart pan. Add onions, carrots, ginger, and garlic. Cook over high heat, stirring often, until liquid has evaporated and vegetables begin to brown (12 to 15 minutes).

2. Add ⅓ cup more broth, stirring to scrape browned bits free. Continue to cook, stirring often, until mixture browns again (about 4 minutes). Repeat 2 or 3 more times, adding about ⅔ cup more broth and cooking until vegetables are richly browned.

3. Stir in split peas, turmeric, chili powder, tomatoes and their liquid, and remaining broth. Reduce heat, cover, and simmer for 1 hour.

4. Add squash; cover and continue to simmer, stirring often, until squash is tender to bite (40 to 50 more minutes). Season to taste with salt.

5. Spoon rice, broccoli, and split pea mixture onto warm plates. Serve with cilantro, yogurt, lime, and red pepper flakes to add to taste. Makes 6 servings.

Per serving: 493 calories (8% calories from fat), 21 g protein, 97 g carbohydrates, 4 g total fat (1 g saturated fat), 1 mg cholesterol, 1,401 mg sodium

Barley, Carrot & Onion Pilaf

Preparation time: About 15 minutes

Cooking time: About 55 minutes

For an attractive presentation, mound this savory pilaf into acorn squash halves. Bake the squash (it takes about 45 minutes) while the pilaf is simmering.

> 2 tablespoons butter or margarine
> 2 tablespoons salad oil
> 2 large onions, thinly sliced
> 4 ounces small mushrooms, quartered
> 1½ cups pearl barley, rinsed and drained
> 2 medium-size carrots, thinly sliced
> ½ teaspoon dry thyme
> 1 clove garlic, minced or pressed
> 3¼ cups homemade (page 33) or canned vegetable broth
> Salt and pepper
> Chopped parsley

1. Heat butter and oil in a wide frying pan over medium-high heat. Add onions and mushrooms. Cook, stirring often, until lightly browned (8 to 10 minutes).

2. Mix in barley and cook, stirring, until lightly toasted (about 3 minutes).

3. Add carrots, thyme, garlic, and broth. Bring to a boil; reduce heat, cover, and simmer until liquid is absorbed and barley is tender to bite (about 45 minutes).

4. Season to taste with salt and pepper. Transfer to a warm bowl. Sprinkle with parsley. Makes 6 servings.

Per serving: 297 calories (28% calories from fat), 6 g protein, 49 g carbohydrates, 10 g total fat (3 g saturated fat), 10 mg cholesterol, 561 mg sodium

Indian-inspired, protein-rich Split Pea Dal, Brown Rice & Broccoli (recipe on facing page) is served like a curry, with yogurt, cilantro, red pepper flakes, and tart lime wedges to add to taste.

Wild Mushroom Polenta Boards

Preparation time: About 1 hour

Cooking and baking time: About 1 hour

●

An assortment of wild mushrooms tumbles over crunchy golden rounds of baked polenta.

- 1 medium-size head garlic
- 2 tablespoons olive oil or salad oil
   Polenta Boards (recipe follows)
- 8 ounces *each* shiitake, chanterelle, and oyster mushrooms
- 1½ teaspoons *each* dry rosemary and dry sage
- 2 teaspoons cornstarch blended with ¾ cup canned vegetable broth
- 2 tablespoons grated Parmesan cheese

1. Cut garlic head in half crosswise. Pour 1 tablespoon of the oil into a small baking pan. Add garlic, cut sides down. Bake in a 350° oven until cut sides are golden brown (about 45 minutes). Meanwhile, prepare Polenta Boards.

2. Let garlic stand until cool enough to handle. Squeeze cloves into a small bowl; mash. Set aside.

3. Discard stems from shiitake mushrooms; thinly slice shiitake mushroom caps and whole chanterelles.

4. Heat remaining 1 tablespoon oil in a 5- to 6-quart pan over medium-high heat. Add sliced shiitake and chanterelle mushrooms, whole oyster mushrooms, rosemary, and sage. Cover and cook until mushrooms are juicy (about 8 minutes). Uncover and continue to cook, stirring often, until liquid has evaporated and mushrooms are browned (15 to 20 more minutes).

5. Stir in cornstarch mixture and garlic. Bring to a boil, stirring constantly.

6. Place Polenta Boards on a large baking sheet. Spoon mushroom sauce into center of each; sprinkle with cheese. Broil 4 to 6 inches below heat until sizzling (about 2 minutes). Transfer to warm plates. Makes 6 servings.

Polenta Boards. In a food processor or bowl, combine ½ cup **unbleached all-purpose flour**, ½ cup **polenta** or yellow cornmeal, ¼ cup **instant nonfat dry milk,** and 1½ teaspoons **baking powder;** whirl or stir until blended. Add 1 tablespoon **butter** or margarine; whirl or rub with your fingers until coarse crumbs form. Add ⅓ cup **water;** whirl or stir with a fork until dough begins to stick together.

Pat dough into a ball and knead briefly on a lightly floured board until smooth. Divide into 6 equal portions; cover with plastic wrap. On a well-floured board, roll each portion into a 6- to 7-inch round. Arrange, slightly apart, on 2 large baking sheets. Bake in a 350° oven until lightly browned (12 to 14 minutes). If made ahead, let cool; then wrap airtight and store at room temperature for up to a day.

Per serving: 218 calories (32% calories from fat), 8 g protein, 31 g carbohydrates, 8 g total fat (2 g saturated fat), 7 mg cholesterol, 308 mg sodium

Mexican Polenta

Preparation time: About 20 minutes

Cooking time: 25 to 30 minutes

●

Accent this piquant, vegetable-dotted dish with salsa.

- 1 tablespoon salad oil
- 1 small onion, finely chopped
- 2 large fresh Anaheim or New Mexico chiles, seeded and finely chopped
- 1 package (about 10 oz.) frozen corn, thawed
- 1½ cups polenta or yellow cornmeal
- 6 cups homemade (page 33) or canned vegetable broth
- ½ cup chopped cilantro
- ½ cup shredded jack cheese
   About 1 cup purchased salsa

1. Heat oil in a 4- to 5-quart pan over medium-high heat. Add onion and chiles. Cook, stirring often, until onion is soft but not browned (about 5 minutes). Stir in corn and polenta.

2. Stir in broth. Bring to a boil over high heat, stirring often with a long-handled wooden spoon (mixture will spatter). Reduce heat and simmer, stirring often, until polenta tastes creamy (15 to 20 minutes). Stir in cilantro.

3. Spoon into wide bowls. Sprinkle with cheese. Serve with salsa to add to taste. Makes 4 to 6 servings.

Per serving: 320 calories (24% calories from fat), 9 g protein, 54 g carbohydrates, 9 g total fat (0.5 g saturated fat), 10 mg cholesterol, 1,569 mg sodium

Cooking Grains

Grains play many roles in menu planning. You can serve them with steamed or richly sauced vegetables, or simply let them stand on their own.

Here are some guidelines for cooking grains:

• **Yield:** 1 cup uncooked grain will yield about 3 cups cooked grain.

• **Salt:** For each cup uncooked grain, add about ¼ teaspoon salt to the cooking water.

• **Cooking option:** For some grains—bulgur, buckwheat, and, of course, rice—one alternative to simple boiling is to cook the grain like a pilaf. Sauté the dry grain first in butter, margarine, or salad oil (about 1 tablespoon per cup); then, instead of water, add boiling vegetable broth. Cover and simmer until grain is done.

• **Doneness:** The doneness test for grains is like that for pasta: tender to bite. At this point, each grain is tender but has a slightly resilient core.

A MEDLEY OF GRAINS

NAME	DESCRIPTION	HOW TO COOK
Barley	*Pearl variety:* mild, starchy flavor. *Hulled variety:* nutty flavor. Use both in soups, stews, casseroles.	2 parts water to 1 part barley. Bring to a boil; reduce heat, cover, and simmer for 40–45 minutes. Let stand, covered, for 5–10 minutes.
Buckwheat (kasha)	Not a true grain but a member of a herbaceous plant family. Available untoasted or toasted; strong, distinct flavor. Use in casseroles or serve with sauces.	Cook as directed for bulgur, but only for 10–12 minutes. Or, in an ungreased frying pan, mix 2 cups buckwheat and 1 large beaten egg; cook over high heat, stirring, for 2 minutes. Then add boiling broth or water; reduce heat, cover, and simmer for 12–15 minutes.
Bulgur (bulgur wheat)	Wheat berries that have been steamed, dried, and cracked; delicate, nutty flavor. Use in casseroles, whole grain breads, salads.	1½ parts water to 1 part bulgur. Bring to a boil; reduce heat, cover, and simmer for 12–15 minutes. Or see "Cooking option," above.
Millet	Mild, nutty flavor. Use in stuffings, casseroles, whole grain breads; serve with sauces.	2½ parts water to 1 part millet. Bring to a boil; reduce heat, cover, and simmer for 18–20 minutes. Or see "Cooking option," above.
Oats	Rolled, quick-cooking, or groats (steel-cut); mild flavor, creamy texture. Use as a cereal or in baked goods.	1 part boiling water to 1 part *rolled* or *quick-cooking oats* (or use up to 2 parts water for a creamier consistency). Reduce heat, cover, and simmer for 3–10 minutes. Soak 1 part *groats* in 2 parts water for 1 hour. Bring to a boil; reduce heat, cover, and simmer for 25–30 minutes.
Rice, brown	Unpolished, long or short grain; sweet, nutty flavor. Use in soups, stews, casseroles; serve with sauces.	2 parts water to 1 part brown rice. Bring to a boil; reduce heat, cover, and simmer for 35–40 minutes. Let stand, covered, for 5–10 minutes. Or see "Cooking option," above.
Rice, white	Long, medium, or short grain, polished or preprocessed (parboiled to remove surface starch); mild, delicate flavor. Use in soups, salads, casseroles, puddings; serve with sauces.	2 parts water to 1 part white rice. Bring to a boil; reduce heat, cover, and simmer for 15–20 minutes. Let stand, covered, for 5–10 minutes. Or see "Cooking option," above. For preprocessed rice, follow package directions.
Rice, wild	Not a true rice, but a grass seed. Nutty flavor, chewy texture. Use in salads, stuffings; serve with sauces.	Rinse in several changes of cold water. For cooking, use 4 parts water to 1 part wild rice. Bring to a boil; reduce heat, cover, and simmer for 40–45 minutes. If too moist, drain well.
Rye & triticale	Both have earthy flavor; triticale (a wheat-rye hybrid containing more protein than either parent grain) is slightly milder than rye. Use in casseroles and whole grain breads.	3 parts water to 1 part rye or triticale. Bring to a boil; reduce heat, cover, and simmer for 1–1¼ hours. If too dry, add water and continue to cook. If too moist, drain well.
Wheat, cracked	Similar to bulgur, but not steamed before being cracked. Same uses as bulgur.	See directions for bulgur.
Wheat, whole kernels (wheat berries)	Nutty, mild flavor; chewy texture. Use in sauces, casseroles, stews, whole grain breads; serve with sauces.	3 parts water to 1 part whole wheat. Bring to a boil; reduce heat, cover, and simmer for 2 hours. If too dry, add water and continue to cook. If too moist, drain well.

Lentil & Golden Squash Pot Pie (recipe on facing page) makes a handsome dinner dish. Roll the pastry trimmings and cut into leaves, if you like, to decorate the crust.

Lentil & Golden Squash Pot Pie

Pictured on facing page

Preparation time: About 45 minutes

Cooking and baking time: 1¼ to 1½ hours

●

This spicy vegetable medley is baked under a flaky pastry.

- 2 **teaspoons coriander seeds**
- 1 **teaspoon cumin seeds**
- 1 **teaspoon whole cardamom, pods removed**
- 2 **large onions, finely chopped**
- 2 **cloves garlic, minced or pressed**
- 2 **tablespoons minced fresh ginger**
- ½ **teaspoon crushed red pepper flakes**
  About 1¼ cups water
- 1 **package (about 12 oz.) or 2 cups lentils, rinsed and drained**
- 6 **cups homemade (page 33) or canned vegetable broth**
  About 2¾ pounds banana, Hubbard, or butternut squash
  Salt and pepper
  Pastry for a 2-crust 9-inch pie
- 1 **tablespoon beaten egg (optional)**
  Yogurt Sauce (recipe follows)

1. Crush coriander, cumin, and cardamom seeds coarsely with a mortar and pestle (or whirl in a blender until coarsely powdered). Transfer to a 5- to 6-quart pan and add onions, garlic, ginger, red pepper flakes, and ½ cup of the water.

2. Cook over medium-high heat, stirring occasionally, until a brown film forms on pan bottom (10 to 12 minutes). Add ¼ cup more water, stirring to loosen film. Repeat about 2 more times, cooking mixture until dry and then adding water, until vegetables are richly browned.

3. Add lentils and broth. Bring to a boil; reduce heat, cover, and simmer for 10 minutes. Meanwhile, peel and seed squash; cut into ¾-inch cubes (you should have about 2 quarts).

4. Add squash and continue to simmer, covered, until lentils and squash are soft when pressed (15 to 20 minutes). Season to taste with salt and pepper. Pour into

a shallow 3- to 3½-quart casserole. (At this point, you may cool, cover, and refrigerate for up to a day.)

5. Roll pastry on a floured board to match shape of casserole plus 1 inch on all sides. Lay over vegetable mixture. Fold edge under and flute firmly against rim. Brush with beaten egg, if desired. Decoratively slash top.

6. Bake in a 400° oven until crust is browned and filling is bubbly (25 to 30 minutes); if pastry browns too rapidly, drape edge with foil. Meanwhile, prepare Yogurt Sauce.

7. Serve with Yogurt Sauce to add to taste. Makes 8 to 10 servings.

Yogurt Sauce. In a bowl, combine 2 cups **plain nonfat yogurt,** ¼ cup chopped **fresh mint** or 2 tablespoons dry mint, and ¼ cup chopped **cilantro;** stir until blended.

Per serving: 447 calories (29% calories from fat), 18 g protein, 64 g carbohydrates, 15 g total fat (3 g saturated fat), 1 mg cholesterol, 969 mg sodium

Hominy, Cheese & Chile Casserole

Preparation time: About 20 minutes

Baking time: About 20 minutes

●

For a bright finishing touch, garnish this piquant combination with tomatoes and green onions.

- 2 **cans (about 14½ oz. *each*) white or yellow hominy, rinsed, drained, and patted dry**
- 1 **medium-size onion, finely chopped**
- 3 **cups (about 12 oz.) shredded Cheddar cheese**
- 1 **can (about 4 oz.) diced green chiles**
- 1 **medium-size tomato, seeded and diced**
  Sliced green onions

1. Spread half the hominy in a greased shallow 2- to 2½-quart casserole. Sprinkle with half the chopped onion and 1½ cups of the cheese. Evenly spoon in chiles. Layer with remaining hominy, chopped onion, and cheese.

2. Bake, covered, in a 400° oven until bubbly and hot in center (about 20 minutes). Garnish with tomato and green onions. Makes 4 to 6 servings.

Per serving: 409 calories (53% calories from fat), 20 g protein, 28 g carbohydrates, 24 g total fat (15 g saturated fat), 71 mg cholesterol, 908 mg sodium

Oven Polenta with Red Peppers & Mushrooms

Pictured on front cover

Preparation time: About 30 minutes

Cooking and baking time: About 1 hour

Savory polenta bakes side by side with its colorful herbed vegetable topping for an easy and satisfying dinner.

    5   large red bell peppers (2½ to 3 lbs. *total*),
        seeded and cut lengthwise into 1-inch strips
    1   pound large mushrooms, sliced ½ inch thick
    2   cloves garlic, minced or pressed
    2   teaspoons homemade (page 97) or purchased
        herbes de Provence
    ¼   cup olive oil
    5   cups homemade (page 33) or canned
        vegetable broth
    1½ cups polenta or yellow cornmeal
    1   medium-size onion, finely chopped
    3   tablespoons butter or margarine, diced
    2   cups (about 8 oz.) shredded jack cheese
        Freshly ground pepper
        Chopped parsley

1. Combine bell peppers and mushrooms in a shallow 3-quart casserole. In a small bowl, mix garlic, herbes de Provence, and oil; drizzle over vegetable mixture.

2. Bake in a 350° oven, stirring about every 15 minutes, until vegetables are tender when pierced and lightly browned (50 minutes to 1 hour). Meanwhile, combine broth, polenta, onion, and butter in another greased 3-quart casserole. Bake in same oven until liquid is absorbed (40 to 45 minutes).

3. Sprinkle polenta with cheese and spoon on vegetable mixture. Season to taste with pepper. Sprinkle with parsley. Makes 4 to 6 servings.

Per serving: 585 calories (51% calories from fat), 19 g protein, 55 g carbohydrates, 34 g total fat (6 g saturated fat), 58 mg cholesterol, 1,336 mg sodium

Minted Wild Rice Pilaf with Feta & Olives

Preparation time: About 20 minutes

Cooking and baking time: About 1¼ hours

Fresh mint, salty olives, and chunks of feta cheese add lively flavors to this butter-toasted pilaf of wild rice and brown rice.

    ¼   cup butter or margarine
    1   cup brown rice
    1   medium-size onion, finely chopped
    ⅔   cup wild rice, rinsed and drained
    4   cups homemade (page 33) or canned
        vegetable broth
    ⅓   cup finely chopped parsley
    2   teaspoons dry rosemary
    6   ounces feta cheese, cut into ½-inch cubes
    ½   cup pitted, chopped calamata or other
        Greek-style salty olives
    ⅓   cup chopped fresh mint
        Mint sprigs

1. Melt butter in a wide frying pan over medium-high heat. Add brown rice and onion. Cook, stirring often, until rice is lightly toasted and opaque (6 to 8 minutes).

2. Add wild rice, broth, parsley, and rosemary. Bring to a boil; reduce heat, cover, and simmer until wild rice is tender to bite (45 to 55 minutes).

3. Transfer rice mixture to a shallow 2- to 2½-quart casserole. Stir in feta, olives, and chopped mint. Cover tightly with foil.

4. Bake in a 400° oven until bubbly and heated through (about 20 minutes). Garnish with mint sprigs. Makes 4 to 6 servings.

Per serving: 460 calories (46% calories from fat), 12 g protein, 52 g carbohydrates, 24 g total fat (12 g saturated fat), 55 mg cholesterol, 1,763 mg sodium

Bulgur Mexicana
Low-Fat

Preparation time: About 20 minutes

Cooking and baking time: About 25 minutes

●

East meets West in this blend of Middle Eastern bulgur and Mexican ingredients.

> 2 tablespoons salad oil
> 1 large onion, finely chopped
> ¾ cup bulgur
> 2 cans (about 10 oz. *each*) enchilada sauce
> 1 can (about 14½ oz.) Mexican-style stewed tomatoes
> ⅔ cup toasted wheat germ
> 1 package (about 10 oz.) frozen chopped Swiss chard or spinach
> 2 fresh jalapeño chiles, seeded and finely chopped
> ½ teaspoon dry oregano
> 1 cup cooked red kidney beans (page 64) or 1 small can (about 8 oz.) red kidney beans, drained and rinsed
> 6 flour tortillas (about 8-inch diameter)
> Cilantro sprigs
> Purchased salsa
> Plain yogurt

1. Heat oil in a wide frying pan over medium heat. Add onion and bulgur. Cook, stirring often, until onion is soft but not browned (8 to 10 minutes).

2. Stir in enchilada sauce, tomatoes and their liquid, wheat germ, Swiss chard, chiles, oregano, and beans. Cover and cook, stirring several times to break up chard, until liquid is absorbed (10 to 15 minutes). Meanwhile, wrap tortillas in foil and heat in a 350° oven until hot (about 15 minutes). Or, to heat in a microwave oven, wrap tortillas in paper towels and loosely enclose in plastic wrap; microwave on HIGH (100%) until hot (30 to 45 seconds).

3. Transfer bulgur mixture to a warm bowl and garnish with cilantro. Spoon into tortillas. Serve with salsa and yogurt to add to taste. Makes 6 servings.

Per serving: 405 calories (22% calories from fat), 15 g protein, 68 g carbohydrates, 10 g total fat (1 g saturated fat), 0 mg cholesterol, 1,600 mg sodium

Black Bean & Fresh Corn Tacos

Pictured on page 7

Preparation time: About 35 minutes

Cooking and baking time: About 20 minutes

●

Warm flour tortillas envelop a mixture of black beans and fresh corn, topped with melted jack cheese.

> Tomato Salsa (recipe follows)
> Savory Black Beans (recipe follows)
> 2 cups fresh corn kernels
> 1 cup (about 4 oz.) shredded jalapeño jack cheese
> 12 flour tortillas (about 7-inch diameter)
> Thin avocado slices
> Cilantro sprigs

1. Prepare Tomato Salsa and Savory Black Beans.

2. Spoon beans onto a large ovenproof platter, spreading into about a 10-inch oval. Layer with corn and cheese.

3. Bake in a 400° oven until heated through (about 10 minutes). Meanwhile, heat tortillas as directed for Bulgur Mexicana (at left), baking for only 10 minutes.

4. Garnish bean mixture with avocado and cilantro. Spoon into tortillas. Serve with Tomato Salsa to add to taste. Makes 4 to 6 servings.

Tomato Salsa. In a medium-size bowl, combine 1 small **fresh hot chile,** seeded and chopped; 2 medium-size **tomatoes** (about 12 oz. *total*), diced; ⅓ cup chopped **yellow bell pepper** or red bell pepper; 1 tablespoon **lime juice;** and 2 teaspoons chopped **cilantro.** Season to taste with **salt.** If made ahead, cover and let stand for up to 6 hours.

Savory Black Beans. Heat 1½ tablespoons **salad oil** in a wide frying pan over medium heat. Add 1 medium-size **onion,** coarsely chopped, and 1 clove **garlic,** minced or pressed. Cook, stirring often, until onion is soft and lightly browned (8 to 10 minutes). Reserving ½ cup of the liquid, drain and rinse 4 cups **cooked black beans** (page 64) or 2 cans (about 15 oz. *each*) black beans. Add beans to onion mixture with the ½ cup liquid and 1 tablespoon **distilled white vinegar.** Coarsely mash beans with a spoon.

Per serving: 748 calories (26% calories from fat), 30 g protein, 112 g carbohydrates, 23 g total fat (5 g saturated fat), 24 mg cholesterol, 1,047 mg sodium

Pinto Bean Cakes with Salsa

Pictured on facing page

Preparation time: About 15 minutes

Cooking time: About 15 minutes

●

Dollop a favorite prepared salsa—or your own fresh, homemade sauce—over these cornmeal-coated bean cakes.

1½ tablespoons salad oil

1 small onion, finely chopped

¼ cup finely chopped red bell pepper

2 cloves garlic, minced or pressed

1 medium-size fresh jalapeño chile, seeded and finely chopped

4 cups cooked pinto beans (page 64) or 2 cans (about 15 oz. *each*) pinto beans, drained and rinsed

⅛ teaspoon liquid smoke

¼ cup chopped cilantro

½ teaspoon ground cumin

¼ teaspoon pepper

⅓ cup yellow cornmeal

Vegetable oil cooking spray (optional)

½ to 1 cup purchased or homemade salsa

1. **Heat** 1½ teaspoons of the oil in a wide nonstick frying pan over medium heat. Add onion, bell pepper, garlic, and chile. Cook, stirring often, until onion is soft but not browned (about 5 minutes).

2. **Place** beans in a large bowl and mash coarsely with a potato masher. Stir in onion mixture, liquid smoke, cilantro, cumin, and pepper; mix well. If mixture is too soft to shape, refrigerate briefly.

3. **Spread** cornmeal on a sheet of wax paper. Divide bean mixture into 8 portions; shape each into a ½-inch-thick cake. Coat with cornmeal.

4. **Heat** remaining 1 tablespoon oil in frying pan over medium-high heat. Add bean cakes and cook, turning once, until golden brown on both sides (8 to 10 minutes total); if necessary, spray pan with cooking spray to prevent sticking. Serve with salsa to add to taste. Makes 4 servings (2 cakes each).

Per serving: 341 calories (16% calories from fat), 16 g protein, 57 g carbohydrates, 6 g total fat (1 g saturated fat), 0 mg cholesterol, 608 mg sodium

Tabbouleh Burritos

Preparation time: About 30 minutes

Standing time: About 2 hours

Baking time: About 10 minutes

●

Roll tangy, minted bulgur in a warm tortilla and garnish with fresh tomato, sprouts, feta cheese, and yogurt.

1 cup bulgur

1½ cups water

1 fresh Anaheim chile, seeded and finely chopped

¼ cup olive oil or salad oil

3 tablespoons *each* lemon juice, minced green onions, and minced fresh mint

Salt and pepper

8 flour tortillas (about 7-inch diameter) or 4 pita breads (about 6-inch diameter)

Condiments (directions follow)

1. **Combine** bulgur and water in a large bowl; let stand until bulgur is tender to bite (about 2 hours). Drain well.

2. **Return** to bowl and add chile, oil, lemon juice, onions, and mint; mix well. Season to taste with salt and pepper.

3. **Wrap** tortillas in foil and heat in a 350° oven until warm (about 10 minutes). Meanwhile, prepare condiments.

4. **Mound** bulgur on a platter. Spoon into tortillas. Serve with condiments to add to taste. Makes 4 servings.

Condiments. Arrange in separate bowls 1 large firm-ripe **tomato,** chopped; 4 ounces **feta cheese,** cut into ¼-inch cubes; and 1 cup *each* **alfalfa sprouts** and **plain yogurt.**

Per serving: 546 calories (35% calories from fat), 13 g protein, 78 g carbohydrates, 22 g total fat (2 g saturated fat), 0 mg cholesterol, 520 mg sodium

Crunchy cornmeal coats smoky tasting patties made of pinto beans, onion, and bell pepper. Pinto Bean Cakes with Salsa (recipe on facing page) are a smart choice for a quick supper.

Black Bean Chilaquiles

Preparation time: About 30 minutes

Cooking and baking time: About 1 hour

●

This savory Mexican casserole features layers of tortilla chips, black beans, a piquant tomato sauce, and cheese.

- 2 tablespoons salad oil
- 1 large onion, thinly sliced
- 1 medium-size carrot, finely chopped
- 2 cloves garlic, minced or pressed
- ¼ cup slivered almonds
- ½ teaspoon *each* crushed red pepper flakes, ground cumin, ground coriander, and salt
- 1 teaspoon dry oregano
- 1 can (about 14½ oz.) diced tomatoes
- 1 large can (about 15 oz.) tomato sauce
- 1 small can (about 4 oz.) diced green chiles
- ½ cup ripe olive wedges
- 4 cups cooked black beans (page 64) or 2 cans (about 15 oz. *each*) black beans, drained and rinsed
- 6 cups whole tortilla chips
- 3 cups (about 12 oz.) shredded jack cheese
- 1 cup light sour cream
- ⅓ cup crushed tortilla chips
- 1 avocado
  Cilantro sprigs

1. **Heat** oil in a wide frying pan over medium heat. Add onion, carrot, garlic, and almonds. Cook, stirring often, until onion is soft but not browned (8 to 10 minutes). Stir in red pepper flakes, cumin, coriander, salt, oregano, tomatoes and their liquid, tomato sauce, chiles, and olives. Bring to a boil; reduce heat, cover, and simmer for 20 minutes.

2. **Increase** heat to medium, uncover, and boil gently until sauce is slightly thickened (about 10 minutes).

3. **Spoon** about a third of the tomato sauce into a shallow 2½- to 3-quart casserole. Layer with a third of the beans, a third of the whole tortilla chips, and ¾ cup of the cheese. Repeat, making 2 more layers. Cover tightly with foil. (At this point, you may refrigerate for up to a day.)

4. **Bake** in a 350° oven for 45 minutes. Uncover and spread evenly with sour cream; sprinkle with remaining

cheese and crushed tortilla chips. Bake, uncovered, until cheese is melted and lightly browned (15 to 20 minutes). Meanwhile, pit, peel, and slice avocado.

5. **Garnish** with avocado and cilantro. Makes 6 servings.

Per serving: 886 calories (50% calories from fat), 34 g protein, 81 g carbohydrates, 51 g total fat (7 g saturated fat), 63 mg cholesterol, 1,739 mg sodium

Four Quarters Bean & Barley Stew

Preparation time: About 25 minutes

Standing time: 1 hour

Cooking time: About 1 hour

●

A quarter cup each of three legumes and barley gives this spicy and nutritious stew its name.

- ¼ cup *each* dry kidney beans, pinto beans, black-eyed peas, and pearl barley
- 5 to 6 cups homemade (page 33) or canned vegetable broth
- 1 medium-size onion, chopped
- 1 cup chopped celery
- 2 cups sliced carrots
- 2 teaspoons curry powder
- 1 teaspoon ground turmeric
- 1½ tablespoons cider vinegar
  Salt and pepper

1. **Rinse** and sort through kidney and pinto beans, peas, and barley, discarding any debris; drain.

2. **Place** beans, peas, and barley in a 4- to 5-quart pan; add enough water to cover by 1 inch. Boil over high heat for 2 minutes. Remove from heat, cover, and let stand for 1 hour. Drain well.

3. **Return** bean mixture to pan and add 5 cups of the broth, onion, celery, carrots, curry powder, and turmeric. Bring to a boil over high heat; reduce heat, cover, and simmer until beans are tender to bite (about 45 minutes).

4. **Stir** in more broth as needed if mixture is too thick. Add vinegar; simmer for 5 more minutes. Season to taste with salt and pepper. Makes 4 servings.

Per serving: 231 calories (9% calories from fat), 10 g protein, 45 g carbohydrates, 2 g total fat (0.1 g saturated fat), 0 mg cholesterol, 1,446 mg sodium

Curried Garbanzos

Preparation time: About 20 minutes

Cooking time: About 40 minutes

Sauté onion and tomato with some spices and then add cooked garbanzo beans to make this distinctive vegetable curry.

> 3 tablespoons salad oil
>
> 1 large onion, finely chopped
>
> 3 cloves garlic, minced or pressed
>
> 1 tablespoon minced fresh ginger
>
> 1 large tomato, chopped
>
> 1½ teaspoons ground cumin
>
> 1 teaspoon ground coriander
>
> ½ teaspoon *each* ground red pepper (cayenne) and ground turmeric
>
> 4 cups cooked garbanzo beans (page 64) or 2 cans (about 1 lb. *each*) garbanzo beans, drained and rinsed
>
> ¾ cup water
>
> 2 large limes
>
> ¼ cup chopped cilantro

1. Heat oil in a wide frying pan over medium heat. Add onion, garlic, and ginger. Cook, stirring often, until onion is lightly browned (8 to 10 minutes).

2. Add tomato and cook, stirring, until almost all liquid has evaporated (about 3 minutes). Mix in cumin, coriander, ground red pepper, and turmeric. Reduce heat to low and cook, stirring, until spices become aromatic (3 to 5 minutes).

3. Stir in garbanzos and water. Cover and simmer, stirring occasionally, until mixture thickens (about 20 minutes). Meanwhile, squeeze juice from half a lime. Cut remaining limes into wedges.

4. Stir lime juice into garbanzo mixture. Sprinkle with cilantro. Serve with lime wedges to add to taste. Makes 4 to 6 servings.

Per serving: 304 calories (33% calories from fat), 12 g protein, 41 g carbohydrates, 12 g total fat (1 g saturated fat), 0 mg cholesterol, 283 mg sodium

Tofu Indonesian-style

Preparation time: About 15 minutes

Baking time: About 25 minutes

Peanut butter flavors the spicy sauce for this baked tofu entrée. Serve it alongside hot cooked rice and tender-crisp steamed green beans or baby bok choy.

> ¼ cup *each* creamy peanut butter, soy sauce, and water
>
> ½ teaspoon *each* Oriental sesame oil and ground ginger
>
> 1 teaspoon rice vinegar
>
> 1 tablespoon brown sugar
>
> 2 cloves garlic, minced or pressed
>
> 1 tablespoon sesame seeds
>
> 3 green onions, thinly sliced
>
> 1 pound regular tofu, drained
>
>   Hot cooked rice
>
>   Major Grey's chutney

1. Combine peanut butter, soy sauce, water, sesame oil, ginger, vinegar, and brown sugar in a small bowl; stir until smooth. Mix in garlic, sesame seeds, and onions.

2. Spoon a fourth of the peanut butter sauce into an 8-inch-square baking pan. Cut tofu into 4 equal slices. Arrange slices in a single layer in pan, trimming to fit if necessary; tuck any trimmings into corners. Spoon remaining sauce over tofu.

3. Bake in a 375° oven until tofu is heated through (about 25 minutes).

4. Lift tofu onto warm plates; spoon rice alongside. Pour sauce over tofu and rice. Serve with chutney to add to taste. Makes 4 servings.

Per serving: 229 calories (56% calories from fat), 15 g protein, 12 g carbohydrates, 15 g total fat (2 g saturated fat), 0 mg cholesterol, 1,116 mg sodium

*Versatile and good tasting, polenta is enjoying newfound favor, and no wonder. Dappled
with corn, it makes a delicious crust for inviting Artichoke Polenta Pie (recipe on page 84).
Drizzle a butter lettuce salad with one of the dressings on page 104.*

VEGETABLES

Artichoke Polenta Pie

Indian-spiced Cauliflower

Carrot-Mushroom Loaf

Asian-style Green Beans

Tofu-filled Asian Pancakes

Sautéed Peppers & Pears

Corn Risotto with Sage

Scalloped Carrots & Turnips with Thyme

Hazelnut-stuffed Baked Mushrooms

Potato & Carrot Oven-Fries

Baked Zucchini with Mushrooms

Potato Pizza

Tomato, Potato & Eggplant Gratin

Chard & Rice Packets

Tian Niçoise

Vegetable-stuffed Acorn Squash

Couscous Platter with Skewered Vegetables

Grilled Radicchio with Gorgonzola & Walnuts

Artichoke Polenta Pie

Pictured on page 82

Preparation time: About 20 minutes

Cooking and baking time: About 55 minutes

●

Corn kernels dot the creamy polenta crust that cradles a bed of fennel-accented sautéed onions and artichokes.

- **6 tablespoons butter or margarine**
- **½ cup finely chopped onion**
- **½ cup polenta or yellow cornmeal**
- **2 cups homemade (page 33) or canned vegetable broth**
- **1 package (about 10 oz.) frozen corn kernels, thawed**
- **2 large onions, thinly sliced**
- **2 cloves garlic, minced or pressed**
- **½ teaspoon fennel seeds**
- **1 package (about 10 oz.) frozen artichoke hearts, thawed**
- **⅛ teaspoon paprika**
- **½ cup soft sourdough bread crumbs**
- **1 tablespoon chopped parsley**
- **¼ cup grated Parmesan cheese**

1. Melt 2 tablespoons of the butter in a 3- to 4-quart pan over medium heat. Add chopped onion and cook, stirring often, until soft but not browned (about 5 minutes). Meanwhile, in a medium-size bowl, mix polenta and 1 cup of the broth; set aside.

2. Add corn and remaining 1 cup broth to onion mixture. Increase heat to high and bring to a boil. Using a long-handled spoon, stir polenta mixture into corn mixture. Reduce heat and boil gently, stirring constantly, until mixture is consistency of soft mashed potatoes (about 10 minutes).

3. Pour mixture into a shallow 2-quart casserole. Using back of a spoon, press polenta over bottom and about 1 inch up sides of dish; set aside.

4. Melt 2 tablespoons more butter in a wide frying pan over medium heat. Add sliced onions, half the garlic, and fennel. Cook, stirring often, until onions are soft and begin to brown (8 to 10 minutes). Spoon into polenta crust. Top with artichokes.

5. Melt remaining 2 tablespoons butter in frying pan over medium heat. Add remaining garlic and paprika. Cook, stirring, until garlic begins to brown (about 1 minute). Mix in crumbs. Remove from heat and stir in parsley. Sprinkle mixture over artichokes; top with cheese. Bake in a 350° oven until heated through (20 to 25 minutes). Makes 4 to 6 servings.

Per serving: 327 calories (44% calories from fat), 8 g protein, 40 g carbohydrates, 17 g total fat (10 g saturated fat), 40 mg cholesterol, 680 mg sodium

Indian-spiced Cauliflower

Preparation time: About 30 minutes

Cooking time: About 20 minutes

●

This distinctive dish features cauliflower, tomatoes, and green onions cooked Indian style.

- **1 tablespoon salad oil**
- **1 medium-size cauliflower (1½ to 2 lbs.), cut into bite-size flowerets**
- **3 tablespoons minced fresh ginger**
- **2 cloves garlic, minced or pressed**
- **4 large pear-shaped (Roma-type) tomatoes (about 12 oz. *total*), chopped**
- **½ teaspoon ground turmeric or paprika**
- **¼ cup dry white wine**
- **⅓ cup water**
- **4 green onions, thinly sliced**
  Salt

1. Heat oil in a wide frying pan over medium-high heat. Add cauliflower, ginger, and garlic. Cook, stirring often, until cauliflower is lightly browned (about 6 minutes).

2. Stir in tomatoes, turmeric, wine, water, and half the onions. Increase heat to high and bring to a boil; boil gently, stirring often, until liquid has evaporated and cauliflower is tender when pierced (about 10 minutes). Season to taste with salt.

3. Transfer to a serving bowl. Sprinkle with remaining onions. Makes 4 to 6 servings.

Per serving: 62 calories (40% calories from fat), 2 g protein, 8 g carbohydrates, 3 g total fat (0.4 g saturated fat), 0 mg cholesterol, 19 mg sodium

Carrot-Mushroom Loaf

Preparation time: About 45 minutes

Cooking time: About 1¾ hours

Standing time: At least 30 minutes

●

Carrot slices decorate the top of this vegetable loaf. Let the loaf rest after steaming to allow the juices to be reabsorbed.

   About 3 large carrots
- ¼ **cup butter or margarine**
- 1 **medium-size onion, finely chopped**
- 2 **cloves garlic, minced or pressed**
- 4½ **cups finely shredded carrots (6 to 7 large)**
- 1 **pound mushrooms, finely chopped**
- 5 **large eggs**
- 1 **cup fine dry bread crumbs**
- ¼ **cup minced parsley**
- ½ **teaspoon dry thyme**
   Salt and pepper

1. Cut thick part of whole carrots into ¼-inch slices (you should have about 1 cup); reserve remaining parts of carrots for other uses. Place carrot slices on a rack in a 2½- to 3-quart pan over 1 inch boiling water. Cover and cook over high heat until tender when pierced (about 10 minutes). Neatly arrange carrot slices, overlapping edges, in a 5- by 9-inch loaf pan; set aside.

2. Melt butter in a 5- to 6-quart pan over medium-high heat. Add onion and garlic. Cook, stirring often, until onion is soft and lightly browned (6 to 8 minutes). Add shredded carrots and mushrooms. Cover and cook, stirring often, until carrots are tender to bite (10 to 12 minutes). Let cool slightly.

3. Combine eggs, bread crumbs, parsley, and thyme in a large bowl; beat until blended. Add vegetable mixture, stirring until evenly blended. Season to taste with salt and pepper. Carefully spoon into pan, pressing mixture down firmly. Rap pan on counter several times to remove air bubbles. Cover tightly with foil.

4. Choose a pan large enough to hold loaf pan. Position a rack just above 1 to 2 inches water in pan. Bring water to a boil over high heat, set loaf pan on rack, and cover larger pan. Cook, keeping water at an active boil, until loaf feels firm when pressed in center and top feels dry (about 1¼ hours); maintain water level, adding boiling water as needed.

5. Let stand for at least 30 minutes. Remove foil and run a knife blade around loaf. Invert onto a serving dish. Serve hot or at room temperature. Slice about ½ inch thick. Makes 6 to 8 servings.

Per serving: 249 calories (40% calories from fat), 9 g protein, 29 g carbohydrates, 11 g total fat (5 g saturated fat), 170 mg cholesterol, 289 mg sodium

Low-Fat

Asian-style Green Beans

Preparation time: About 20 minutes

Cooking time: 10 to 15 minutes

●

Steam slender young green beans and then spoon on a colorful fat-free sauté of red bell pepper and mushrooms.

- 1 **large onion, finely chopped**
- 8 **ounces mushrooms, thinly sliced**
- 1 **large red bell pepper (8 to 10 oz.), seeded and cut into thin bite-size strips**
- 1 **clove garlic, minced or pressed**
- ¾ **to 1 cup water**
- 3 **tablespoons soy sauce**
- 1½ **tablespoons honey**
- 1 **pound slender green beans, ends removed**
- ¼ **cup salted roasted peanuts, chopped**

1. Combine onion, mushrooms, bell pepper, garlic, and ⅓ cup of the water in a wide frying pan. Bring to a boil over high heat; cook, stirring often, until liquid has evaporated and mixture begins to brown (8 to 10 minutes).

2. Add ¼ cup more water, stirring to scrape browned bits free. Continue to cook, stirring occasionally, until liquid has evaporated and mixture begins to brown again (about 1 minute). Repeat 1 or 2 more times, cooking until mixture is richly browned. Add soy sauce and honey; keep warm.

3. Place beans on a rack in a 2½- to 3-quart pan over 1 inch boiling water. Cover and cook over high heat just until tender-crisp (about 10 minutes).

4. Arrange beans on a warm platter. Spoon mushroom sauce over beans. Sprinkle with nuts. Makes 4 servings.

Per serving: 167 calories (25% calories from fat), 7 g protein, 28 g carbohydrates, 5 g total fat (0.7 g saturated fat), 0 mg cholesterol, 857 mg sodium

Tofu-filled Asian Pancakes

Pictured on facing page

Preparation time: About 1 hour

Standing time: 30 minutes

Cooking time: About 40 minutes

Wrap a spicy vegetable stir-fry in puffy Peking-style pancakes for a hand-held supper treat.

> Mandarin Pancakes (recipe follows)
>
> Spicy Sauce (recipe follows)
>
> 3 tablespoons salad oil
>
> 1 medium-size onion, finely chopped
>
> 1 cup thinly sliced celery
>
> 1½ cups chopped broccoli
>
> 2 cups thinly sliced mushrooms
>
> 2½ cups diced medium-firm tofu
>
> 1½ cups bean sprouts

1. Prepare Mandarin Pancakes and Spicy Sauce.

2. Heat oil in a wide frying pan over medium heat. Add onion and celery; cook, stirring often, for 3 to 4 minutes. Add broccoli and cook, stirring, for 2 to 3 more minutes. Add mushrooms and cook, stirring, until liquid has evaporated and mushrooms are soft (5 to 7 minutes).

3. Add tofu and cook, stirring gently, until heated through (1 to 2 minutes). Stir in Spicy Sauce. Add bean sprouts and cook just until heated through. Spoon filling down center of Mandarin Pancakes; roll to enclose. Makes 6 servings.

Mandarin Pancakes. In a bowl, mix 1½ cups **unbleached all-purpose flour** and ½ cup **whole wheat flour** (not stone ground). Add ¾ cup **boiling water;** with a fork, stir until dough holds together. On a lightly floured board, knead until smooth and satiny (about 10 minutes). Cover and let stand for 30 minutes. Shape into a 12-inch log. Slice 1 inch thick; cover.

For each pancake, halve a slice of dough (keep remaining dough covered). Shape each half into a ball, flatten slightly, and roll on a lightly floured board into a 3-inch circle. Lightly brush **Oriental sesame oil** or salad oil on one circle and cover with other circle (you will need about 2 tablespoons oil total). Press firmly.

On a lightly floured board, roll double circle of dough, turning often, into a 7- to 8-inch circle. Repeat until you have made 2 or 3 pancakes.

Heat a wide frying pan over medium-high heat. Add a pancake and cook, turning every 15 seconds, just until blistered and dry. Carefully separate halves and stack. Keep covered while shaping and cooking remaining pancakes. Serve warm. Makes 24 pancakes.

Spicy Sauce. In a small bowl, combine 5 tablespoons **soy sauce;** 3 tablespoons **cider vinegar;** 2 teaspoons **cornstarch;** 3 large cloves **garlic,** minced or pressed; 3 tablespoons chopped **cilantro;** and ½ teaspoon **crushed red pepper flakes.** Stir until blended.

Per serving: 413 calories (40% calories from fat), 20 g protein, 45 g carbohydrates, 19 g total fat (3 g saturated fat), 0 mg cholesterol, 897 mg sodium

Sautéed Peppers & Pears

Preparation time: About 25 minutes

Cooking time: About 15 minutes

Hot pears laced with sweet pepper strips are a delicious accompaniment to baked winter squash and a steamed vegetable, such as cauliflower or Brussels sprouts.

> 3 tablespoons butter or margarine
>
> 4 medium-size fresh pimentos or small red or yellow bell peppers (about 1 lb. *total*), seeded and cut into ¼-inch-wide strips
>
> 3 medium-size firm-ripe pears or Golden Delicious apples, peeled, cored, and sliced ¼ inch thick
>
> ¾ cup shredded jack or Münster cheese

1. Melt 2 tablespoons of the butter in a wide frying pan over medium heat. Add pimentos and cook, stirring often, until pimentos begin to soften (7 to 10 minutes).

2. Add pears and remaining 1 tablespoon butter. Cook, stirring often, until pears are tender when pierced (5 to 7 more minutes).

3. Transfer mixture to a warm serving dish. Sprinkle with cheese. Makes 6 servings.

Per serving: 169 calories (53% calories from fat), 4 g protein, 17 g carbohydrates, 10 g total fat (4 g saturated fat), 28 mg cholesterol, 136 mg sodium

Spicy, exotic, yet supremely simple, Tofu-filled Asian Pancakes (recipe on facing page) are a Chinese-style treat. You can make the pancakes ahead and reheat them, wrapped in a damp towel, over simmering water on a steamer rack.

Tempting Grilled Vegetables

When vegetables are cooked on the barbecue, they take on a delicate smoky flavor and become streaked with brown from contact with the hot grill.

Some vegetables cook best when they're blanched first. Other less dense vegetables, such as mushrooms and peppers, can go on the grill raw; to prevent them from drying and burning, put them on the cooler parts of the grill and keep a watchful eye, turning them often.

Enhance grilled vegetables with a flavorful sauce (see at right). Or offer with Green Sauce (page 96).

Grilled Vegetables

Preparation time: 10 to 15 minutes
Cooking time: 6 to 10 minutes for blanched vegetables, 10 to 15 minutes for unblanched

---

2 pounds vegetables (use one or a combination; directions follow)

⅓ cup olive oil or salad oil

---

2 tablespoons minced fresh thyme, fresh oregano, fresh rosemary, or fresh tarragon; or 2 teaspoons dry thyme, dry oregano, dry rosemary, or dry tarragon

---

Salt and pepper

---

1. **Prepare** vegetables.

2. **Blanch** vegetables, if necessary, by bringing 3 quarts water to a boil in a 6- to 8-quart pan over high heat. Add up to a pound of one kind of vegetable. Return to a boil and cook until vegetable is barely tender when pierced (see times at right). Lift out, immerse in cold water, and drain well. Repeat with remaining vegetables, using same pan of water. (At this point, you may cover and refrigerate vegetables for up to a day.)

3. **Coat** raw or blanched vegetables with some of the oil; sprinkle with thyme. Place on a grill 4 to 6 inches above a solid bed of hot coals for blanched vegetables, medium-hot for raw vegetables.

4. **Cook,** turning often and brushing with more oil, until vegetables are hot and streaked with brown (4 to 6 minutes for blanched vegetables, 10 to 15 minutes for raw vegetables). Season to taste with salt and pepper. Serve hot or at room temperature. Makes 6 servings.

Bell peppers (red, yellow, green; fresh pimentos). Cook raw whole peppers and pimentos directly on grill.

Broccoli. Cut off and discard tough ends of stalks; peel remaining stalks, if desired. If heads are thicker than 2 inches, cut in half lengthwise. Blanch for 2 to 3 minutes.

Eggplant. Cut small Oriental eggplants in half lengthwise; cut small standard eggplants (about 12 oz. *each*) lengthwise into 1½-inch wedges. Blanch for 2 to 3 minutes.

Leeks. Cut off and discard root ends. Trim tops, leaving about 3 inches of green leaves. Discard coarse outer leaves. Split lengthwise to within ½ inch of root ends and rinse well. Blanch for 1 to 2 minutes.

Mushrooms (button, shiitake, oyster). Thread 1- to 1½-inch button mushrooms through stems on skewers. Cut off tough stems of shiitake mushrooms. Grill raw mushrooms whole, placing shiitake and oyster mushrooms, unskewered, directly on grill.

Onions (red, yellow, white). Cut small unpeeled onions in half lengthwise; cut large peeled onions into quarters. Thread through layers onto slender skewers. Grill onions raw. Or first blanch unpeeled halves for 3 to 4 minutes; if large, peel, cut in half again, and thread onto skewers.

Potatoes (sweet, russet, thin-skinned; yams). Cut potatoes lengthwise into 1-inch wedges. Blanch for 4 to 5 minutes.

Summer squash (zucchini, crookneck, pattypan). If thicker than 1 inch, cut in half lengthwise. Blanch for 2 to 3 minutes.

Per serving broccoli and sweet potato combination: 207 calories (52% calories from fat), 4 g protein, 23 g carbohydrates, 12 g total fat (2 g saturated fat), 0 mg cholesterol, 31 mg sodium

Basil Salsa

Preparation time: About 10 minutes

---

1 large firm-ripe tomato, coarsely chopped

⅓ cup chopped fresh basil

---

1 to 2 tablespoons balsamic vinegar or red wine vinegar

Salt and pepper

---

1. **Combine** tomato and basil in a small bowl; mix well. Season to taste with vinegar, salt, and pepper. Makes about 1½ cups.

Per tablespoon: 3 calories (9% calories from fat), 0.1 g protein, 0.6 g carbohydrates, 0 g total fat (0 g saturated fat), 0 mg cholesterol, 1 mg sodium

Corn Risotto with Sage

Preparation time: About 15 minutes

Cooking time: About 30 minutes

●

Complement fresh corn with savory fresh sage to make this luscious Italian-style entrée. Imported arborio rice lends an especially creamy texture.

> 3 medium-size ears yellow or white corn, husks and silk removed
> 1 tablespoon butter or margarine
> 1 large onion, finely chopped
> 1 cup arborio or short-grain rice
> 3½ cups homemade (page 33) or canned vegetable broth
> ¼ cup grated Parmesan cheese
> ¼ cup shredded fontina cheese
> 3 tablespoons chopped fresh sage or 2 teaspoons dry sage
> Fresh sage sprigs

1. Cut corn kernels from cobs; set kernels and cobs aside separately.

2. Melt butter in a wide frying pan over medium heat. Add onion and cook, stirring often, until soft but not browned (about 5 minutes). Add rice and cook, stirring, until opaque and milky (about 2 minutes). Stir in about three-fourths of the corn kernels.

3. Pour in broth. Bring to a boil, stirring often. Reduce heat to low and simmer, stirring occasionally, until rice is tender and most of the liquid is absorbed (20 to 25 minutes); as mixture thickens, reduce heat to very low and stir more often.

4. Remove pan from heat. Holding cobs over pan, use dull side of a knife to scrape cobs so corn juices fall into rice mixture. Gently stir in Parmesan, fontina, and chopped sage. Let stand until cheese is melted (about 2 minutes).

5. Transfer to a warm serving dish. Sprinkle with remaining corn. Garnish with sage sprigs. Makes 4 servings.

Per serving: 355 calories (22% calories from fat), 10 g protein, 61 g carbohydrates, 9 g total fat (4 g saturated fat), 20 mg cholesterol, 1,078 mg sodium

Scalloped Carrots & Turnips with Thyme

Preparation time: About 45 minutes

Cooking and baking time: About 1 hour and 10 minutes

●

This root vegetable and apple medley, swathed in a creamy sauce, makes a comforting winter main dish.

> White Sauce (recipe follows)
> 2 medium-large carrots (about 12 oz. *total*), thinly sliced
> 3 medium-size turnips (about 1 lb. *total*), thinly sliced
> 1 large Golden Delicious apple
> 1 cup (about 4 oz.) shredded Cheddar cheese

1. Prepare White Sauce.

2. Arrange half the carrots in an even layer in a greased shallow 2½- to 3-quart casserole. Cover with half the turnips.

3. Peel, core, and thinly slice apple; arrange half the apple slices over turnips. Spoon on half the White Sauce. Repeat layers.

4. Cover and bake in a 400° oven for 30 minutes. Uncover, sprinkle with cheese, and continue to bake until cheese begins to brown and vegetables are tender when pierced (25 to 30 more minutes). Makes 4 to 6 servings.

White Sauce. Melt ¼ cup **butter** or margarine in a 1½- to 2-quart pan over medium heat. Blend in ½ teaspoon **dry thyme** and ¼ cup **unbleached all-purpose flour.** Cook, stirring constantly, until bubbly. Remove from heat and gradually stir in 2 cups **milk;** return to heat and continue to cook, stirring, until sauce boils and thickens (3 to 5 minutes). Season to taste with **salt** and **pepper.**

Per serving: 326 calories (55% calories from fat), 11 g protein, 27 g carbohydrates, 20 g total fat (13 g saturated fat), 62 mg cholesterol, 367 mg sodium

Enjoy guilt-free snacking with crispy Potato & Carrot Oven-Fries (recipe on facing page). The vegetable sticks are roasted in a hot oven with only a fraction of the fat of traditional fries.

Hazelnut-stuffed Baked Mushrooms

Preparation time: About 25 minutes

Cooking and baking time: 35 to 45 minutes

●

Look for generous 2½- to 3-inch-diameter mushrooms to fill with this savory and satisfying vegetable-nut mixture.

- ½ cup hazelnuts
- 16 large mushrooms (*each* at least 2½ inches in diameter)
- 6 tablespoons butter or margarine
- 1 medium-size carrot, finely shredded
- ¼ cup thinly sliced shallots
- 2 large eggs
- 2 tablespoons finely chopped parsley
- ¼ cup fine dry bread crumbs
- ¼ teaspoon salt
- ⅛ teaspoon *each* ground white pepper and ground nutmeg
- 1 tablespoon brandy (optional)
- ⅓ cup grated Parmesan cheese

1. Spread hazelnuts in a shallow baking pan and toast in a 350° oven until pale golden beneath skins (about 10 minutes). Let cool slightly; then use your fingers to rub off skins. Chop nuts coarsely and set aside.

2. Remove mushroom stems and chop finely; set caps aside. Melt 3 tablespoons of the butter in a wide frying pan over medium-high heat. Add chopped stems, carrot, and shallots. Cook, stirring often, until lightly browned (8 to 10 minutes). Meanwhile, beat eggs in a medium-size bowl until blended. Stir in parsley, bread crumbs, salt, pepper, nutmeg, and, if desired, brandy. Mix in vegetable mixture and nuts.

3. Fill mushroom caps with stuffing mixture and arrange in a single layer in a greased shallow 2- to 2½-quart casserole. Sprinkle with cheese. Melt remaining 3 tablespoons butter in pan over medium heat; drizzle over mushrooms. (At this point, you may cover and refrigerate for up to 8 hours.)

4. Bake, uncovered, in a 375° oven until heated through and lightly browned (about 15 minutes; 25 minutes if cold). Makes 4 servings.

Per serving: 389 calories (70% calories from fat), 12 g protein, 18 g carbohydrates, 32 g total fat (14 g saturated fat), 158 mg cholesterol, 538 mg sodium

Low-Fat

Potato & Carrot Oven-Fries

Pictured on facing page

Preparation time: About 10 minutes

Baking time: About 45 minutes

●

Because they're baked rather than fried, these crunchy French fries have little fat. Carrots add color, flavor, and nutrients.

- 3 large white thin-skinned potatoes (about 2 lbs. *total*), cut into ½- by 4-inch sticks
- 2 pounds carrots, cut into ½- by 4-inch sticks
- 2 tablespoons salad oil
  Salt and pepper
  Cider vinegar (optional)

1. Mix potatoes, carrots, and 1½ tablespoons of the oil in a large bowl.

2. Grease two 10- by 15-inch rimmed baking pans with remaining oil and place in a 425° oven for 5 minutes. Spread vegetables evenly in pans and bake, turning once with a spatula, until lightly browned and tender when pierced (about 45 minutes total); if using one oven, switch position of pans halfway through baking.

3. Transfer vegetables to a napkin-lined basket. Season to taste with salt and pepper. Sprinkle with vinegar, if desired. Makes 4 servings.

Per serving: 337 calories (19% calories from fat), 7 g protein, 64 g carbohydrates, 7 g total fat (1 g saturated fat), 0 mg cholesterol, 93 mg sodium

Baked Zucchini with Mushrooms

Low-Fat

Preparation time: *About 30 minutes*

Cooking and baking time: *About 1 hour*

●

This savory casserole makes a good main dish with Red & Orange Ginger Salad (page 110) or Spicy Red Coleslaw (page 101).

- 1 **pound mushrooms, thinly sliced**
- 1 **medium-size onion, finely chopped**
- ½ **cup water**
  About 1⅓ cups homemade (page 33) or canned vegetable broth
- 3 **large eggs**
- 4 **large zucchini (about 2 lbs. *total*), shredded**
- ½ **cup fine dry bread crumbs**
- ¼ **cup grated Parmesan cheese**
- ½ **teaspoon *each* pepper and dry oregano**
- 2 **tablespoons thinly sliced green onion**

1. Combine mushrooms, chopped onion, and water in a wide frying pan. Cook over high heat, stirring often, until liquid has evaporated and browned bits cling to pan.

2. Add ⅓ cup of the broth, stirring to scrape browned bits free. Bring to a boil and cook, stirring often, until liquid has evaporated and onion begins to brown. Repeat 2 or 3 more times, using ⅓ cup more broth each time and cooking until onion is golden brown. Meanwhile, beat eggs in a large bowl until blended.

3. Stir zucchini, bread crumbs, cheese, pepper, oregano, and mushroom mixture into eggs. Pour into a greased shallow 2½- to 3-quart casserole.

4. Bake in a 325° oven until mixture is set in center when shaken (about 45 minutes). Sprinkle with green onion. Makes 6 to 8 servings.

Per serving: 124 calories (28% calories from fat), 8 g protein, 16 g carbohydrates, 4 g total fat (1 g saturated fat), 93 mg cholesterol, 347 mg sodium

Potato Pizza

Preparation time: *About 40 minutes*

Cooking and baking time: *About 55 minutes*

●

Potatoes pizza style are a lively oven entrée you can put together easily, especially if you use your food processor to slice the potatoes.

- 1¼ **to 1½ pounds thin-skinned potatoes**
- 3 **tablespoons butter or margarine**
  Salt and pepper
- 1 **small onion, finely chopped**
- 1 **clove garlic, minced or pressed**
- ½ **teaspoon *each* dry thyme, dry oregano, and dry basil**
- 8 **ounces mushrooms, thinly sliced**
- 2 **cups (about 8 oz.) shredded Cheddar cheese**
- 1 **can (about 2¼ oz.) sliced ripe olives, drained**
- ¼ **cup sliced green onions**

1. Peel potatoes, if desired, and slice ⅛ inch thick.

2. Melt butter in a wide frying pan over medium heat. Brush a 12- to 14-inch pizza pan with about 1 teaspoon of the butter. Arrange potato slices, overlapping slightly, in a single layer in pan. Brush with about 2 teaspoons more butter. Season to taste with salt and pepper.

3. Bake on bottom rack of a 425° oven until potatoes are dappled with brown and some edges are crisp (about 50 minutes). Meanwhile, add chopped onion, garlic, thyme, oregano, and basil to remaining butter in pan. Cook over medium-high heat, stirring occasionally, until onion is soft (5 to 8 minutes). Add mushrooms and continue to cook, stirring often, until mushrooms are limp (about 10 more minutes).

4. Remove pizza pan from oven. Evenly distribute mushroom mixture over potatoes. Top with cheese and olives. Return to oven and continue to bake until cheese is melted (3 to 5 more minutes). Sprinkle with green onions. Cut into wedges. Makes 4 to 6 servings.

Per serving: 383 calories (55% calories from fat), 15 g protein, 29 g carbohydrates, 24 g total fat (14 g saturated fat), 66 mg cholesterol, 476 mg sodium

Tomato, Potato & Eggplant Gratin

Preparation time: About 45 minutes

Cooking and baking time: About 1½ hours

●

This hearty baked vegetable dish is redolent with flavors of the Mediterranean. Serve it with crusty bread and a crisp romaine salad.

>   Olive oil cooking spray
> 1 large eggplant (1¼ to 1½ lbs.), unpeeled, sliced crosswise ¼ inch thick
> 3 tablespoons olive oil
> 1 large onion, thinly sliced
> 1 medium-size red bell pepper, seeded and finely chopped
> 3 large tomatoes, peeled, seeded, and chopped
> 3 cloves garlic, minced or pressed
> ¼ teaspoon sugar
> ½ teaspoon dry thyme
> 5 medium-size russet potatoes (about 2½ lbs. *total*)
>   Salt and pepper
>   Chopped parsley

1. Spray a large shallow baking pan with cooking spray. Arrange eggplant slices in a single layer in pan; spray with more cooking spray. Broil about 4 inches below heat until well browned (6 to 8 minutes). Turn eggplant, spray other sides, and broil until browned (5 to 6 more minutes). Set aside.

2. Heat 2 tablespoons of the olive oil in a wide frying pan over medium heat. Add onion and bell pepper. Cook, stirring often, until vegetables are soft but not browned (8 to 10 minutes). Stir in tomatoes, garlic, sugar, and thyme. Cook, stirring often, until tomatoes are soft (3 to 5 minutes). Set aside.

3. Peel potatoes and thinly slice. Spread a third of the potatoes in a greased shallow 3-quart casserole; season to taste with salt and pepper. Add half each of the eggplant and tomato sauce. Cover with a third more of the potatoes, season to taste with salt and pepper, and add remaining eggplant and tomato sauce. Top with remaining potatoes; season to taste with salt and pepper. Drizzle with remaining 1 tablespoon oil.

4. Bake in a 375° oven until potatoes are tender when pierced and top is lightly browned (1 to 1¼ hours). Sprinkle with parsley. Makes 4 to 6 servings.

Per serving: 322 calories (27% calories from fat), 7 g protein, 54 g carbohydrates, 10 g total fat (1 g saturated fat), 0 mg cholesterol, 31 mg sodium

Chard & Rice Packets

Preparation time: About 20 minutes

Cooking and baking time: 25 to 30 minutes

●

Fill blanched Swiss chard leaves with brown rice, spicy kuminost cheese, and green chiles for a zesty main dish to serve with tender-crisp green beans, cherry tomatoes, and hot corn muffins.

> 8 large Swiss chard leaves (1 to 1½ lbs. *total*), well rinsed
> 1½ cups cooked brown rice (page 73)
> 1 large can (about 7 oz.) diced green chiles
> 1½ cups (about 6 oz.) finely diced kuminost or jalapeño jack cheese
> 3 tablespoons coarsely chopped cilantro
>   Salt and pepper

1. Cut off chard stems, placing leaves and stems in separate piles. In a 5- to 6-quart pan, bring 3 quarts water to a boil over high heat. Add stems and cook until tender when pierced (4 to 5 minutes); lift out and set aside. Add leaves to pan and cook until limp (1 to 2 minutes); drain and set aside.

2. Chop stems coarsely. In a large bowl, mix stems, rice, chiles, cheese, and cilantro. Season to taste with salt and pepper.

3. Place an eighth of the rice mixture in center of each chard leaf. Wrap to enclose. Place, seam sides down, in a greased shallow 3-quart casserole. Cover and bake in a 400° oven until heated through (about 20 minutes). Makes 4 servings.

Per serving: 288 calories (43% calories from fat), 15 g protein, 27 g carbohydrates, 14 g total fat (8 g saturated fat), 45 mg cholesterol, 934 mg sodium

Tian Niçoise

Preparation time: About 20 minutes

Baking time: About 1¼ hours

●

This versatile vegetable dish hails from the little Mediterranean port of Menton.

- 1 **cup long-grain white rice**
- 1 **medium-size onion, finely chopped**
- 3 **medium-size zucchini (about 1 lb. *total*), quartered lengthwise and sliced ¼ inch thick**
- ¼ **cup chopped parsley**
- 2 **tablespoons chopped fresh basil or 1 teaspoon dry basil**
- ¼ **teaspoon salt**
- ⅛ **teaspoon ground nutmeg**
- 2 **cups (about 8 oz.) shredded Swiss cheese**
- ¾ **cup half-and-half**
- 1 **can (about 14 oz.) vegetable broth**
- 1 **tablespoon olive oil**
- 4 **medium-size pear-shaped (Roma-type) tomatoes, sliced ¼ inch thick**

1. Mix rice, onion, zucchini, parsley, basil, salt, nutmeg, and 1 cup of the cheese in a shallow 2- to 2½-quart casserole. Stir in half-and-half and broth. Drizzle with oil.

2. Cover and bake in a 350° oven, stirring lightly after 45 minutes, until rice is almost tender (about 1 hour).

3. Remove casserole from oven. Arrange tomato slices over rice mixture and sprinkle with remaining 1 cup cheese. Return to oven and continue to bake, uncovered, until cheese is melted and lightly browned (about 15 more minutes). Makes 6 servings.

Per serving: 351 calories (43% calories from fat), 15 g protein, 35 g carbohydrates, 17 g total fat (9 g saturated fat), 46 mg cholesterol, 505 mg sodium

Vegetable-stuffed Acorn Squash

Pictured on facing page

Preparation time: About 30 minutes

Cooking and baking time: About 1 hour

●

Carrots, red pepper, and celery, accented with ginger and soy sauce, make a colorful filling for baked acorn squash halves.

- 2 **acorn squash (1½ to 2 lbs. *each*)**
- 3 **tablespoons butter or margarine**
- 1 **medium-size onion, finely chopped**
- 3 **medium-size carrots, chopped**
- 3 **stalks celery, finely chopped**
- ½ **cup chopped red bell pepper**
- 2 **tablespoons minced fresh ginger**
- 1 **clove garlic, minced or pressed**
- ¼ **cup dry white wine**
- 2 **tablespoons soy sauce**
- ½ **cup shredded jack cheese**

1. Cut each squash in half lengthwise; scoop out and discard seeds. Rub 1½ teaspoons of the butter over cut sides. Arrange, cut sides down, in a shallow baking pan.

2. Bake in a 350° oven for 30 minutes. Turn squash and continue to bake until tender when pierced (15 to 20 more minutes). Meanwhile, melt remaining 2½ tablespoons butter in a wide frying pan over medium heat. Add onion, carrots, celery, bell pepper, ginger, and garlic. Cook, stirring often, until onion is soft but not browned (8 to 10 minutes). Stir in wine and soy sauce. Increase heat to medium-high and bring to a boil; cook, stirring, until liquid has evaporated (about 3 minutes).

3. Remove squash from oven and spoon a quarter of the filling into cavity of each squash half. Sprinkle with cheese. Return to oven and continue to bake until cheese is melted and lightly browned (about 10 more minutes). Makes 4 servings.

Per serving: 255 calories (46% calories from fat), 7 g protein, 28 g carbohydrates, 13 g total fat (5 g saturated fat), 36 mg cholesterol, 730 mg sodium

For contrasting colors and textures, pair the baked goodness of Vegetable-stuffed Acorn Squash (recipe on facing page) with slender green beans and buttery Soft Sesame Biscuits (recipe on page 133).

Couscous Platter with Skewered Vegetables

Preparation time: About 35 minutes

Cooking time: About 15 minutes

•

While couscous steeps in vegetable broth, quickly grill skewered shallots, cherry tomatoes, and zucchini.

> **Green Sauce (recipe follows)**
> 12 ounces small shallots, peeled
> 3 medium-size zucchini, sliced ½ inch thick
> 12 ounces cherry tomatoes
> 2 tablespoons olive oil
> 2¼ cups homemade (page 33) or canned vegetable broth
> 1 tablespoon lemon juice
> ¼ teaspoon ground turmeric
> 1½ cups couscous
> ¼ cup coarsely chopped fresh mint
>   Mint sprigs

1. Prepare Green Sauce.

2. Thread shallots, zucchini, and tomatoes separately on 9 metal skewers (9 to 10 inches long), making 3 skewers of each vegetable. Brush vegetables with oil.

3. Place skewers on a grill 4 to 6 inches above a solid bed of hot coals. Cook, turning as needed, until vegetables are lightly browned (10 to 15 minutes for shallots and zucchini, 8 to 10 minutes for tomatoes). Meanwhile, bring broth to a boil in a 2- to 3-quart pan over high heat. Stir in lemon juice, turmeric, and couscous. Cover pan and remove from heat; let stand for 5 to 10 minutes.

4. Fluff couscous with a fork and stir in chopped mint. Spoon couscous onto a warm platter. Push vegetables off skewers and arrange over couscous. Garnish with mint sprigs. Serve with Green Sauce to add to taste. Makes 4 to 6 servings.

Per serving: 449 calories (34% calories from fat), 11 g protein, 64 g carbohydrates, 18 g total fat (2 g saturated fat), 0 mg cholesterol, 510 mg sodium

Green Sauce. In a food processor or blender, combine 1⅔ cups **parsley,** ¼ cup **olive oil,** 2 cloves **garlic,** 1½ teaspoons **capers,** and 1½ tablespoons **lemon juice;** whirl until smooth. If made ahead, cover and refrigerate for up to 3 days. Makes about ½ cup.

Per tablespoon: 66 calories (91% calories from fat), 0.3 g protein, 1 g carbohydrates, 7 g total fat (1 g saturated fat), 0 mg cholesterol, 19 mg sodium

Grilled Radicchio with Gorgonzola & Walnuts

Preparation time: About 20 minutes

Cooking time: 15 to 20 minutes

•

Grilling halved radicchio heads on the barbecue intensifies the flavor of this distinctive reddish purple member of the endive family. Top the hot radicchio with pungent cheese, toasted nuts, and a drizzling of vinaigrette.

> ⅓ cup coarsely chopped walnuts
> ⅓ cup olive oil
> 4 teaspoons red wine vinegar
> 1 clove garlic, minced or pressed
> 1 teaspoon Dijon mustard
>   Salt and pepper
> 3 heads radicchio (*each* 4- to 5-inch diameter, 1 to 1¼ lbs. *total*), halved lengthwise
> ⅓ cup crumbled Gorgonzola cheese

1. Spread nuts in a small baking pan and toast in a 350° oven until golden brown (8 to 10 minutes). Set aside.

2. Combine oil, vinegar, garlic, and mustard in a small bowl; mix well. Season to taste with salt and pepper.

3. Brush radicchio halves with some of the oil mixture; reserve remaining mixture. Place, cut sides down, on a greased grill about 6 inches above a solid bed of medium-hot coals. Cook, turning once, until hot and lightly browned (5 to 8 minutes total).

4. Arrange, cut sides up, on a serving platter. Sprinkle with cheese and nuts. Drizzle with remaining oil mixture. Makes 6 servings.

Per serving: 191 calories (83% calories from fat), 4 g protein, 5 g carbohydrates, 18 g total fat (3 g saturated fat), 6 mg cholesterol, 137 mg sodium

Spicing Up Vegetarian Fare

One of the secrets of creating tempting vegetarian fare is to use herbs and spices in new and unusual ways. Singly or in combination, fresh or dried, herbs and spices can bring distinctive flavor to the simplest dish.

If you purchase more fresh herbs than you can use at one time, dry them in your microwave oven (see below), preserving their fragrance and color.

Enjoy the Provençal herbs on sautéed and steamed vegetables and with tomatoes and grilled eggplant. Try Chinese Five Spice with stir-fried vegetables (look for Szechwan peppercorns and star anise in Asian markets) and Cajun Spice with bell peppers and okra. Sweet Curry is good with cauliflower, rice, and lentils. Best of all, these mixtures have little or no fat.

Dried Herbs. Scatter 2 cups loosely packed washed and dried **fresh herb leaves** or sprigs on paper towels. Microwave, uncovered, on HIGH (100%) for 4 minutes or until herbs look dry. Let cool. Store airtight. Makes ½ to ⅔ cup.

Herbes de Provence

Preparation time: About 10 minutes

2 tablespoons dry basil

4 teaspoons dry oregano

2 teaspoons *each* dry marjoram, dry tarragon, dry thyme, and dry savory

1½ teaspoons crushed bay leaves

1 teaspoon *each* fennel seeds, dry mint, ground sage, and dry rosemary

1 teaspoon dry lavender (optional)

1. Combine basil, oregano, marjoram, tarragon, thyme, savory, bay leaves, fennel, mint, sage, rosemary, and, if desired, lavender in a blender or food processor; whirl until fine. Store airtight. Makes about 7 tablespoons.

Per ¼ teaspoon: 1 calorie (0% calories from fat), 0 g protein, 0.2 g carbohydrates, 0 g total fat (0 g saturated fat), 0 mg cholesterol, 0.1 mg sodium

Chinese Five Spice

Preparation time: About 10 minutes

2 tablespoons *each* fennel seeds and Szechwan peppercorns

4 star anise or 1 teaspoon anise seeds

1¼ teaspoons whole cloves or 1 teaspoon ground cloves

1 cinnamon stick (about 2 inches long), broken into several pieces, or 1 teaspoon ground cinnamon

1. Combine fennel, peppercorns, star anise, cloves, and cinnamon stick in a blender or food processor; whirl until coarsely powdered. Store airtight. Makes about 5 tablespoons.

Per ¼ teaspoon: 2 calories (12% calories from fat), 0.1 g protein, 0.3 g carbohydrates, 0 g total fat (0 g saturated fat), 0 mg cholesterol, 0.3 mg sodium

Cajun Spice

Preparation time: About 10 minutes

1 tablespoon *each* ground red pepper (cayenne) and garlic salt

2 teaspoons dry basil

1½ teaspoons *each* crushed bay leaves and coarsely ground black pepper

1 teaspoon *each* dry sage, dry thyme, and ground white pepper

½ teaspoon ground allspice

1. Combine ground red pepper, garlic salt, basil, bay leaves, ground black pepper, sage, thyme, ground white pepper, and allspice in a blender or food processor; whirl until fine. Store airtight. Makes about 5 tablespoons.

Per ¼ teaspoon: 1 calorie (10% calories from fat), 0 g protein, 0.2 g carbohydrates, 0 g total fat (0 g saturated fat), 0 mg cholesterol, 92 mg sodium

Sweet Curry

Preparation time: About 10 minutes

2 tablespoons *each* ground coriander and ground cumin

1 tablespoon ground mace

2 teaspoons *each* ground cardamom and ground cinnamon

1 teaspoon *each* ground cloves, ground nutmeg, and ground turmeric

½ teaspoon ground red pepper (cayenne)

1 teaspoon coarsely ground black pepper (optional)

1. Combine coriander, cumin, mace, cardamom, cinnamon, cloves, nutmeg, turmeric, ground red pepper, and, if desired, ground black pepper in a small bowl. Stir well. Store airtight. Makes about 6 tablespoons.

Per ¼ teaspoon: 2 calories (35% calories from fat), 0 g protein, 0.2 g carbohydrates, 0.1 g total fat (0 g saturated fat), 0 mg cholesterol, 0.5 mg sodium

*Crisp spinach, tangy feta cheese, and gleaming red peppers all play starring roles in
Roasted Pepper, Spinach & Feta Salad (recipe on page 100). Whether you serve it as a first course
or as a light main dish, it will surely win rave reviews.*

98

SALADS

Jicama & Avocado Salad with Orange Vinaigrette

Roasted Pepper, Spinach & Feta Salad

Peking Spinach Salad

Spicy Red Coleslaw

Warm Goat Cheese Salad

Green & White Sesame Salad

Cauliflower with Toasted Mustard Seeds

Cucumber & Green Onion Salad

Squash Salad Provençal

Shredded Zucchini Salad

Zucchini & Cauliflower with Tahini

Spaghetti Squash & Broccoli

Soy-braised Eggplant Salad

Fresh Corn on Romaine with Parmesan

Bok Choy with Ginger Vinaigrette

Red & Orange Ginger Salad

Peppered Potato & Two-Bean Salad

Avocado Fans with Pistachios

Summer Fruit & Almond Salad

Wilted Waldorf Salad

Red Potato Salad with Yogurt

White Bean Salad

Cool Pasta Platter with Olives & Cheese

Minted Lentils with Goat Cheese

Spinach Pesto Pasta Salad

Warm Wild Rice & Asparagus Salad

Indonesian Brown Rice Salad

Chive & Egg Salad

Jicama & Avocado Salad with Orange Vinaigrette

Preparation time: About 20 minutes

●

This refreshing salad, which combines favorite Mexican flavors, is good with black bean dishes and casseroles that call for tortillas.

- 1 teaspoon *each* **Dijon mustard and grated orange peel**
- ¼ **cup orange juice**
- 2 **tablespoons salad oil**
- 1 **medium-size firm-ripe avocado**
- 6 **cups thinly slivered romaine lettuce, rinsed and crisped**
- 1 **cup thinly slivered jicama**
  Salt and pepper

1. Combine mustard, orange peel, orange juice, and oil in a small bowl; mix well. Set dressing aside.

2. Pit, peel, and slice avocado. Place romaine, avocado, and jicama in a large bowl.

3. Pour dressing over salad; mix gently. Season to taste with salt and pepper. Makes 6 servings.

Per serving: 117 calories (72% calories from fat), 2 g protein, 7 g carbohydrates, 10 g total fat (1 g saturated fat), 0 mg cholesterol, 34 mg sodium

Roasted Pepper, Spinach & Feta Salad

Pictured on page 98

Preparation time: About 25 minutes

Standing time: At least 1 hour

●

Offer this pretty, colorful salad either as a first course or as a light main dish.

- 2 **tablespoons** *each* **frozen orange juice concentrate, thawed, and white wine vinegar**
- 1 **tablespoon minced shallot or red onion**
- ¼ **cup olive oil or salad oil**
- 2 **jars (about 7 oz.** *each***) roasted red peppers or whole pimentos, rinsed and drained, cut into 1-inch-wide strips**
- 2 **cups lightly packed tender spinach leaves, rinsed and crisped**
- 1 **cup lightly packed fresh basil**
- 8 **ounces feta cheese, sliced ¼ inch thick**
- 2 **tablespoons pine nuts (optional)**
  Freshly ground pepper

1. Combine orange juice concentrate, vinegar, shallot, and oil in a medium-size bowl; mix well. Gently mix in peppers. Cover and let stand for at least an hour or up to a day.

2. Remove and discard stems from spinach. Arrange a fourth each of the spinach and basil on each of 4 salad plates. Using a slotted spoon, lift peppers from dressing and arrange over spinach mixture, dividing evenly.

3. Top with cheese and drizzle with remaining dressing. Sprinkle with pine nuts, if desired. Season to taste with pepper. Makes 4 servings.

Per serving: 331 calories (68% calories from fat), 11 g protein, 16 g carbohydrates, 26 g total fat (10 g saturated fat), 50 mg cholesterol, 677 mg sodium

Peking Spinach Salad

Low-Fat

Preparation time: About 30 minutes

Baking time: About 3 minutes

●

Crisp won ton squares add appealing crunch to this light and lively salad of fresh spinach, mushrooms, carrots, and rosy plums. To keep the won tons crisp, wait to add the dressing until just before you serve the salad.

- 12　won ton skins (*each* about 3 inches square)
- ⅓　cup plum jam
- 1　tablespoon soy sauce
- 3　tablespoons lemon juice
- ½　teaspoon ground cinnamon
- 1½　quarts (about 12 oz.) lightly packed spinach leaves, rinsed and crisped
- 4　ounces mushrooms, thinly sliced
- ¾　cup *each* shredded carrots and lightly packed cilantro sprigs
- 2　medium-size red-skinned plums, pitted and thinly sliced

1. Cut each won ton skin into quarters. Arrange in a single layer on a greased baking sheet; spray or brush with water. Bake in a 500° oven, watching carefully to prevent burning, until golden (about 3 minutes).

2. Combine jam, soy sauce, lemon juice, and cinnamon in a small bowl; mix well. Set dressing aside.

3. Place spinach in a large bowl. Top with mushrooms, carrots, cilantro, plums, and won tons.

4. Add dressing just before serving; mix gently. Makes 8 servings.

Per serving: 100 calories (4% calories from fat), 3 g protein, 22 g carbohydrates, 1 g total fat (0 g saturated fat), 1 mg cholesterol, 238 mg sodium

Spicy Red Coleslaw

Preparation time: About 30 minutes

Chilling time: At least 30 minutes

●

This red cabbage salad, a colorful mélange of carrots, radishes, and red onion, glistens with a celery seed–speckled vinaigrette dressing.

- 3　tablespoons lemon juice
- 2　tablespoons red wine vinegar
- 2　teaspoons sugar
- 1　teaspoon Dijon mustard
- ½　teaspoon celery seeds
- ¼　teaspoon ground cumin
- 3　tablespoons olive oil
- 　Salt and pepper
- 6　cups finely shredded red cabbage
- 1　cup *each* thinly sliced radishes and shredded carrots
- ¼　cup minced parsley
- 1　tablespoon finely chopped red onion
- 6　to 8 large lettuce leaves, rinsed and crisped

1. Combine lemon juice, vinegar, sugar, mustard, celery seeds, cumin, and oil in a small bowl; mix well. Season to taste with salt and pepper. Set dressing aside.

2. Place cabbage, radishes, carrots, parsley, and onion in a large bowl. Add dressing and mix lightly. Cover and refrigerate for at least 30 minutes or up to 6 hours.

3. Mix slaw again just before serving. Line a serving bowl with lettuce leaves; mound slaw in bowl. Makes 6 servings.

Per serving: 102 calories (59% calories from fat), 2 g protein, 10 g carbohydrates, 7 g total fat (1 g saturated fat), 0 mg cholesterol, 47 mg sodium

Warm Goat Cheese Salad

Pictured on facing page

Preparation time: About 15 minutes

Baking and broiling time: 7 to 10 minutes

●

A thick slice of warm goat cheese nestles in a bed of mixed salad greens, anointed with a mustardy walnut oil dressing and toasted nuts.

- ¾ **cup walnut halves or pieces**
- ¼ **cup white wine vinegar**
- 1 **tablespoon Dijon mustard**
- ¼ **cup walnut oil or olive oil**
   Salt and pepper
- 6 **to 8 ounces round or log-shaped medium-firm goat cheese (chèvre)**
- 12 **ounces mixed salad greens, such as red leaf, oak leaf, and butter lettuces, rinsed and crisped**

1. Spread nuts in a large shallow baking pan and toast in a 400° oven until dark golden brown (5 to 6 minutes). Set pan aside.

2. Combine vinegar, mustard, and oil in a small bowl; mix well. Season to taste with salt and pepper. Set dressing aside.

3. Cut cheese into 6 equal pieces and place in pan with nuts. Broil about 3 inches below heat until cheese is speckled brown and slightly melted (2 to 4 minutes). Meanwhile, tear lettuce into large pieces and arrange on 6 salad plates.

4. Place a piece of cheese on each salad; sprinkle with nuts. Serve with dressing to add to taste. Makes 6 servings.

Per serving: 275 calories (81% calories from fat), 9 g protein, 5 g carbohydrates, 26 g total fat (7 g saturated fat), 22 mg cholesterol, 226 mg sodium

---

Low-Fat

Green & White Sesame Salad

Preparation time: About 20 minutes

Cooking time: 4 to 6 minutes

●

A trio of crunchy vegetables—cool cooked asparagus, slim green beans, and matchstick pieces of jicama—bathe in a piquant hoisin dressing.

- ⅓ **cup seasoned rice vinegar, or ⅓ cup distilled white vinegar plus 1 teaspoon sugar**
- 1 **tablespoon *each* sugar, hoisin sauce, and Dijon mustard**
- 3 **tablespoons sesame seeds**
- 1 **pound slender asparagus, tough ends removed**
- 10 **to 12 ounces slender green beans, ends removed**
- 12 **ounces jicama, peeled and cut into long matchstick pieces**

1. Combine vinegar, sugar, hoisin, and mustard in a small bowl; mix well. Set dressing aside.

2. Toast sesame seeds in a wide frying pan over medium-high heat, stirring often, until golden (2 to 4 minutes). Add to dressing.

3. Pour water into same pan to a depth of ½ inch and bring to a boil over high heat. Add asparagus and beans. Cover and cook just until tender-crisp (about 2 minutes). Drain, immerse in cold water until cool, and drain again.

4. Arrange asparagus, beans, and jicama on a platter. Stir dressing well; drizzle over vegetables. Makes 6 servings.

Per serving: 105 calories (21% calories from fat), 5 g protein, 18 g carbohydrates, 3 g total fat (0.4 g saturated fat), 0 mg cholesterol, 430 mg sodium

Here's a splendid version of a dish that's become a classic in a few short years. Warm Goat Cheese Salad (recipe on facing page) features broiled goat cheese and mixed greens garnished with toasted walnuts. A mustard-based vinaigrette is drizzled over all.

103

Make-Ahead Dressings

Hectic weekday schedules often leave little time for dinner preparation. That's why it's good to have recipes you can make ahead, when you have a few extra moments. These dressings, which keep in the refrigerator, fit the bill perfectly, allowing you to dress a salad in piquant flavors on a moment's notice.

Sample the dressings with simple combinations of one or more greens, or with fresh young spinach leaves. Or drizzle a little dressing over cool vegetables; it's a fine way to revive leftovers when you've cooked more than you need. These convenient dressings are also good for transforming cold cooked legumes (page 64) into tempting salads.

Berry Vinegar Vinaigrette

Preparation time: About 10 minutes

5 tablespoons raspberry or blueberry vinegar, or ¼ cup red wine vinegar plus 1 tablespoon berry jelly

½ cup olive oil or salad oil

2 tablespoons minced shallots

1 teaspoon *each* honey and Dijon mustard

Freshly ground pepper

1. Combine vinegar, oil, shallots, honey, and mustard in a small bowl; mix well. Season to taste with pepper.

2. Pour into a jar, cover, and refrigerate for up to 2 weeks. Shake well before using. Makes about 1 cup.

Per tablespoon: 66 calories (91% calories from fat), 0 g protein, 2 g carbohydrates, 7 g total fat (1 g saturated fat), 0 mg cholesterol, 10 mg sodium

Chinese Mustard Dressing

Preparation time: About 10 minutes

4 teaspoons prepared Chinese mustard or Dijon mustard

¼ cup lemon juice

1 teaspoon Worcestershire

½ cup olive oil or salad oil

3 tablespoons grated Parmesan cheese

Freshly ground pepper

1. Combine mustard, lemon juice, Worcestershire, oil, and cheese in a small bowl; whisk until dressing is creamy and slightly thickened. Season to taste with pepper.

2. Pour into a jar, cover, and refrigerate for up to 2 weeks. Shake well before using. Makes about 1 cup.

Per tablespoon: 67 calories (95% calories from fat), 0.4 g protein, 0.5 g carbohydrates, 7 g total fat (1 g saturated fat), 0.7 mg cholesterol, 59 mg sodium

Honey Mustard Vinaigrette

Preparation time: About 5 minutes

2 tablespoons *each* honey and sherry vinegar

1 tablespoon *each* Dijon mustard, coarse-grained mustard, and dry thyme

2 teaspoons lemon juice

¼ cup olive oil

6 tablespoons salad oil

1. Combine honey, vinegar, Dijon and coarse mustards, thyme, and lemon juice

in a food processor or blender; whirl briefly. With motor running, add olive oil and salad oil in a thin, steady stream, whirling until well combined.

2. Pour into a jar, cover, and refrigerate for up to a week. Shake well before using. Makes about ¾ cup.

Per tablespoon: 115 calories (88% calories from fat), 0.1 g protein, 3 g carbohydrates, 11 g total fat (1 g saturated fat), 0 mg cholesterol, 51 mg sodium

Mixed Oil & Vinegar Dressing

Preparation time: About 10 minutes

¼ cup *each* extra-virgin olive oil, safflower oil, soy oil, and peanut oil

3 tablespoons *each* balsamic vinegar and cider vinegar

1 clove garlic, minced or pressed

1½ tablespoons crumbled blue-veined cheese

1 teaspoon soy sauce

½ teaspoon dry mustard

¼ teaspoon *each* pepper and dry basil

1. Combine olive oil, safflower oil, soy oil, peanut oil, balsamic vinegar, cider vinegar, garlic, cheese, soy sauce, mustard, pepper, and basil in a small bowl; mix well.

2. Pour into a jar, cover, and refrigerate for up to a week. Shake well before using. Makes about 1⅓ cups.

Per tablespoon: 95 calories (98% calories from fat), 0.1 g protein, 0.3 g carbohydrates, 11 g total fat (2 g saturated fat), 0.5 mg cholesterol, 25 mg sodium

Cauliflower with Toasted Mustard Seeds

Preparation time: *About 15 minutes*

Cooking time: *About 15 minutes*

●

Cauliflower makes a delicious foil for a sprightly mustard-spiked yogurt dressing in this low-fat salad.

    3 **tablespoons mustard seeds**

  1½ **cups plain low-fat or nonfat yogurt**

    ¼ **cup minced fresh mint or 2 tablespoons crumbled dry mint**

    2 **teaspoons sugar**

    1 **teaspoon ground cumin**

    1 **large cauliflower (about 2 lbs.), stem and leaves trimmed**

    1 **small head romaine lettuce (8 to 10 oz.), rinsed and crisped**

      Mint sprigs (optional)

1. Toast mustard seeds in a small frying pan over medium heat, stirring often, until seeds turn gray (about 5 minutes).

2. Combine yogurt, minced mint, sugar, cumin, and 2 tablespoons of the mustard seeds in a large bowl; mix well. Set aside.

3. Cut cauliflower into bite-size flowerets. Place on a rack in a 5- to 6-quart pan over 1 inch boiling water. Cover and cook over high heat until tender when pierced (about 8 minutes). Immerse in cold water until cool; drain well on paper towels.

4. Add cauliflower to yogurt mixture, mixing gently. (At this point, you may cover and refrigerate for up to 4 hours.)

5. Arrange lettuce leaves on a platter. Spoon cauliflower mixture on lettuce. Sprinkle with remaining 1 tablespoon mustard seeds. Garnish with mint sprigs, if desired. Makes 4 servings.

Per serving: 134 calories (26% calories from fat), 9 g protein, 17 g carbohydrates, 4 g total fat (1 g saturated fat), 5 mg cholesterol, 79 mg sodium

Cucumber & Green Onion Salad

Preparation time: *About 20 minutes*

Standing time: *About 30 minutes*

●

This refreshing sliced cucumber salad has a lean rice vinegar dressing. Offer it with brown rice or Asian dishes.

    3 **large English cucumbers (about 3 lbs. *total*), thinly sliced**

    1 **tablespoon salt**

    ½ **cup thinly sliced green onions**

    1 **tablespoon sugar**

    ⅓ **cup seasoned rice vinegar, or ⅓ cup rice vinegar plus 1 tablespoon sugar**

1. Mix cucumbers and salt in a large bowl. With your hands, lightly crush cucumbers. Let stand for about 30 minutes.

2. Transfer cucumbers to a colander and squeeze gently; let drain briefly. Rinse with cold water, squeeze gently, and drain again. (At this point, you may cover and refrigerate for up to a day.)

3. Combine cucumbers, onions, sugar, and vinegar in a large bowl; mix well. If desired, transfer with a slotted spoon to a rimmed platter. Makes 8 to 10 servings.

Per serving: 34 calories (5% calories from fat), 1 g protein, 8 g carbohydrates, 0.2 g total fat (0 g saturated fat), 0 mg cholesterol, 300 mg sodium

*Part salad and part salsa, Squash Salad Provençal (recipe on facing page) can be served
as a salad course or as a topping for grilled Oriental eggplant and other vegetables. It's even good
spooned into a fluffy baked potato.*

Squash Salad Provençal

Pictured on facing page

Preparation time: About 25 minutes

●

This colorful medley of green and yellow summer squash with tomatoes and olives can also be served as a salsa to accent grilled vegetables, such as eggplant and small red-skinned potatoes.

- 2 **medium-size zucchini (about 8 oz.** *total***), diced**
- 2 **large yellow crookneck squash (8 to 10 oz.** *total***), diced**
- 2 **large pear-shaped (Roma-type) tomatoes, seeded and finely chopped**
- ¼ **cup dried tomatoes packed in oil, drained and finely chopped**
- ¼ **cup oil-cured ripe olives, pitted and minced**
- 3 **green onions, thinly sliced**
- 3 **tablespoons cider vinegar**
- 1½ **teaspoons minced fresh oregano or ½ teaspoon dry oregano**
   Salt and pepper
   Oregano sprig (optional)

1. **Combine** zucchini, crookneck squash, pear-shaped tomatoes, dried tomatoes, olives, and onions in a large bowl. Drizzle with vinegar and sprinkle with minced oregano. Mix lightly.

2. **Season** to taste with salt and pepper. Garnish with oregano sprig, if desired. Makes 4 to 6 servings.

Per serving: 93 calories (57% calories from fat), 2 g protein, 9 g carbohydrates, 7 g total fat (1 g saturated fat), 0 mg cholesterol, 503 mg sodium

Shredded Zucchini Salad

Preparation time: About 20 minutes

Cooking time: About 3 minutes

Standing time: About 30 minutes

●

Shred raw zucchini into long, thin strands—an Oriental shredder works well—to make this refreshing almond-topped salad.

- ¼ **cup sliced almonds**
- 3 **large zucchini (about 1¼ lbs.** *total***)**
- 3 **tablespoons cider vinegar**
- 2 **tablespoons extra-virgin olive oil**
   Salt and pepper
- 2 **ounces thinly shaved Parmesan cheese**

1. **Toast** almonds in a small frying pan over medium-high heat, stirring often, until golden brown (about 3 minutes). Set aside.

2. **Shred** zucchini into long, thin strands. Place in a colander and let stand for about 30 minutes to drain. Squeeze gently.

3. **Transfer** zucchini to a large bowl; fluff with a fork. Add vinegar and oil; mix lightly. Season to taste with salt and pepper.

4. **Mound** zucchini mixture on salad plates. Sprinkle with almonds and cheese. Makes 4 to 6 servings.

Per serving: 137 calories (69% calories from fat), 6 g protein, 5 g carbohydrates, 11 g total fat (3 g saturated fat), 8 mg cholesterol, 186 mg sodium

Zucchini & Cauliflower with Tahini

Preparation time: About 20 minutes

Cooking time: 10 to 15 minutes

●

A thick sesame tahini sauce with garbanzos, yogurt, and lemon juice cloaks cool cooked zucchini and cauliflower.

> 1 **small can (about 8¾ oz.) garbanzo beans**
>
> ½ **cup *each* plain low-fat yogurt, lemon juice, and canned tahini**
>
> ½ **teaspoon ground cumin**
>
> 1 **clove garlic**
>
> **Salt and pepper**
>
> 1 **small cauliflower (about 1 lb.), stem and leaves trimmed**
>
> 4 **medium-size zucchini (about 1 lb. *total*), sliced ½ inch thick**
>
> **Parsley sprigs and lemon slices**

1. Drain garbanzos, reserving liquid. In a food processor or blender, combine garbanzos, yogurt, lemon juice, tahini, cumin, and garlic; whirl until smooth. Add a little bean liquid to make sauce pourable; whirl again. Season to taste with salt and pepper. (At this point, you may cover and refrigerate for up to a week; stir before using.)

2. Cut cauliflower into bite-size flowerets. Bring 3 quarts water to a boil in a 4- to 5-quart pan over high heat. Add cauliflower and cook until tender when pierced (6 to 8 minutes). Lift out with a slotted spoon, drain, and arrange on a platter.

3. Add zucchini to boiling water and cook just until tender when pierced (4 to 6 minutes). Drain, immerse in cold water until cool, and drain again. Add to platter.

4. Pour tahini sauce over vegetables. Garnish with parsley and lemon slices. Makes 8 servings.

Per serving: 153 calories (48% calories from fat), 6 g protein, 15 g carbohydrates, 9 g total fat (1 g saturated fat), 0.9 mg cholesterol, 128 mg sodium

Spaghetti Squash & Broccoli

Preparation time: About 25 minutes

Cooking and baking time: 1¼ to 1½ hours

●

Lean spaghetti squash makes an appealing salad with lightly cooked broccoli and a delicate orange and rice vinegar dressing.

> 1 **medium-size spaghetti squash (3 to 4 lbs.)**
>
> ½ **cup walnuts or pecans, coarsely chopped**
>
> 2 **cups broccoli flowerets**
>
> 2 **tablespoons grated orange peel**
>
> ½ **cup seasoned rice vinegar, or ½ cup rice vinegar plus 1 teaspoon sugar**
>
> **Salt**
>
> **Butter lettuce leaves, rinsed and crisped**

1. Pierce shell of squash in several places. Set squash on an 8-inch-square sheet of foil and bake in a 350° oven for 45 minutes; turn squash over and continue to bake until shell yields to pressure (15 to 25 more minutes). Let stand until cool enough to handle.

2. Cut squash in half horizontally. Scoop out and discard seeds. Remove strands of squash with a fork. (At this point, you may cover and refrigerate for up to 2 days.)

3. Toast nuts in a small frying pan over medium-high heat, stirring often, until lightly browned (6 to 8 minutes). Pour into a small bowl and set aside.

4. Bring 3 cups water to a boil in a 1½- to 2-quart pan over high heat. Add broccoli and cook just until tender when pierced (about 2 minutes). Drain, immerse in cold water until cool, and drain again.

5. Combine broccoli, squash, and orange peel in a large bowl. Pour in vinegar and mix lightly. Season to taste with salt.

6. Arrange lettuce on 6 salad plates. Mound salad on lettuce. Sprinkle with nuts. Makes 6 servings.

Per serving: 158 calories (39% calories from fat), 4 g protein, 22 g carbohydrates, 7 g total fat (0.8 g saturated fat), 0 mg cholesterol, 439 mg sodium

Soy-braised Eggplant Salad

Preparation time: About 15 minutes

Cooking time: About 40 minutes

Cooling time: At least 30 minutes

●

You can serve this Hunan-style salad at room temperature or cold, as a side dish with stir-fried vegetables or as the first course of an Asian meal.

- 1 **medium-size eggplant (about 1 lb.)**
- 3 **to 6 tablespoons salad oil**
- 1 **cup water**
- ¼ **cup soy sauce**
- 6 **thin slices ginger (*each* about 1-inch diameter)**
- 2 **cloves garlic, minced or pressed**
- 1 **teaspoon sugar**
- 3 **tablespoons red wine vinegar**
- ⅓ **cup coarsely chopped cilantro**
- 2 **teaspoons minced fresh ginger**
- ¼ **to ½ teaspoon crushed red pepper flakes**

1. **Remove** and discard eggplant stem. Cut unpeeled eggplant lengthwise into 1-inch-thick wedges.

2. **Pour** 2 tablespoons of the oil into a wide frying pan. Place over medium-high heat until oil is hot. Add eggplant, cut sides down, several pieces at a time (do not crowd pan). Cook, turning often, until lightly browned on all sides (10 to 15 minutes total); add more oil as needed. When all eggplant is browned, return to pan.

3. **Add** water, soy sauce, ginger slices, garlic, and sugar. Bring to a boil; reduce heat, cover, and simmer, turning eggplant occasionally, until it mashes easily when pressed (25 to 30 minutes). Stir in vinegar. Let cool to room temperature, turning occasionally. (At this point, you may cover and refrigerate for up to a day.)

4. **Remove** and discard ginger slices. Transfer eggplant and sauce to a serving dish. Sprinkle with cilantro and minced ginger. Season to taste with red pepper flakes. Makes 4 servings.

Per serving: 184 calories (73% calories from fat), 2 g protein, 11 g carbohydrates, 15 g total fat (2 g saturated fat), 0 mg cholesterol, 1,034 mg sodium

Fresh Corn on Romaine with Parmesan

Preparation time: About 30 minutes

Cooking time: 4 to 6 minutes

●

This red, green, and gold first-course salad highlights the delicate sweetness of fresh corn.

- 2 **tablespoons balsamic vinegar or red wine vinegar**
- 2 **tablespoons mayonnaise**
- 1 **teaspoon coarse-grained mustard**
- 1½ **teaspoons minced shallot**
- 3 **tablespoons olive oil**
  Pepper
  About 2 ounces Parmesan cheese
- 2 **medium-size ears corn**
- 2 **small heads romaine lettuce (about 1¼ lbs. *total*), rinsed and crisped**
- 1 **small red bell pepper, seeded and cut into bite-size slivers**

1. **Combine** vinegar, mayonnaise, mustard, shallot, and oil in a small bowl; mix well. Season to taste with pepper. Set dressing aside.

2. **Pull** a cheese-shaving slicer or vegetable peeler over cheese to make thin strips; set aside.

3. **Remove** and discard corn husks and silk. Bring 2 quarts water to a boil in a 5- to 6-quart pan over high heat. Add corn and cook until hot (4 to 6 minutes). Drain and let cool. Cut corn kernels from cobs.

4. **Reserve** large romaine leaves for other uses. Arrange small leaves on 4 salad plates. Spoon on bell pepper slivers and corn. Gently top with a layer of shaved cheese. Drizzle with dressing. Makes 4 servings.

Per serving: 263 calories (66% calories from fat), 9 g protein, 14 g carbohydrates, 20 g total fat (5 g saturated fat), 14 mg cholesterol, 297 mg sodium

Bok Choy with Ginger Vinaigrette

Pictured on facing page

Preparation time: About 15 minutes

Cooking time: About 10 minutes

•

Tender young bunches of lightly cooked baby bok choy are served as a salad with a piquant fresh ginger dressing.

2 tablespoons white wine vinegar

2 teaspoons *each* Dijon mustard and soy sauce

1 clove garlic, minced or pressed

1 tablespoon minced fresh ginger

½ teaspoon sugar

⅓ cup salad oil

1½ pounds baby bok choy or bok choy hearts (*each* 6 to 8 inches long), well rinsed

Sliced kumquats (optional)

1. Combine vinegar, mustard, soy sauce, garlic, ginger, sugar, and oil in a small bowl; mix well. Set dressing aside.

2. Use small heads bok choy whole, or, if thicker than 3 inches, cut in half lengthwise. Place bok choy in a single layer on a rack in a wide pan over 1 inch boiling water. Cover and cook over medium-high heat until stems begin to turn translucent and are just soft when pierced (4 to 5 minutes). Immerse in cold water until cool; drain well.

3. Arrange in a single layer in a shallow serving dish. Pour dressing over bok choy. Garnish with kumquats, if desired. Makes 6 to 8 servings.

Per serving: 109 calories (83% calories from fat), 2 g protein, 3 g carbohydrates, 11 g total fat (1 g saturated fat), 0 mg cholesterol, 204 mg sodium

Red & Orange Ginger Salad

Preparation time: About 35 minutes

Cooking time: About 40 minutes

Cooling time: About 20 minutes

•

This colorful beet and potato salad includes juicy nectarines. Accent its summertime appeal with bright nasturtium blossoms, if you wish.

3 medium-size thin-skinned potatoes (about 1 lb. *total*), peeled

4 medium-size beets (about 1 lb. *total*), well scrubbed

¼ cup coarsely chopped preserved ginger in syrup (including about 1 teaspoon syrup)

¼ cup distilled white vinegar

2 tablespoons water

⅛ teaspoon ground red pepper (cayenne)

2 medium-size nectarines (about 12 oz. *total*)

Salt

Nasturtium flowers (optional)

1. Place potatoes in a 3- to 4-quart pan; add water to cover. Bring to a boil; reduce heat, cover, and boil gently just until tender when pierced (about 15 minutes). Lift out, drain, and let cool.

2. Add beets to pan. Return to a boil over high heat; reduce heat, cover, and boil gently until tender when pierced (about 20 minutes). Meanwhile, in a blender or food processor, combine ginger, vinegar, water, and ground red pepper; whirl until smooth. Set dressing aside.

3. Drain beets and let cool; peel. Pit nectarines. Cut potatoes, beets, and nectarines into ½-inch cubes and arrange in a wide bowl. Drizzle with dressing. Season to taste with salt. Decorate with nasturtiums, if desired. Makes 6 servings.

Per serving: 120 calories (3% calories from fat), 3 g protein, 28 g carbohydrates, 0.4 g total fat (0 g saturated fat), 0 mg cholesterol, 49 mg sodium

Glistening baby bok choy becomes an enticing salad offering when bathed in an Asian-inspired dressing. Serve Bok Choy with Ginger Vinaigrette (recipe on facing page) as a preface to an Oriental dinner.

Roasted Vegetable Salads

Oven-roasting intensifies the flavors and natural sweetness of vegetables. In the chart below are directions for roasting a variety of fresh vegetables. Use them in the low-fat recipes that appear on the facing page, serve them by themselves, or make your own roasted vegetable combinations. The vegetables will keep in the refrigerator for up to a day. For best flavor, bring them to room temperature before serving.

Vegetable & Preparation	Pan Size	Roasting Directions
Potatoes, thin-skinned: 1 pound small (about 1½-inch diameter). Cut into 1-inch chunks.	8 to 10 inches square; 10 by 15 inches for 2 batches or 2 vegetables	Mix with 2 teaspoons **olive oil.** Bake in a 475° oven, turning occasionally, until richly browned (35 to 45 minutes).
Potatoes, russet: 2 large (about 1½ lbs. *total*). Peel and cut into 1-inch chunks.	8 to 10 inches square; 10 by 15 inches for 2 batches or 2 vegetables	As directed for thin-skinned potatoes (above); allow 1 to 1¼ hours.
Carrots: 4 large (about 1 lb. *total*). Cut into 1-inch chunks.	8 to 10 inches square; 10 by 15 inches for 2 batches or 2 vegetables	As directed for thin-skinned potatoes (above); allow 45 to 55 minutes.
Garlic: 3 large heads (about 12 oz. *total*). Separate into cloves; peel.	8 to 10 inches square; 10 by 15 inches for 2 batches or 2 vegetables	As directed for thin-skinned potatoes (above); bake until tinged with brown (20 to 30 minutes).
Fennel: 2 large heads (*each* about 3 inches wide). Rinse; trim bases and tops of stalks. Cut bulbs into 1-inch chunks.	10 inches square or 9 by 13 inches; 10 by 15 inches for 2 batches or 2 vegetables	As directed for thin-skinned potatoes (above); bake until tinged with brown (about 1 hour).
Onion, red: 1 large (about 12 oz.). Peel; cut into ¾-inch-thick chunks.	8 to 10 inches square; 10 by 15 inches for 2 batches or 2 vegetables	Mix with ½ teaspoon **olive oil** and 2 tablespoons **balsamic vinegar** or wine vinegar. Roast as directed for thin-skinned potatoes (above); bake until edges are dark brown (40 to 50 minutes).
Tomatoes, pear-shaped (Roma-type): 12 to 14 medium-size (about 1¾ lbs. *total*). Halve lengthwise.	9 by 13 inches; 10 by 15 inches for 2 batches. Do not combine with other vegetables.	Drizzle with about 1¾ teaspoons **olive oil;** arrange, cut sides up, in pan. Season to taste with **salt.** Bake in a 475° oven until edges are dark brown (about 1 hour and 10 minutes).
Peppers, red bell: 2 medium-size (about 1 lb. *total*). Halve lengthwise.	10 inches square or 9 by 13 inches. Do not combine with other vegetables.	Broil, cut sides down, 4 to 6 inches below heat until skins are charred (about 8 minutes). Drape with foil and let cool. Pull off and discard skins and seeds; save juice. Cut into strips or chunks.
Eggplants, Oriental: 5 or 6 slender (about 1 lb. *total*). Cut off stems. Halve lengthwise; cut each half lengthwise into thirds.	10 by 15 inches. Do not combine with other vegetables.	Rub skin very lightly with about 1 teaspoon *total* **olive oil.** Arrange, skin sides down, in an oiled pan. Bake in a 475° oven until richly browned and soft when pressed (20 to 30 minutes).

Roasted Potato & Carrot Salad

Preparation time: About 30 minutes
Baking time: 35 to 45 minutes

Citrus Dressing (recipe follows)

2 batches roasted thin-skinned potatoes (see chart)

2 batches roasted carrots (see chart)

Salt and pepper

Basil sprigs

1. Prepare Citrus Dressing. Mix lightly with potatoes and carrots in a shallow bowl. Season to taste with salt and pepper. Garnish with basil. Makes 8 servings.

Citrus Dressing. In a small bowl, combine 2 teaspoons grated **orange peel**; ½ cup **orange juice**; 2 tablespoons **white wine vinegar**; 2 tablespoons chopped **fresh basil**; 1 tablespoon **honey**; 2 teaspoons **Dijon mustard**; 1 teaspoon **ground cumin**; 2 cloves **garlic**, minced or pressed; and 1 fresh **jalapeño chile**, seeded and finely chopped. Mix well.

Per serving: 196 calories (23% calories from fat), 3 g protein, 36 g carbohydrates, 5 g total fat (0.6 g saturated fat), 0 mg cholesterol, 83 mg sodium

Broccoli & Roasted Garlic Salad

Preparation time: About 30 minutes
Cooking and baking time: 20 to 30 minutes

9 cups (about 1¼ lbs.) broccoli flowerets

2 tablespoons soy sauce

1 teaspoon Oriental sesame oil

1 batch roasted garlic (see chart)

1. Bring 3 quarts water to a boil in a 5- to 6-quart pan over high heat. Add broccoli and cook just until tender (about 5 minutes). Drain, immerse in cold water until cool, and drain again. Pat dry.

2. Mix soy sauce and oil in a shallow bowl. Add broccoli and garlic; mix lightly. Makes 6 servings.

Per serving: 123 calories (18% calories from fat), 6 g protein, 22 g carbohydrates, 3 g total fat (0.3 g saturated fat), 0 mg cholesterol, 372 mg sodium

Roasted Pepper & Black Bean Salad

Preparation time: About 30 minutes
Broiling time: About 8 minutes

Cilantro Dressing (recipe follows)

6 cups cooked black beans (page 64) or 3 cans (about 15 oz. *each*) black beans, rinsed and drained

1 batch roasted bell peppers (see chart)

Salt and pepper

1. Prepare Cilantro Dressing.

2. Mix beans, bell peppers and their juices, and dressing in a large bowl. Season to taste with salt and pepper. Makes 8 to 10 servings.

Cilantro Dressing. In a medium-size bowl, combine ½ cup **seasoned rice vinegar**, or ½ cup rice vinegar plus 1 tablespoon sugar; ¼ cup **olive oil**; 1 tablespoon **honey**; and ½ teaspoon **chili oil**. Mix well. Just before using, stir in ¼ cup minced **cilantro** and 2 tablespoons chopped **green onion**.

Per serving: 240 calories (25% calories from fat), 10 g protein, 36 g carbohydrates, 7 g total fat (1 g saturated fat), 0 mg cholesterol, 487 mg sodium

Roasted Eggplant Salad

Preparation time: About 40 minutes
Baking time: 40 minutes to 1 hour
Broiling time: About 8 minutes

1 batch roasted eggplants (see chart)

1 batch roasted bell peppers (see chart)

1 batch roasted garlic (see chart)

3 tablespoons balsamic vinegar, or 3 tablespoons red wine vinegar plus 2 teaspoons sugar

Salt and pepper

2 tablespoons chopped parsley

1. Mix eggplants, bell peppers, garlic, and vinegar in a shallow bowl. Season to taste with salt and pepper. Sprinkle with parsley. Makes 6 servings.

Per serving: 137 calories (16% calories from fat), 5 g protein, 27 g carbohydrates, 3 g total fat (0.4 g saturated fat), 0 mg cholesterol, 13 mg sodium

Tomato & White Bean Salad

Preparation time: About 20 minutes
Cooking and baking time: About 1 hour and 10 minutes

3 cans (about 15 oz. *each*) white kidney beans (cannellini)

2 tablespoons chopped fresh thyme or 2 teaspoons dry thyme

2 tablespoons chopped fresh basil or 2 teaspoons dry basil

1 batch roasted tomatoes (see chart)

1 batch roasted red onion (see chart)

Salt and pepper

1. Place beans and their liquid in a 2- to 3-quart pan. Add thyme and, if used, dry basil. Bring to a boil, stirring often; reduce heat and simmer for 3 minutes.

2. Pour into a strainer, reserving liquid. Transfer beans to a large bowl; tap herbs from strainer into beans.

3. Chop 8 of the tomato halves coarsely. Stir into beans with fresh basil, if used, and onion. Stir in some of the reserved liquid to moisten, if desired. Season to taste with salt and pepper.

4. Arrange remaining tomato halves over salad. Makes 6 to 8 servings.

Per serving: 205 calories (10% calories from fat), 11 g protein, 37 g carbohydrates, 2 g total fat (0.3 g saturated fat), 0 mg cholesterol, 648 mg sodium

When is potato salad a meal in itself? When it's summer-fresh Peppered Potato & Two-Bean Salad
(recipe on facing page), a colorful mélange of potatoes, black beans, spinach, bell pepper,
and slender green beans.

Peppered Potato & Two-Bean Salad

Low-Fat

Pictured on facing page

Preparation time: About 25 minutes

Cooking time: 25 to 30 minutes

●

Green beans, black beans, and red bell pepper mingle with fresh herbs in this multicolored potato salad.

> 5 **large red thin-skinned potatoes (about 2 lbs. *total*)**
> **Yogurt & Herb Dressing (recipe follows)**
> 2 **cups cooked black beans (page 64) or 1 can (about 14½ oz.) black beans, rinsed and drained**
> ½ **cup chopped red onion**
> **Salt**
> 8 **ounces spinach leaves, rinsed and crisped**
> 1 **medium-size red bell pepper, seeded and chopped**
> 4 **cups cold cooked green beans**

1. Place potatoes in a 5- to 6-quart pan; add water to cover. Bring to a boil; reduce heat, cover, and boil gently until tender when pierced (25 to 30 minutes). Meanwhile, prepare Yogurt & Herb Dressing.

2. Drain potatoes, immerse in cold water until cool, and drain again. Cut into ¾-inch cubes. Add to Yogurt & Herb Dressing along with black beans and onion; mix gently. Season to taste with salt.

3. Line a platter with some of the spinach; sliver remaining spinach. Mound slivered spinach on platter and top with potato salad. Sprinkle with bell pepper and surround with green beans. Makes 8 servings.

Yogurt & Herb Dressing. In a large bowl, combine 1 cup **plain nonfat yogurt,** or ½ cup *each* plain nonfat yogurt and reduced-calorie mayonnaise; 3 tablespoons *each* minced **cilantro** and minced **fresh basil;** and 2 tablespoons **lemon juice.** Mix well.

Per serving: 202 calories (3% calories from fat), 10 g protein, 41 g carbohydrates, 1 g total fat (0.1 g saturated fat), 0.6 mg cholesterol, 140 mg sodium

Avocado Fans with Pistachios

Pictured on front cover

Preparation time: About 25 minutes

●

A sprinkling of crisp pistachios adds color, flavor, and texture contrast to this salad of sliced oranges and avocados.

> ¼ **teaspoon grated orange peel**
> 3 **tablespoons orange juice**
> 1 **tablespoon white wine vinegar**
> 1 **teaspoon Dijon mustard**
> ¼ **cup salad oil**
> 2 **large oranges**
> 2 **large avocados**
> **Watercress sprigs**
> ¼ **cup shelled roasted salted or unsalted pistachios, coarsely chopped**

1. Combine orange peel, orange juice, vinegar, mustard, and oil in a small bowl; mix well. Set dressing aside.

2. Cut and discard peel and white membrane from oranges. Slice each orange crosswise into 6 to 8 rounds.

3. Cut avocados in half lengthwise. Remove and discard pits and peel. Set each avocado half, cut side down, on a dinner plate or large salad plate. Starting at large end of avocado, cut lengthwise to within ¾ inch of top, spacing cuts about ½ inch apart. Press down gently to fan slices slightly apart.

4. Arrange 3 or 4 orange slices and a few watercress sprigs alongside each avocado half. Spoon dressing over salads. Sprinkle with pistachios. Makes 4 servings.

Per serving: 421 calories (74% calories from fat), 5 g protein, 24 g carbohydrates, 37 g total fat (5 g saturated fat), 0 mg cholesterol, 85 mg sodium

Summer Fruit & Almond Salad

Preparation time: *About 45 minutes*

Cooking time: *About 3 minutes*

●

Celebrate summer's bounty with style! Serve a rainbow of melons, grapes, and berries in a slightly sweet, almond-flavored citrus dressing.

- ½ **cup sliced almonds**
- 8 **ounces jicama, peeled and cut into matchstick pieces**
- ¼ **cup orange juice**
- 2 **tablespoons lemon juice**
- 1 **teaspoon** *each* **poppy seeds and sugar**
- ¼ **teaspoon almond extract**
- 2 **cups** *each* **cubed, seeded watermelon and cubed cantaloupe**
- 1 **cup seedless grapes, halved**
- 1 **cup strawberries, hulled and sliced**
- 12 **to 16 large lettuce leaves, rinsed and crisped**
- 1 **large kiwi fruit (about 4 oz.), peeled and thinly sliced**

1. Toast almonds in a wide frying pan over medium-high heat, stirring often, until golden brown (about 3 minutes). Remove from pan and set aside.

2. Mix jicama, orange juice, lemon juice, poppy seeds, sugar, and almond extract in a large bowl. Add watermelon, cantaloupe, grapes, and strawberries; mix gently.

3. Arrange lettuce on salad plates. Mound fruit mixture on lettuce. Garnish with kiwi slices and sprinkle with almonds. Makes 6 to 8 servings.

Per serving: 128 calories (29% calories from fat), 3 g protein, 21 g carbohydrates, 4 g total fat (0.4 g saturated fat), 0 mg cholesterol, 12 mg sodium

Wilted Waldorf Salad

Preparation time: *About 20 minutes*

Cooking time: *14 to 17 minutes*

●

Quickly wilt shredded red cabbage in a hot frying pan to make the colorful main ingredient of this salad, a variation on a classic theme.

- ⅓ **cup slivered almonds or chopped walnuts**
- 2 **tablespoons sugar**
- 6 **tablespoons cider vinegar**
- 1 **large tart apple**
- 1 **tablespoon salad oil**
- 1 **large onion, thinly sliced**
- 1 **clove garlic, minced or pressed**
- ½ **teaspoon caraway seeds**
- 1 **quart finely shredded red cabbage**
  Salt

1. Toast nuts in a wide frying pan over medium heat, stirring often, until lightly browned (8 to 10 minutes). Pour out of pan; set nuts and pan aside.

2. Mix sugar and 4 tablespoons of the vinegar in a medium-size bowl until sugar is dissolved. Core apple and cut into ½-inch cubes. Stir into vinegar mixture; set aside.

3. Heat oil in pan over high heat. Add onion, garlic, and caraway seeds. Cook, stirring occasionally, until onion begins to soften (4 to 5 minutes). Add cabbage and remaining 2 tablespoons vinegar. Cook, stirring, until cabbage is barely wilted (about 2 minutes).

4. Transfer cabbage mixture to a shallow bowl. Add apple mixture and nuts; mix lightly. Season to taste with salt. Makes 6 servings.

Per serving: 128 calories (42% calories from fat), 3 g protein, 17 g carbohydrates, 6 g total fat (1 g saturated fat), 0 mg cholesterol, 7 mg sodium

Red Potato Salad with Yogurt

Preparation time: About 25 minutes

Cooking time: 25 to 30 minutes

●

Yogurt and rice vinegar contribute refreshingly tangy taste; celery and green onions lend crisp texture. You can make this salad up to a day in advance of serving it.

> 5 large red thin-skinned potatoes (about 2 lbs. *total*)
>
> ½ cup *each* mayonnaise and plain yogurt
>
> 3 tablespoons seasoned rice vinegar, or 3 tablespoons white wine vinegar plus 1 teaspoon sugar
>
> 2 cloves garlic, minced or pressed
>
> 1 tablespoon minced fresh thyme or 1 teaspoon dry thyme
>
> ½ cup *each* thinly sliced green onions and thinly sliced celery
>
>   Salt and pepper

1. **Place** potatoes in a 5- to 6-quart pan; add water to cover. Bring to a boil; reduce heat, cover, and boil gently until tender when pierced (25 to 30 minutes).

2. **Drain,** immerse in cold water until cool, and drain again. Cut into ¾-inch cubes.

3. **Combine** mayonnaise, yogurt, vinegar, garlic, and thyme in a large bowl; mix well. Add potatoes, onions, and celery; mix gently. Season to taste with salt and pepper. If made ahead, cover and refrigerate for up to a day. Makes 6 servings.

Per serving: 278 calories (48% calories from fat), 4 g protein, 32 g carbohydrates, 15 g total fat (2 g saturated fat), 12 mg cholesterol, 288 mg sodium

White Bean Salad

Pictured on page 55

Preparation time: About 15 minutes

Standing time: About 1 hour

●

A garlicky, herb-flecked marinade imparts tangy flavor to these beans. They make a grand picnic lunch with crusty bread, deviled eggs, and a selection of cheeses.

> ½ cup olive oil
>
> 3 tablespoons red wine vinegar
>
> 2 tablespoons chopped chives
>
> 3 cloves garlic, minced or pressed
>
> 1 tablespoon minced fresh tarragon or 1 teaspoon dry tarragon
>
> ⅛ teaspoon freshly grated nutmeg or ground nutmeg
>
> ½ teaspoon *each* salt and honey
>
>   Dash of liquid hot pepper seasoning
>
> 5 cups cooked small white beans (page 64), rinsed and drained
>
> ⅓ cup finely chopped parsley
>
>   Butter lettuce leaves, rinsed and crisped

1. **Combine** oil, vinegar, chives, garlic, tarragon, nutmeg, salt, honey, and hot pepper seasoning in a large bowl; mix well.

2. **Add** beans and parsley to dressing; mix well. Let stand at room temperature for about an hour. (At this point, you may cover and refrigerate for up to 6 hours; bring to room temperature before continuing.)

3. **Line** a bowl or platter with lettuce. Mound beans on lettuce. Makes 4 to 6 servings.

Per serving: 429 calories (46% calories from fat), 15 g protein, 44 g carbohydrates, 22 g total fat (3 g saturated fat), 0 mg cholesterol, 560 mg sodium

Cool Pasta Platter with Olives & Cheese

Pictured on facing page

Preparation time: About 20 minutes

Cooking time: About 10 minutes

Flavorful Roma tomatoes team up with fancifully shaped pasta, pungent calamata olives, and goat cheese for this colorful supper salad.

2 cups (about 6 oz.) bite-size dry pasta, such as penne or rotelle
  Tarragon Dressing (recipe follows)

2 quarts bite-size pieces red leaf lettuce, rinsed and crisped

8 medium-size pear-shaped (Roma-type) tomatoes (about 1 lb. *total*), thinly sliced

⅔ cup (about 3 oz.) crumbled soft goat cheese

½ cup calamata or other Greek-style salty olives
  Freshly ground pepper

1. Bring 3 quarts water to a boil in a 5- to 6-quart pan. Add pasta and cook just until tender to bite (about 10 minutes); or cook according to package directions. Drain, rinse with cold water, and drain again.

2. Prepare Tarragon Dressing. In a large bowl, combine pasta and ⅓ cup of the dressing; mix lightly.

3. Arrange lettuce on 4 dinner plates. Mound pasta on lettuce and top with tomatoes. Sprinkle with cheese and olives.

4. Drizzle remaining Tarragon Dressing over salads. Season to taste with pepper. Makes 4 to 6 servings.

Tarragon Dressing. In a small bowl, combine ⅓ cup **white wine vinegar,** 1½ tablespoons **Dijon mustard,** 2 teaspoons **dry tarragon,** and 3 tablespoons **olive oil;** mix well.

Per serving: 255 calories (34% calories from fat), 10 g protein, 34 g carbohydrates, 10 g total fat (3 g saturated fat), 8 mg cholesterol, 555 mg sodium

Minted Lentils with Goat Cheese

Preparation time: About 20 minutes

Cooking time: 25 to 30 minutes

Cooling time: At least 20 minutes

Red cabbage leaves frame this handsome salad of tender lentils, pink onion rings, tangy goat cheese, and fresh mint.

1 package (about 12 oz.) or 2 cups lentils, rinsed and drained

3 cups homemade (page 33) or canned vegetable broth

½ teaspoon dill seeds

1 teaspoon dry thyme
  Rosy Onion Rings (recipe follows)

3 tablespoons red wine vinegar

2 to 3 tablespoons olive oil
  Red cabbage leaves, rinsed and crisped
  About 4 ounces medium-firm goat cheese (chèvre), coarsely crumbled

¼ cup chopped fresh mint
  Mint sprigs

1. Combine lentils, broth, dill seeds, and thyme in a 2- to 3-quart pan. Bring to a boil; reduce heat, cover, and boil gently, stirring occasionally, until lentils are tender to bite (20 to 25 minutes). Meanwhile, prepare Rosy Onion Rings.

2. Drain lentils, reserving liquid. Let lentil mixture and liquid cool. (At this point, you may cover and refrigerate lentils and liquid for up to 2 days.)

3. Mix lentils and enough of the reserved liquid to moisten (4 to 6 tablespoons) in a large bowl. Gently stir in vinegar and 1 tablespoon of the oil.

4. Line a platter or bowl with cabbage. Mound lentils on cabbage. Top with Rosy Onion Rings, cheese, and chopped mint. Drizzle with 1 to 2 tablespoons more oil. Garnish with mint sprigs. Makes 6 servings.

Rosy Onion Rings. Peel and thinly slice 1 large **red onion** (about 12 oz.). In a 2- to 3-quart pan, combine 3 cups **water** and 2 tablespoons **red wine vinegar.** Bring to a boil over high heat. Push onion into boiling liquid and cook until mixture returns to a boil; drain well. If made ahead, cover and refrigerate for up to 2 days.

Per serving: 345 calories (31% calories from fat), 21 g protein, 40 g carbohydrates, 12 g total fat (5 g saturated fat), 15 mg cholesterol, 616 mg sodium

Pasta needn't be predictable, at least not when you serve Cool Pasta Platter with Olives & Cheese (recipe on facing page). Break chunks from a crusty loaf of onion bread to munch with the salad.

Spinach Pesto Pasta Salad

Preparation time: About 25 minutes

Cooking time: About 7 minutes

●

Purée fresh spinach and dry basil to make the bright pesto dressing for this linguine and cherry tomato salad.

- 1 **pound dry linguine**
- 1 **cup (about 2 oz.) firmly packed chopped spinach**
- 3 **tablespoons dry basil**
- 1 or 2 **cloves garlic**
- ⅓ **cup grated Parmesan cheese**
- ⅓ **cup olive oil**
- 1 **can (about 2¼ oz.) sliced ripe olives, drained**
- 2 **cups cherry tomatoes, halved**
- ½ **cup dried tomatoes packed in oil, drained and finely chopped (optional)**

  Salt and pepper

1. **Bring** 3 quarts water to a boil in a 5- to 6-quart pan. Add linguine and cook just until tender to bite (about 7 minutes); or cook according to package directions. Drain, rinse with cold water until cool, and drain again.

2. **Place** spinach, basil, garlic, cheese, and oil in a food processor or blender; whirl until smooth.

3. **Combine** linguine, spinach mixture, olives, cherry tomatoes, and, if desired, dried tomatoes in a large bowl; mix lightly. Season to taste with salt and pepper. Makes 8 to 10 servings.

Per serving: 289 calories (33% calories from fat), 8 g protein, 41 g carbohydrates, 10 g total fat (2 g saturated fat), 2 mg cholesterol, 128 mg sodium

Warm Wild Rice & Asparagus Salad

Low-Fat

Preparation time: About 25 minutes

Cooking time: About 50 minutes

●

Cook wild rice, asparagus, and mushrooms to make this elegant spring salad. Unlike most salads, this one is served warm.

- 1 **cup wild rice, rinsed and drained**
- 4 **cups water**
- 1 **pound mushrooms, thinly sliced**
- 1 **large onion, finely chopped**

  About 2½ cups homemade (page 33) or canned vegetable broth
- 1 **pound asparagus**
- 3 **tablespoons balsamic vinegar**
- 1 **tablespoon olive oil**

  Salt and pepper

1. **Combine** rice and water in a 3- to 3½-quart pan. Bring to a boil; reduce heat, cover, and simmer until rice is tender to bite (about 50 minutes). Meanwhile, combine mushrooms, onion, and ¾ cup of the broth in a wide frying pan. Boil over high heat, stirring often, until liquid has evaporated and vegetables begin to brown (about 12 minutes).

2. **Add** ⅓ cup more broth, stirring to scrape browned bits free. Continue to cook, stirring often, until liquid has evaporated and mixture begins to brown again (2 to 4 minutes). Repeat 3 or 4 more times, cooking until vegetables are well browned. Meanwhile, break off and discard tough ends of asparagus; slice spears thinly.

3. **Stir** ⅓ cup more broth into vegetables. Add asparagus and cook, stirring often, until asparagus is tender-crisp (about 2 minutes).

4. **Drain** rice well; transfer to a serving bowl. Stir in asparagus mixture, vinegar, and oil. Season to taste with salt and pepper. Makes 8 servings.

Per serving: 126 calories (17% calories from fat), 5 g protein, 22 g carbohydrates, 3 g total fat (0.3 g saturated fat), 0 mg cholesterol, 322 mg sodium

Indonesian Brown Rice Salad

Preparation time: *About 30 minutes*

Cooking time: *About 45 minutes*

Standing time: *At least 15 minutes*

●

The dressing for this rice, raisin, and crunchy vegetable salad is accented with lime, fresh ginger, and full-flavored sesame oil.

>   2   cups long-grain brown rice
> 4½   cups water
>   Lime Dressing (recipe follows)
>   1   medium-size red or green bell pepper, seeded and chopped
>   6   ounces Chinese pea pods (also called snow peas), ends and strings removed, thinly sliced
>   5   green onions, thinly sliced
>   1   can (about 8 oz.) water chestnuts, drained and chopped
>   ¼   cup *each* raisins and chopped cilantro
>   Cilantro sprigs

1. Combine rice and water in a 2½- to 3-quart pan. Bring to a boil; reduce heat, cover, and simmer until rice is tender to bite (about 45 minutes). Meanwhile, prepare Lime Dressing; set aside.

2. Transfer rice to a large bowl and let stand until cooled slightly (at least 15 minutes). Lightly mix in Lime Dressing. Add bell pepper, pea pods, green onions, water chestnuts, raisins, and chopped cilantro; mix lightly until well combined.

3. Spoon salad into a serving bowl. Garnish with cilantro sprigs. Makes 8 servings.

Lime Dressing. In a medium-size bowl, combine ⅔ cup **rice vinegar** or cider vinegar, 2 tablespoons *each* **lime juice** and **reduced-sodium soy sauce,** 1 tablespoon minced **fresh ginger,** 2 teaspoons minced **garlic,** and 1 teaspoon **Oriental sesame oil;** mix well.

Per serving: 225 calories (8% calories from fat), 5 g protein, 48 g carbohydrates, 2 g total fat (0.3 g saturated fat), 0 mg cholesterol, 160 mg sodium

Chive & Egg Salad

Preparation time: *About 35 minutes*

Cooking time: *18 minutes*

●

This salad arrives at the table in an edible bell pepper boat. Accompany it with red or yellow cherry tomatoes and crisp breadsticks.

>   6   large eggs
>   1   tablespoon Dijon mustard
>   1   teaspoon white wine vinegar
>   ½   teaspoon pepper
>   ¾   cup sour cream
> 1½   cups *each* thinly sliced chives and thinly sliced celery
>   Salt
>   3   large green or red bell peppers, halved lengthwise and seeded
>   Whole chives or chive blossoms

1. Place eggs in a 2- to 3-quart pan. Add enough water to cover eggs by 1 inch. Bring just to a simmer over high heat; reduce heat to medium-low and cook eggs for 18 minutes.

2. Drain eggs and cover with cold water; let cool for about 5 minutes. Peel and discard shells. Separate whites from yolks.

3. Chop whites with a knife or in a food processor; set aside. Mash yolks with a potato masher or fork, or in a food processor. Add mustard, vinegar, and pepper to yolks; mash or whirl until smooth.

4. Stir in sour cream, egg whites, sliced chives, and celery. Season to taste with salt. Spoon into bell pepper halves. Garnish with whole chives. Makes 6 servings.

Per serving: 164 calories (63% calories from fat), 8 g protein, 7 g carbohydrates, 12 g total fat (5 g saturated fat), 225 mg cholesterol, 180 mg sodium

ANDREA

Home-baked breads are always impressive, even when they're as simple to make as these marmalade-filled Siena Muffins (recipe on page 125). Here they add luster to a brunch menu featuring
Red & Yellow Pepper Flat Omelet (recipe on page 56).

BREADS

Sweet Potato Muffins

Cheese-Red Pepper Corn Muffins

Siena Muffins

Apricot Granola Muffins

Breakfast Tea Bread

Summer-Winter Peach Coffee Cake

Mango Bread

Cheddar Cheese Popovers

Cranberry Cornmeal Scones

Cinnamon Flatbread

Soft Sesame Biscuits

Blueberry Whole Grain Pancakes

Oat & Cornmeal Waffles

Ginger Whole Wheat Pancakes

Honey Multigrain Hearth Bread

Cornbread Fuego

Polenta Cheese Bread

Mediterranean Olive Bread

Sage Cracker Breads

Garlic Cheese Bread

Cinnamon Slashed Flatbread

Chili-Cornmeal Breadsticks

Upside-Down Nut Buns

Apple & Prune Swirls

Sweet Potato Muffins

Preparation time: About 20 minutes

Baking time: About 25 minutes

●

These spicy, raisin-studded muffins bring welcome warmth to cool-weather breakfasts. You'll also enjoy them with puréed vegetable soups.

- 1⅓ cups unbleached all-purpose flour
- 2 teaspoons baking powder
- 1¼ teaspoons ground cinnamon
- ¼ teaspoon ground nutmeg
- ¼ cup *each* raisins and chopped walnuts
- ½ teaspoon salt
- 1 cup mashed cooked sweet potatoes
- 1 cup plus 1 tablespoon sugar
- ½ cup milk
- ⅓ cup butter or margarine, melted and cooled
- 1 large egg

1. Combine flour, baking powder, ½ teaspoon of the cinnamon, nutmeg, raisins, walnuts, and salt in a large bowl; stir well.

2. Combine sweet potatoes, 1 cup of the sugar, milk, butter, and egg in a medium-size bowl; beat well.

3. Add sweet potato mixture to flour mixture, stirring just until moistened.

4. Spoon batter into 12 greased or paper-lined 2½-inch muffin cups, filling each about three-quarters full. In a small bowl, stir together remaining ¾ teaspoon cinnamon and the 1 tablespoon sugar. Sprinkle over batter.

5. Bake in a 350° oven until muffins spring back when lightly touched (about 25 minutes). Serve warm. Makes 12 muffins.

Per muffin: 253 calories (33% calories from fat), 3 g protein, 40 g carbohydrates, 10 g total fat (4 g saturated fat), 33 mg cholesterol, 239 mg sodium

Cheese–Red Pepper Corn Muffins

Preparation time: About 30 minutes

Baking time: About 20 minutes

●

To transform a simple salad into a satisfying supper, offer these colorful muffins as accompaniments. They're also good with your favorite vegetarian chili.

- ⅓ cup salad oil
- 1 medium-size onion, finely chopped
- ½ cup finely chopped red bell pepper
- 1¼ cups unbleached all-purpose flour
- ¾ cup yellow cornmeal
- ⅓ cup sugar
- 1 tablespoon baking powder
- ½ teaspoon salt
- 2 large eggs
- 1 cup milk
- 1¼ cups (about 5 oz.) shredded sharp Cheddar cheese

1. Heat 2 tablespoons of the oil in a medium-size frying pan over medium heat. Add onion and bell pepper. Cook, stirring often, until onion is soft but not browned (6 to 8 minutes).

2. Remove pan from heat and let cool briefly. Meanwhile, combine flour, cornmeal, sugar, baking powder, and salt in a large bowl; stir well. In a medium-size bowl, combine eggs, milk, and remaining oil; beat well.

3. Add egg mixture to flour mixture, stirring just until moistened. With last few strokes, stir in onion mixture and ¾ cup of the cheese.

4. Spoon batter into greased or paper-lined 2½-inch muffin cups, filling each about two-thirds full. Sprinkle with remaining cheese.

5. Bake in a 400° oven until muffins are golden brown (about 20 minutes). Serve warm. Makes 16 to 18 muffins.

Per muffin: 174 calories (48% calories from fat), 5 g protein, 18 g carbohydrates, 9 g total fat (3 g saturated fat), 36 mg cholesterol, 217 mg sodium

Siena Muffins

Pictured on page 122

Preparation time: About 20 minutes

Baking time: About 20 minutes

●

Marmalade-filled wells are the surprise feature of these stylish spiced and sugar-dusted muffins.

- 1½ **cups unbleached all-purpose flour**
- 1 **cup sliced almonds**
- 1 **teaspoon baking powder**
- ½ **teaspoon baking soda**
- 1¼ **teaspoons ground cinnamon**
- ½ **teaspoon** *each* **ground nutmeg and ground coriander**
- ¼ **teaspoon ground cloves**
- ½ **cup** *each* **honey and milk**
- ¼ **cup butter or margarine, melted and cooled**
- 1 **large egg**
- 1 **teaspoon grated lemon peel**
- ¼ **cup orange marmalade**
- 2 **tablespoons sugar**

1. Combine flour, almonds, baking powder, baking soda, 1 teaspoon of the cinnamon, nutmeg, coriander, and cloves in a large bowl; stir well.

2. Combine honey, milk, butter, egg, and lemon peel in a medium-size bowl; beat well.

3. Add honey mixture to flour mixture, stirring just until moistened.

4. Spoon batter into 10 greased or paper-lined 2½-inch muffin cups, filling each about three-quarters full. Using a teaspoon, gently press 1 rounded teaspoon marmalade into center of each muffin.

5. Bake in a 350° oven until golden in color and firm when lightly touched (about 20 minutes). Let cool in pan for 5 minutes. Meanwhile, in a small bowl, stir together sugar and remaining ¼ teaspoon cinnamon.

6. Remove muffins from pan and transfer to a rack. Sprinkle with cinnamon-sugar. Serve warm. Makes 10 muffins.

Per muffin: 273 calories (37% calories from fat), 5 g protein, 39 g carbohydrates, 12 g total fat (4 g saturated fat), 35 mg cholesterol, 174 mg sodium

Apricot Granola Muffins

Preparation time: About 20 minutes

Baking time: 25 to 30 minutes

●

Scented with almonds and cinnamon, these chunky muffins offer the nutritional benefits of dried apricots, granola, and whole wheat flour.

- ¾ **cup unbleached all-purpose flour**
- ½ **cup whole wheat flour**
- 2 **teaspoons baking powder**
- 1 **teaspoon ground cinnamon**
- 1 **cup granola cereal**
- ½ **cup dried apricots, chopped**
- ½ **cup slivered almonds, chopped**
- ¼ **cup butter or margarine, at room temperature**
- ½ **cup firmly packed brown sugar**
- 2 **large eggs**
- ½ **cup nonfat milk**
- ¼ **teaspoon almond extract**

1. Combine all-purpose flour, whole wheat flour, baking powder, cinnamon, granola, apricots, and almonds in a large bowl; stir well.

2. Combine butter and brown sugar in a medium-size bowl; beat until smooth. Beat in eggs, one at a time. Stir in milk and almond extract.

3. Add egg mixture to flour mixture, stirring just until moistened.

4. Spoon batter into 12 greased or paper-lined 2½-inch muffin cups, filling each about three-quarters full.

5. Bake in a 325° oven until muffins are browned and spring back when lightly touched (25 to 30 minutes). Serve warm. Makes 12 muffins.

Per muffin: 232 calories (41% calories from fat), 5 g protein, 30 g carbohydrates, 11 g total fat (4 g saturated fat), 46 mg cholesterol, 145 mg sodium

Breakfast Tea Bread

Preparation time: About 15 minutes

Baking time: 1 to 1¼ hours

●

Quick to prepare, this orange-laced bread brimming with raisins is long on satisfaction. Serve it at breakfast or in the afternoon with a cup of spiced tea.

    2 cups unbleached all-purpose flour
    1 teaspoon baking powder
    3 large eggs
    ¾ cup sugar
    ½ cup butter or margarine, at room temperature
    1 tablespoon finely shredded orange peel
    1 cup sour cream
    2 cups *each* seedless raisins and golden raisins
    ½ cup chopped almonds

1. Combine flour and baking powder in a medium-size bowl; stir well.

2. Combine eggs, sugar, butter, and orange peel in a large bowl; beat well. Stir in sour cream.

3. Add flour mixture to egg mixture; beat just until blended. Stir in seedless raisins, golden raisins, and almonds.

4. Spread mixture in a greased or nonstick 5- by 9-inch loaf pan, smoothing top with a rubber spatula.

5. Bake in a 325° oven until a wooden pick inserted in center comes out clean and loaf begins to pull away from sides of pan (1 to 1¼ hours).

6. Let cool in pan on a rack for 15 minutes. Invert onto rack and let cool thoroughly. Slice thinly. Makes 1 loaf (about 16 slices).

Per slice: 325 calories (33% calories from fat), 5 g protein, 52 g carbohydrates, 12 g total fat (6 g saturated fat), 62 mg cholesterol, 114 mg sodium

Summer-Winter Peach Coffee Cake

Pictured on facing page

Preparation time: About 30 minutes

Baking time: 45 minutes to 1 hour

●

This quick coffee cake can be made with juicy fresh peaches in summer, canned peach halves in winter.

    6 medium-size firm-ripe peaches (about 2¼ lbs. *total*), peeled, halved, and pitted, or 2 cans (about 1 lb. *each*) peach halves in light syrup, drained
    1 small package (about 3 oz.) cream cheese
    ⅔ cup sugar
    6 tablespoons butter or margarine
    1 large egg
    ½ teaspoon almond extract
    1½ cups unbleached all-purpose flour
    1 teaspoon *each* baking soda and baking powder
    2 tablespoons finely chopped almonds
    1 teaspoon ground cinnamon

1. Combine 3 of the peach halves, cream cheese, ½ cup of the sugar, 5 tablespoons of the butter, egg, and almond extract in a food processor or blender; whirl until smooth.

2. Combine flour, baking soda, and baking powder in a medium-size bowl; stir well. Add to cream cheese mixture and whirl until blended.

3. Spread batter in a greased 9-inch spring-form pan or 9-inch-round cake pan with a removable bottom.

4. Place remaining peaches, cut sides down, over batter. Dot with remaining 1 tablespoon butter. In a small bowl, stir together almonds, cinnamon, and remaining sugar. Sprinkle over peaches.

5. Bake in a 350° oven until cake is well browned and begins to pull away from sides of pan (45 minutes to 1 hour). Remove pan sides. Serve warm or at room temperature. Makes 8 servings.

Per serving: 333 calories (39% calories from fat), 5 g protein, 46 g carbohydrates, 15 g total fat (8 g saturated fat), 62 mg cholesterol, 347 mg sodium

*No matter what the season, you can bake rich and spicy Summer-Winter Peach Coffee Cake
(recipe on facing page) to enjoy with a cup of your favorite coffee. Use fresh peaches when they're
in the market, convenient canned peach halves when they're not.*

Frozen bread dough—white or whole wheat—saves time when you want to make yeasty treats like these. Follow the package directions for thawing the dough in the refrigerator or at room temperature.

Yellow Bell Pizza

Pictured on page 159
Preparation time: About 20 minutes
Rising time: About 20 minutes
Baking time: About 16 minutes

---

1 loaf (about 1 lb.) frozen white bread dough, thawed

1 cup (about 4 oz.) shredded part-skim mozzarella cheese

2 medium-size yellow bell peppers (about 12 oz. *total*), seeded and thinly sliced

4 teaspoons grated Parmesan cheese

1 tablespoon chopped fresh basil or 1 teaspoon dry basil

---

1. Cut dough into quarters. Shape each piece into a ball. On a lightly floured surface, roll each into a 6-inch round. Place rounds, about 1 inch apart, on 2 lightly greased 12- by 15-inch baking sheets. With your hands, flatten rounds to about ¼ inch thick (make edges slightly thicker) and 7 inches in diameter. Let rise, uncovered, at room temperature until puffy (about 20 minutes).

2. Sprinkle each round to within ¼ inch of edges with 2 tablespoons of the mozzarella cheese; top with bell pepper slices. Sprinkle with Parmesan cheese, basil, and remaining ½ cup mozzarella cheese.

3. Bake pizzas in a 400° oven until crust is browned on bottom (about 16 minutes); if using one oven, switch position of baking sheets halfway through baking. Cut pizzas into quarters. Makes 4 servings.

Per serving: 424 calories (28% calories from fat), 17 g protein, 59 g carbohydrates, 13 g total fat (5 g saturated fat), 23 mg cholesterol, 712 mg sodium

Spinach Pizza

Pictured on page 159
Preparation time: About 20 minutes
Rising time: About 20 minutes
Baking time: About 16 minutes

---

1 loaf (about 1 lb.) frozen white bread dough, thawed

¼ cup chopped shallots

½ cup homemade (page 33) or canned vegetable broth

2 packages (about 10 oz. *each*) frozen chopped spinach, thawed and squeezed dry

¼ teaspoon ground nutmeg

½ cup shredded reduced-fat Jarlsberg cheese

---

1. Prepare dough and let rise as directed for Yellow Bell Pizza (at left). While dough is rising, combine shallots and broth in a wide frying pan. Cook over medium-high heat, stirring occasionally, until shallots are soft and golden and liquid has evaporated (about 10 minutes). Add spinach and nutmeg to shallots; mix well. Remove from heat and let cool.

2. Cover each round of dough to within ¼ inch of edges with a fourth of the spinach mixture; sprinkle with cheese.

3. Bake pizzas as directed for Yellow Bell Pizza (at left). Makes 4 servings.

Per serving: 394 calories (19% calories from fat), 17 g protein, 62 g carbohydrates, 8 g total fat (3 g saturated fat), 12 mg cholesterol, 840 mg sodium

Lentil, Vegetable & Cheese Pizza

Preparation time: About 45 minutes
Cooking time: About 45 minutes
Baking time: 35 to 40 minutes

⅓ cup lentils, rinsed and drained

1⅓ cups water

Tomato-Herb Sauce (recipe follows)

Cooked Vegetable Mixture (recipe follows)

1 loaf (about 1 lb.) frozen white or whole wheat bread dough, thawed

1½ cups sliced mushrooms

1½ cups (about 6 oz.) *each* shredded mozzarella and Cheddar cheese

---

1. Combine lentils and water in a 1- to 1½-quart pan. Bring to a boil; reduce heat, cover, and boil gently until lentils are tender to bite (about 25 minutes). Meanwhile, prepare Tomato-Herb Sauce and Cooked Vegetable Mixture.

2. Drain lentils and set aside.

3. Shape dough into a ball. On a lightly floured surface, roll into a 16-inch round, turning dough and adding flour as needed to prevent sticking. Transfer dough to a greased 14-inch-round pizza pan; fold under edge of dough. With a fork, pierce crust all over.

4. Bake in a 375° oven until lightly browned (about 20 minutes). Remove crust from oven. (At this point, you may cool, cover, and refrigerate lentils, sauce, vegetables, and crust separately for up to a day.)

5. Spread sauce over crust. Top with layers of vegetables, mushrooms, mozzarella, Cheddar, and lentils.

6. Bake in a 400° oven until cheese is bubbly (about 15 minutes). Cut into wedges and serve hot. Makes 3 to 5 servings.

Tomato-Herb Sauce. Heat 1 tablespoon **salad oil** in a 3- to 4-quart pan over medium heat. Add ½ cup chopped **onion** and 2 cloves **garlic,** minced or pressed; cook, stirring often, until onion is very soft but not browned (about 5 minutes).

Add 1 large can (about 15 oz.) **tomato sauce;** 2 tablespoons **Italian herb seasoning,** or 1½ teaspoons *each* dry basil, dry marjoram, dry oregano, and dry thyme; ½ teaspoon **pepper;** and ⅛ teaspoon **ground red pepper** (cayenne). Increase heat to high and bring to a boil; cook, stirring often, until reduced to 1⅓ cups (about 8 minutes).

Cooked Vegetable Mixture. Bring 1 quart **water** to a boil in a 3- to 4-quart pan. Add 1½ cups **cauliflower flowerets;** reduce heat, cover, and boil gently until tender when pierced (about 4 minutes). Lift cauliflower from pan with a slotted spoon, immerse in cold water until cool, and drain well; set aside.

To boiling water add 2 cups **broccoli flowerets** and boil gently, uncovered, until barely tender when pierced (about 3 minutes). Lift from pan, immerse in cold water until cool, and drain well.

Per serving: 766 calories (38% calories from fat), 37 g protein, 83 g carbohydrates, 33 g total fat (16 g saturated fat), 83 mg cholesterol, 1,663 mg sodium

Asparagus Breadsticks

Preparation time: About 25 minutes
Rising time: 45 minutes to 1 hour
Baking time: 20 to 25 minutes

2 loaves (about 1 lb. *each*) frozen white or whole wheat bread dough, thawed

1 large egg white (about 2 tablespoons)

¼ cup grated Parmesan cheese

1 teaspoon *each* dry tarragon and dry dill weed

1. Place dough on a lightly floured surface and pat each loaf into a 5- by 10-inch rectangle. Cover and let rise until puffy (45 minutes to 1 hour).

2. Cut each loaf crosswise into 9 equal pieces. Gently stretch each piece until about 15 inches long; place on 3 greased 12- by 15-inch baking sheets, spacing about 1½ inches apart (if dough snaps back, let rest for a few minutes and stretch again).

3. Snip dough with scissors at a 45° angle to make cuts about ½ inch apart along about 4 inches at one end of each stick to resemble asparagus.

4. Beat egg white just until frothy; brush dough lightly with egg white. In a small bowl, mix cheese, tarragon, and dill; sprinkle over breadsticks.

5. Bake in a 350° oven until breadsticks

are browned (20 to 25 minutes); if using one oven, switch position of baking sheets halfway through baking (refrigerate one sheet while baking others). Transfer breadsticks to racks. Serve warm or at room temperature. Makes 18 breadsticks.

Per breadstick: 142 calories (18% calories from fat), 4 g protein, 24 g carbohydrates, 3 g total fat (1 g saturated fat), 3 mg cholesterol, 267 mg sodium

Bread Blossoms

Preparation time: About 15 minutes
Rising time: About 30 minutes
Baking time: About 25 minutes

1 loaf (about 1 lb.) frozen whole wheat or white bread dough, thawed

2 tablespoons beaten egg

½ teaspoon sesame seeds

1. Place dough on a lightly floured surface; cut into 6 equal pieces. Shape each piece into a ball. Place each ball of dough in a greased 2½-inch muffin cup.

2. Cover and let rise in a warm place until almost doubled (about 30 minutes). With scissors, make 4 cuts in top half of each ball, forming a cross; separate cuts to form petals.

3. Brush dough gently with egg and sprinkle center of cuts with sesame seeds.

4. Bake in a 375° oven until golden brown (about 25 minutes). Serve warm or at room temperature. Makes 6 rolls.

Per roll: 225 calories (24% calories from fat), 6 g protein, 36 g carbohydrates, 6 g total fat (1 g saturated fat), 25 mg cholesterol, 371 mg sodium

*Even the simplest green salad turns into a feast when accompanied by hot and crusty
Cheddar Cheese Popovers (recipe on facing page). Best of all, you can whip up the batter in no
time in your food processor or blender.*

Mango Bread

Low-Fat

Preparation time: About 30 minutes

Baking time: 50 to 55 minutes

●

You'll need a 1-pound or larger mango to make the purée for this golden bread. Mangoes arrive in markets sporadically from January through August, peaking in June. When ripe, a mango gives to gentle pressure like a ripe avocado.

- 1 cup puréed mango
- ¾ teaspoon baking soda mixed with 2 teaspoons water
- 1 cup sugar
- 2 large eggs
- ½ cup sweetened flaked coconut, minced
- ¼ cup salad oil
- 2½ cups unbleached all-purpose flour
- 1½ teaspoons baking powder

1. Combine mango purée and baking soda mixture in a large bowl; let stand for 5 minutes.

2. Add sugar, eggs, coconut, and oil; beat until blended.

3. Combine flour and baking powder in a medium-size bowl; stir well. Add to mango mixture; beat well. Pour into a greased or nonstick 5- by 9-inch loaf pan.

4. Bake in a 350° oven until loaf is richly browned and begins to pull away from sides of pan (50 to 55 minutes).

5. Let stand in pan on a rack for 10 minutes. Invert onto rack. Serve warm or at room temperature. Slice thinly. Makes 1 loaf (about 16 slices).

Per slice: 182 calories (26% calories from fat), 3 g protein, 31 g carbohydrates, 5 g total fat (1 g saturated fat), 27 mg cholesterol, 119 mg sodium

Cheddar Cheese Popovers

Pictured on facing page

Preparation time: About 15 minutes

Baking time: About 50 minutes

●

Crisp-crusted popovers flavored with Cheddar cheese star at brunch or lunch with a hearty spinach or mixed green salad.

- 3 large eggs
- 1 cup *each* milk and unbleached all-purpose flour
- 2 tablespoons butter or margarine, melted
- ¾ cup shredded sharp Cheddar cheese

1. Combine eggs, milk, flour, and 1 tablespoon of the butter in a food processor or blender; whirl until smooth, scraping sides of container with a spatula several times. (At this point, you may cover and refrigerate for up to a day; whirl again before using.)

2. Brush six 6-ounce custard cups or eight 2¾-inch muffin cups with remaining butter. Divide cheese equally among cups. Pour popover batter over cheese.

3. Bake in a 375° oven until puffed and well browned (about 50 minutes). Let cool for 1 minute. Loosen with a sharp knife and turn out. Serve warm. Makes 6 to 8 popovers.

Per popover: 242 calories (53% calories from fat), 10 g protein, 18 g carbohydrates, 14 g total fat (7 g saturated fat), 137 mg cholesterol, 179 mg sodium

Cranberry Cornmeal Scones

Pictured on page 42

Preparation time: About 25 minutes

Baking time: 20 to 25 minutes

●

Quick to make, these colorful scones are a delightful addition to a brunch or a fruit salad lunch. Look for dried cranberries at farm stands or in stores that sell natural foods.

- 1¾ cups unbleached all-purpose flour
- ¾ cup yellow cornmeal
- ¼ cup powdered sugar
- 1 tablespoon baking powder
- ½ cup firm butter or margarine
- ¾ cup dried cranberries
- 1 tablespoon grated orange peel
- 1 large egg
- ¾ cup milk
- 1 to 2 tablespoons granulated sugar

1. Combine flour, cornmeal, powdered sugar, and baking powder in a large bowl; stir well. Using a pastry blender or your fingers, cut or rub in butter until coarse crumbs form. Stir in cranberries and orange peel.

2. Beat egg with ⅔ cup of the milk in a small bowl until blended. Add egg mixture to cranberry mixture, stirring just until moistened.

3. Turn dough out onto a lightly floured surface and knead just until dough holds together. Pat into a ½-inch-thick round.

4. Cut scones with a 2½-inch-diameter cutter. Place slightly apart on a lightly greased baking sheet. Brush tops with remaining milk. Sprinkle with granulated sugar.

5. Bake in a 375° oven until golden brown (20 to 25 minutes). Serve warm. Makes 12 scones.

Per serving: 222 calories (37% calories from fat), 4 g protein, 32 g carbohydrates, 9 g total fat (5 g saturated fat), 41 mg cholesterol, 214 mg sodium

Cinnamon Flatbread

Preparation time: About 25 minutes

Baking time: 15 to 20 minutes

●

Mixed in the style of biscuits and scones, this raisin-studded flatbread made with whole wheat and all-purpose flour goes together in a jiffy.

- About 1¼ cups unbleached all-purpose flour
- ¾ cup whole wheat flour
- 3 tablespoons sugar
- 2 teaspoons baking powder
- ½ teaspoon baking soda
- ⅓ cup sesame seeds
- 4 tablespoons firm butter or margarine
- ½ cup raisins
- 1 cup plain yogurt
- 1½ teaspoons ground cinnamon

1. Combine 1¼ cups of the all-purpose flour, whole wheat flour, 1 tablespoon of the sugar, baking powder, baking soda, and sesame seeds in a large bowl; stir well.

2. Add 2 tablespoons of the butter. Using a pastry blender or your fingers, cut or rub in butter until fine crumbs form. Add raisins and yogurt to dough, stirring just until moistened.

3. Turn dough out onto a floured surface and knead just until dough holds together, adding more flour as needed to prevent sticking. With floured hands, pat dough into a ¼-inch-thick round. Transfer to a greased baking sheet.

4. Bake in a 425° oven until lightly browned (about 10 minutes). Meanwhile, melt remaining 2 tablespoons butter in a small pan over medium heat. In a small bowl, stir together cinnamon and remaining 2 tablespoons sugar.

5. Brush partially baked bread with butter. Sprinkle with cinnamon-sugar. Return to oven and continue to bake until well browned at edges (5 to 10 more minutes). Cut into wedges and serve warm. Makes 8 servings.

Per serving: 264 calories (33% calories from fat), 6 g protein, 39 g carbohydrates, 10 g total fat (4 g saturated fat), 17 mg cholesterol, 282 mg sodium

Soft Sesame Biscuits

Pictured on page 95

Preparation time: About 30 minutes

Baking time: 12 to 14 minutes

●

The texture of these tender, buttery sesame-sprinkled rolls may strike you as a cross between drop biscuits and muffins.

- 1 cup *each* **whole wheat flour and unbleached all-purpose flour**
- 2 **tablespoons sugar**
- 1 **teaspoon baking soda**
- ¼ **teaspoon salt**
- 2 **tablespoons sesame seeds**
- ⅓ **cup firm butter or margarine, diced**
- 1 **cup buttermilk**

1. Combine whole wheat flour, all-purpose flour, sugar, baking soda, salt, and 1 tablespoon of the sesame seeds in a large bowl; stir well. Using a pastry blender or your fingers, cut or rub in butter until coarse crumbs form.

2. Pour in buttermilk, stirring with a fork just until moistened.

3. Divide dough into 12 equal portions. With oiled hands, shape each into a ball. Place about 1 inch apart on a well-greased baking sheet. Pat each ball into a 1-inch-thick round. Sprinkle with remaining 1 tablespoon sesame seeds.

4. Bake in a 450° oven until deep golden brown (12 to 14 minutes). Serve warm. Makes 12 biscuits.

Per biscuit: 148 calories (42% calories from fat), 3 g protein, 19 g carbohydrates, 7 g total fat (3 g saturated fat), 14 mg cholesterol, 224 mg sodium

Blueberry Whole Grain Pancakes

Preparation time: About 25 minutes

Cooking time: 10 to 15 minutes total

●

Serve these hearty pancakes as they're cooked; or, if made ahead, place in a single layer on racks in a warm oven until all are ready.

- 2 **large firm-ripe peaches (about 1¼ lbs.** *total***)**
- 1 **tablespoon lemon juice**
- ¾ cup *each* **whole wheat flour and unbleached all-purpose flour**
- ½ **cup regular rolled oats**
- ⅓ **cup yellow cornmeal**
- 1 **tablespoon** *each* **sugar and baking powder**
- ½ **teaspoon salt**
- 3 **large eggs, separated**
- 1¾ **cups milk**

  About 3 tablespoons salad oil
- 3 **cups blueberries, rinsed and drained**

1. Peel, pit, and slice peaches into a medium-size bowl. Lightly mix in lemon juice; set aside.

2. Combine whole wheat flour, all-purpose flour, oats, cornmeal, sugar, baking powder, and salt in a large bowl; stir well. In a deep bowl, beat egg whites until stiff peaks form; set aside. To flour mixture add egg yolks, milk, and 3 tablespoons of the oil; whisk just until smooth.

3. Stir 1½ cups of the blueberries into batter. Gently fold in egg whites.

4. Heat 2 regular or nonstick griddles or wide frying pans over medium heat. Lightly oil griddles, if needed. For each pancake, scoop ⅓ cup batter from bottom of bowl onto griddle, spreading slightly. Cook until tops of pancakes are bubbly and almost dry; turn and continue to cook until bottoms are browned.

5. Stir remaining blueberries into peach mixture. Serve pancakes hot with peach mixture to add to taste. Makes 6 servings (about 18 pancakes).

Per serving: 397 calories (32% calories from fat), 12 g protein, 58 g carbohydrates, 14 g total fat (3 g saturated fat), 116 mg cholesterol, 499 mg sodium

Oat & Cornmeal Waffles

Pictured on facing page

Preparation time: About 20 minutes

Cooking time: About 30 minutes total

●

Top these crunchy waffles with sour cream and sliced fresh fruit, such as strawberries, kiwi fruit, and bananas. Pour a fragrant tea, such as Earl Grey, as a beverage.

- 1 **large egg**
- 2⅔ **cups buttermilk**
- 1⅓ **cups unbleached all-purpose flour**
- ⅔ **cup** *each* **regular rolled oats and yellow cornmeal**
- 1¼ **teaspoons baking soda**
- ¼ **teaspoon salt**
- 3 **tablespoons sugar**
- ⅓ **cup butter or margarine, melted and cooled**

1. Beat egg in a large bowl until blended. Add buttermilk, stirring well.

2. Combine flour, oats, cornmeal, baking soda, salt, and sugar in another large bowl; stir well.

3. Add flour mixture and butter to egg mixture, stirring just until moistened.

4. Heat a waffle iron according to manufacturer's directions. Grease iron. For each waffle, fill iron half full with batter. Bake until waffle is well browned and crisp (7 to 8 minutes). If made ahead, keep warm on a rack in a 200° oven until all are cooked. Serve waffles hot. Makes 4 servings (about four 8-inch-square waffles).

Per serving: 562 calories (35% calories from fat), 16 g protein, 76 g carbohydrates, 22 g total fat (11 g saturated fat), 101 mg cholesterol, 872 mg sodium

Ginger Whole Wheat Pancakes

Low-Fat

Preparation time: About 25 minutes

Cooking time: 10 to 15 minutes total

●

Crystallized ginger accents these wholesome griddle cakes made with cider and yogurt. The hot and spicy topping combines maple syrup and apple butter.

- 1⅓ **cups unbleached all-purpose flour**
- 1 **cup whole wheat flour**
- ⅓ **cup powdered sugar**
- 3 **tablespoons minced crystallized ginger**
- 1½ **teaspoons baking soda**
- 1 **teaspoon** *each* **baking powder and ground cinnamon**
- 1 **cup** *each* **apple cider and vanilla-flavored yogurt**
- 2 **large eggs**
- 2 **tablespoons butter or margarine, melted Salad oil Spiced Apple Syrup (recipe follows)**

1. Combine all-purpose flour, whole wheat flour, sugar, ginger, baking soda, baking powder, and cinnamon in a large bowl; stir well.

2. Combine cider, yogurt, eggs, and butter in a medium-size bowl; beat well. Add to flour mixture, stirring just until moistened.

3. Heat a regular or nonstick griddle or wide frying pan over medium heat. Lightly oil griddle, if needed. For each pancake, scoop ¼ cup batter onto griddle, spreading to make a 4-inch round. Cook until top of pancake is bubbly and bottom is browned (about 1 minute); turn and continue to cook until bottom is browned (about 1 more minute). Meanwhile, prepare Spiced Apple Syrup.

4. Serve pancakes hot with Spiced Apple Syrup to add to taste. Makes 6 to 8 servings (about 24 pancakes).

Spiced Apple Syrup. In a 1-quart pan, combine ½ cup **apple butter** and 1 cup **maple syrup.** Cook over medium heat, stirring often, until heated through (3 to 5 minutes). Makes about 1½ cups.

Per serving: 448 calories (14% calories from fat), 8 g protein, 90 g carbohydrates, 7 g total fat (3 g saturated fat), 71 mg cholesterol, 424 mg sodium

Richly browned Oat & Cornmeal Waffles (recipe on facing page) offer no end of topping possibilities. Here they're crowned with sliced fresh fruits and sour cream, but the more traditional finishing touch of butter and warm maple syrup is also perfectly delicious.

Vegetarian Sandwiches

Whole grain breads make a fine foundation for a variety of hearty vegetarian sandwiches. Even French toast can be made with whole wheat bread; our version, piquant Chile-Cheese French Toast with Salsa, is baked instead of pan-fried to decrease the amount of fat and make cleanup easier.

Whole wheat flour tortillas enfold a cheese and sautéed onion filling to make quesadillas. Or roll the tortillas around a vegetable filling to produce attractive pinwheel sandwiches.

Broiled Reuben Muffins demonstrate a savory and nutritious topping for whole wheat English muffins. Zucchini-Mushroom Sandwiches, open-faced on pumpernickel, derive their flavor from oven-browned, puréed vegetables.

Chile-Cheese French Toast with Salsa

Preparation time: About 15 minutes
Baking time: About 22 minutes

3 large eggs

1 cup nonfat or low-fat milk

8 diagonally cut slices whole wheat French bread (*each* about ⅓ inch thick)

1⅓ cups (about 5½ oz.) shredded jack cheese

1 can (about 4 oz.) diced green chiles

¼ cup minced cilantro

About 2 cups purchased salsa

1. **Beat** eggs and milk in a wide bowl until well blended. Dip 4 slices of the bread into egg mixture; turn to saturate both sides. Arrange slices on a greased 12- by 15-inch baking sheet.

2. **Top** bread evenly with cheese, chiles, and cilantro. Dip remaining bread slices into egg mixture, coating both sides. Cover each sandwich with a second bread slice, making 4 sandwiches.

3. **Bake** in a 400° oven until sandwiches begin to brown (about 12 minutes). Turn carefully with a wide spatula and continue to bake until sandwiches are puffed and evenly browned (about 10 more minutes).

4. **Transfer** sandwiches to plates; cut each in half. Serve with salsa to add to taste. Makes 4 sandwiches.

Per sandwich: 399 calories (39% calories from fat), 21 g protein, 39 g carbohydrates, 17 g total fat (2 g saturated fat), 195 mg cholesterol, 1,486 mg sodium

Hot Spinach Quesadillas

Preparation time: About 30 minutes
Cooking time: 18 to 20 minutes

Curried Onions (recipe follows)

1 package (about 10 oz.) frozen chopped spinach, thawed and squeezed dry

½ cup part-skim ricotta cheese

¼ cup slivered roasted red peppers or pimentos

Salt and pepper

4 whole wheat flour tortillas (about 7-inch diameter), at room temperature

Plain nonfat yogurt (optional)

Sliced green onions (optional)

1. **Prepare** Curried Onions; set aside.

2. **Combine** spinach, ricotta, and red peppers in a medium-size bowl; mix lightly. Season to taste with salt and pepper.

3. **Place** a fourth of the spinach mixture on half of one of the tortillas. Spoon on a fourth of the onion mixture. Fold tortilla in half gently to make a turnover. Repeat to make remaining quesadillas.

4. **Cook** quesadillas on a greased or well-seasoned wide griddle or nonstick frying pan over medium heat until lightly browned (about 5 minutes); turn carefully and cook other sides until lightly browned (about 3 more minutes).

5. **Serve** hot. If desired, top with yogurt and green onions. Makes 4 servings.

Curried Onions. Heat 2 teaspoons **salad oil** in a wide nonstick frying pan over medium heat. Add 1 large **onion**, thinly sliced; 1 clove **garlic**, minced or pressed; and 1½ teaspoons **curry powder.** Cook, stirring often, for 5 minutes. Stir in ¼ cup **dry white wine** or water; reduce heat and continue to cook, stirring often, until most of the liquid has evaporated and onion is very soft (5 to 7 more minutes). Stir in ¼ cup sliced **green onions.**

Per serving: 253 calories (36% calories from fat), 10 g protein, 31 g carbohydrates, 10 g total fat (2 g saturated fat), 10 mg cholesterol, 264 mg sodium

Broiled Reuben Muffins

Preparation time: About 25 minutes
Baking and broiling time: 12 to 14 minutes

1 small can (about 8 oz.) sauerkraut, well drained

1 cup cooked red kidney beans (page 64) or 1 small can (about 8 oz.) kidney beans, drained and rinsed

¼ cup mayonnaise

1 tablespoon *each* catsup, Dijon mustard, and sweet pickle relish

1 teaspoon caraway seeds

4 whole wheat English muffins, split

1 cup (about 4 oz.) shredded Swiss cheese

2 tablespoons thinly sliced green onion

1. Combine sauerkraut, beans, mayonnaise, catsup, mustard, pickle relish, and caraway seeds in a large bowl; mix lightly. Set aside.

2. Place muffin halves, cut sides up, on a 12- by 15-inch baking sheet. Bake in a 375° oven until crisp and lightly browned (about 10 minutes).

3. Top each muffin half with an eighth of the sauerkraut mixture and sprinkle with 2 tablespoons of the cheese.

4. Broil muffins about 6 inches below heat until topping is heated through and cheese is bubbly and lightly browned (2 to 4 minutes). Sprinkle with green onion. Makes 4 servings (2 halves each).

Per serving: 418 calories (43% calories from fat), 17 g protein, 42 g carbohydrates, 20 g total fat (7 g saturated fat), 34 mg cholesterol, 815 mg sodium

---

Low-Fat

Zucchini-Mushroom Sandwiches

Preparation time: About 30 minutes
Baking time: 30 to 40 minutes

About 2 tablespoons olive oil

1 large red onion (about 12 oz.), sliced ½ inch thick

1¼ pounds zucchini, cut lengthwise into ¼-inch-thick slices

2 tablespoons balsamic vinegar or red wine vinegar

1¼ pounds mushrooms, sliced ½ inch thick

Salt and pepper

6 to 8 butter lettuce leaves, rinsed and crisped

6 to 8 thin slices pumpernickel bread

1. Line two 10- by 15-inch baking pans with foil; brush lightly with a little of the oil. Place onion and zucchini slices, overlapping slightly, in one of the pans. Sprinkle vinegar over onion slices; brush onion and zucchini slices with more of the oil.

2. Arrange mushroom slices in second pan; brush with remaining oil.

3. Bake in a 475° oven until mushrooms are lightly browned (about 30 minutes) and onion and zucchini are well browned (30 to 40 minutes).

4. Combine roasted onion, zucchini, and mushrooms in a food processor or blender; whirl until coarsely puréed. Season to taste with salt and pepper. (At this point, you may cool, cover, and refrigerate for up to 2 days.)

5. Place a lettuce leaf on each bread slice; spread generously with vegetable mixture. Makes 6 to 8 servings.

Per serving: 167 calories (27% calories from fat), 6 g protein, 26 g carbohydrates, 5 g total fat (1 g saturated fat), 0 mg cholesterol, 226 mg sodium

---

Tomato-Spinach Wheels

Preparation time: About 20 minutes

1 package (about 10 oz.) frozen chopped spinach, thawed and squeezed dry

1 large package (8 oz.) Neufchâtel or light cream cheese, at room temperature

2 tablespoons prepared horseradish

¼ cup dried tomatoes packed in oil, well drained and chopped

⅛ teaspoon *each* ground allspice and pepper

6 whole wheat flour tortillas (about 7-inch diameter), at room temperature

1. Combine spinach, cheese, horseradish, dried tomatoes, allspice, and pepper in a large bowl; mix well.

2. Spread spinach mixture on tortillas, using a sixth of the mixture for each.

3. Roll each tortilla tightly to enclose filling. If made ahead, enclose in plastic wrap and refrigerate for up to a day.

4. Cut each roll diagonally into 4 slices. Makes 6 servings.

Per serving: 243 calories (45% calories from fat), 9 g protein, 25 g carbohydrates, 12 g total fat (6 g saturated fat), 29 mg cholesterol, 362 mg sodium

When the weather turns cool and the leaves begin to fall, bring on flavorful Honey Multigrain Hearth Bread (recipe on facing page), robust Roasted Golden Squash Bisque (recipe on page 28), and glasses of sparkling cider.

Honey Multigrain Hearth Bread

Pictured on facing page

Preparation and rising time: 2¾ to 3½ hours

Baking time: About 50 minutes

●

Plump, round, and flavorful, this fine-textured bread contains a variety of grains. Look for soy flour in a specialty market or health-food store.

- **1 package active dry yeast**
- **1½ cups warm water (about 110°F)**
- **3 tablespoons honey**
- **¾ cup milk, at room temperature**
  About 1½ cups stone-ground whole wheat flour or graham flour
  About 3¾ cups unbleached all-purpose flour
- **3 tablespoons *each* yellow cornmeal and regular rolled oats**
- **3 tablespoons *each* soy flour and salad oil**
- **½ teaspoon salt**

1. Combine yeast, 1 cup of the water, and honey in a large bowl; let stand until softened (about 5 minutes). Add milk, whole wheat flour, and ¾ cup of the all-purpose flour; stir until moistened.

2. Cover and let stand in a warm place for 1 to 2 hours. Meanwhile, in a small bowl, combine remaining ½ cup warm water, cornmeal, and oats; let stand until grains are softened (1 to 2 hours).

3. Add cornmeal mixture to yeast mixture along with 2¾ cups more all-purpose flour, soy flour, oil, and salt. Beat until stretchy. To knead by hand, turn dough out onto a surface coated with all-purpose flour. Knead until smooth and elastic (about 10 minutes), adding more flour as needed. To knead with a dough hook, beat on high speed until dough pulls away from sides of bowl (5 to 8 minutes), adding more all-purpose flour, 1 tablespoon at a time, as needed.

4. Turn dough over in a greased bowl. Cover and let rise in a warm place until doubled (about 1 hour).

5. Knead dough briefly on a lightly floured surface. Shape into a ball. Place on a greased 12- by 15-inch baking sheet and flatten to a 7-inch round. Cover and let rise until puffy (15 to 20 minutes).

6. Bake, uncovered, in a 350° oven until deep golden brown (about 50 minutes). Let cool on a rack for 10 minutes. Makes 1 loaf (about 3 lbs.).

Per ounce: 69 calories (17% calories from fat), 2 g protein, 12 g carbohydrates, 1 g total fat (0.2 g saturated fat), 0.5 mg cholesterol, 25 mg sodium

Cornbread Fuego

Preparation time: About 20 minutes

Baking time: 20 to 25 minutes

●

Three grains give this distinctive cornbread a dense, coarse texture; salsa contributes the fiery flavor that gives it its name.

- **1 cup yellow cornmeal**
- **⅔ cup whole wheat flour**
- **½ cup oat bran cereal or wheat bran cereal**
- **3 tablespoons sugar**
- **1 tablespoon baking powder**
- **1 teaspoon salt**
- **½ cup canned green chile salsa**
- **⅔ cup ¼-inch cubes sharp Cheddar cheese**
- **⅓ cup butter or margarine, melted and cooled**
- **⅓ cup milk**
- **1 large egg**

1. Combine cornmeal, whole wheat flour, cereal, sugar, baking powder, and salt in a large bowl; stir well.

2. Combine salsa, cheese, butter, milk, and egg in a medium-size bowl; mix well.

3. Add salsa mixture to cornmeal mixture; stir just until moistened. Spread batter in a greased 8- or 9-inch-round or square baking pan.

4. Bake in a 400° oven until cornbread feels firm when pressed lightly in center (20 to 25 minutes). Serve warm. Makes 6 to 8 servings.

Per serving: 304 calories (44% calories from fat), 9 g protein, 35 g carbohydrates, 15 g total fat (8 g saturated fat), 67 mg cholesterol, 798 mg sodium

Polenta Cheese Bread

Pictured on page 2

Preparation and rising time: 2½ to 3 hours

Baking time: About 35 minutes

●

Mix and knead this full-flavored bread in your food processor. Don't process for more than 60 seconds or the dough will overheat.

- 1 **package active dry yeast**
- 1 **cup warm water (about 110°F)**
- 2 **tablespoons sugar**
- 4 **ounces sharp Cheddar cheese, cut into small chunks**

  About 3½ cups unbleached all-purpose flour
- ½ **cup polenta or yellow cornmeal**
- 1 **teaspoon salt**
- 1 **large egg**

1. Combine yeast, water, and 1 teaspoon of the sugar in a small bowl; let stand until softened (about 5 minutes).

2. Combine cheese, 3¼ cups of the flour, polenta, salt, and remaining 1⅔ tablespoons sugar in a food processor; whirl until cheese is finely chopped. Add egg. With motor running, add yeast mixture in a slow, steady stream. Whirl for 45 seconds to knead (dough should be slightly sticky; if too wet, add flour, 1 tablespoon at a time, using short on-off bursts).

3. Shape dough into a smooth ball. Turn over in a greased bowl. Cover and let rise in a warm place until doubled (1 to 1½ hours).

4. Punch dough down and knead briefly on a floured surface. Shape into a smooth ball. Place on a greased baking sheet; flatten to a 7-inch round. Lightly cover and let rise until about 2½ inches high (about 1 hour).

5. Sprinkle with 1 to 2 teaspoons more all-purpose flour. Bake in a 375° oven until well browned (about 35 minutes). Let cool. Makes 1 loaf (about 2 lbs.).

Per ounce: 80 calories (20% calories from fat), 3 g protein, 13 g carbohydrates, 2 g total fat (0.8 g saturated fat), 10 mg cholesterol, 93 mg sodium

Mediterranean Olive Bread

Pictured on front cover

Preparation and rising time: About 3 hours

Baking time: About 45 minutes

●

Black and green olives stud this golden-crusted loaf of Venetian origin.

- 1 **package active dry yeast**
- ¾ **cup warm water (about 110°F)**
- ¼ **cup sugar**
- ½ **cup butter or margarine, at room temperature**
- 4 **large eggs**

  About 5 cups unbleached all-purpose flour
- 1 **cup *each* Spanish-style pimento-stuffed olives and pitted ripe olives, drained and patted dry**
- 1 **egg yolk, lightly beaten**

1. Combine yeast and water in a small bowl; let stand until softened (about 5 minutes). Meanwhile, combine sugar and butter in large bowl of an electric mixer; beat well. Add eggs, one at a time, beating after each addition.

2. Stir in yeast mixture. To knead by hand, add 2½ cups of the flour and beat on medium speed for 10 minutes. Stir in 1½ cups more flour until moistened. Transfer dough to a floured surface and knead until smooth (8 to 10 minutes), adding more flour as needed. To knead with a dough hook, add 4½ cups flour to yeast mixture. Beat on medium speed until dough pulls away from sides of bowl (about 10 minutes), adding flour, 1 tablespoon at a time, as needed.

3. Turn dough over in a greased bowl. Cover and let rise in a warm place until doubled (about 1½ hours).

4. Knead dough briefly on a lightly floured surface. Pat into a 14- to 16-inch square. Sprinkle with olives, pressing in lightly. Roll up and place, seam side down, on a greased 12- by 15-inch baking sheet. Tuck ends under and pat into an oval about 2 inches thick. Lightly cover and let stand in a warm place until puffy (about 30 minutes).

5. Brush loaf with egg yolk. Bake in a 325° oven until richly browned (about 45 minutes). Let cool on a rack. Makes 1 loaf (about 3 lbs.).

Per ounce: 84 calories (36% calories from fat), 2 g protein, 11 g carbohydrates, 3 g total fat (1 g saturated fat), 27 mg cholesterol, 118 mg sodium

Sage Cracker Breads

Preparation and rising time: 2 to 2¼ hours

Baking time: About 30 minutes

●

Break off pieces of this flatbread to munch with soup or salad.

  1 **package active dry yeast**
  2 **cups warm water (about 110°F)**
  2 **tablespoons sugar**
  1 **teaspoon salt**
  2 **tablespoons olive oil**
  2 **tablespoons minced fresh sage leaves or
    1 tablespoon dry sage**
  3 **to 3¾ cups unbleached all-purpose flour**
  2⅓ **cups whole wheat flour**
    Wheat germ
    Coarse salt
  36 **to 48 damp fresh sage leaves or
    3 teaspoons dry sage**

1. Combine yeast and water in large bowl of an electric mixer; let stand until softened (about 5 minutes). Stir in sugar, the 1 teaspoon salt, oil, and minced sage. Add 3 cups of the all-purpose flour. Beat with a heavy-duty mixer on high speed until stretchy (about 5 minutes).

2. Stir in whole wheat flour. To knead by hand, place on a floured surface and knead until smooth (about 8 minutes), adding more all-purpose flour as needed. To knead with a dough hook, beat on medium speed until dough pulls away from sides of bowl (about 5 minutes), adding more all-purpose flour, 1 tablespoon at a time, as needed.

3. Turn dough over in a greased bowl. Cover and let rise in a warm place until doubled (about 1 hour). Meanwhile, grease 3 rimless 14- by 17-inch baking sheets; dust with wheat germ.

4. Punch dough down and knead on a floured surface until smooth. Divide into three 14-inch logs. Roll each ½ inch thick; lay on a baking sheet. Sprinkle with coarse salt and sage leaves. Roll ⅛ inch thick. Bake, one at a time, in a 375° oven until browned and crisp (15 to 20 minutes). Let cool on racks. Makes 3 loaves (about 9 oz. each).

Per ounce: 107 calories (11% calories from fat), 3 g protein, 21 g carbohydrates, 1 g total fat (0.2 g saturated fat), 0 mg cholesterol, 82 mg sodium

Garlic Cheese Bread

Pictured on page 39

Preparation and rising time: About 2¼ hours

Baking time: 15 to 18 minutes

●

Garlicky, cheesy, and with the consistency of pizza, this flatbread is also known as focaccia.

  1 **package active dry yeast**
  1 **cup warm water (about 110°F)**
  2 **teaspoons sugar**
  ¾ **teaspoon salt**
  ½ **cup olive oil**
  2⅔ **to 3 cups unbleached all-purpose flour**
  3 **or 4 large cloves garlic, minced**
  ¼ **cup grated Parmesan cheese**

1. Combine yeast and water in a large bowl; let stand until softened (about 5 minutes). Stir in sugar, salt, and ¼ cup of the oil. Add 2 cups of the flour. With a wooden spoon or a heavy-duty electric mixer, beat on medium speed until batter is elastic and pulls away from sides of bowl (about 5 minutes). Stir in about ⅔ cup more flour to make a soft dough.

2. Knead on a floured surface until smooth and satiny (10 to 15 minutes), adding more flour as needed.

3. Turn dough over in a greased bowl. Cover and let rise in a warm place until doubled (about 1 hour).

4. Heat remaining ¼ cup oil in a small pan over low heat. Add garlic and cook, stirring occasionally, until soft and golden (10 to 15 minutes); set aside.

5. Punch dough down and knead briefly on a lightly floured surface. Roll with a rolling pin and stretch with your hands to fit a well-greased 10- by 15-inch rimmed baking pan. Place dough in pan. With your fingers or tip of a spoon, pierce dough at 1-inch intervals. Drizzle with garlic mixture; sprinkle with cheese. Let rise until puffy (10 to 15 minutes).

6. Bake in a 400° oven until golden brown (15 to 18 minutes). Cut into strips. Serve warm or at room temperature. Makes 16 servings.

Per serving: 156 calories (46% calories from fat), 3 g protein, 18 g carbohydrates, 8 g total fat (1 g saturated fat), 1 mg cholesterol, 127 mg sodium

Cinnamon Slashed Flatbread

Pictured on facing page

Preparation and rising time: About 2 hours

Baking time: 20 to 25 minutes

Slashes in this sweet cinnamon bread catch and hold the buttery topping so it penetrates the bread as it bakes.

 1 package active dry yeast
 ¼ cup warm water (110°F)
 1 cup warm milk (110°F)
 ½ cup sugar
 ¾ teaspoon salt
 1 large egg
 ½ cup butter or margarine, melted and cooled
 4¼ to 4¾ cups unbleached all-purpose flour
 1 teaspoon ground cinnamon

1. Combine yeast and water in a large bowl; let stand until softened (about 5 minutes). Add milk, 5 tablespoons of the sugar, salt, egg, 2 tablespoons of the butter, and 2½ cups of the flour. Beat with a heavy spoon or dough hook until elastic (about 5 minutes).

2. Mix in 1 cup more flour. To knead by hand, place on a floured surface and knead until smooth and springy (about 10 minutes), adding more flour as needed. To knead with a dough hook, beat on medium speed until dough pulls away from sides of bowl (6 to 8 minutes), adding more flour, 1 tablespoon at a time, as needed.

3. Turn dough over in a greased bowl. Cover and let rise in a warm place until doubled (about 1 hour).

4. Punch dough down and knead briefly on a lightly floured surface. Pat and stretch dough to fit a greased shallow 10- by 15-inch baking pan. With a sharp knife, make ½-inch-deep slashes about 1 inch apart diagonally across surface in a diamond pattern.

5. Mix cinnamon, remaining 6 tablespoons butter, and 2 tablespoons sugar in a small bowl. Drizzle over dough. Let rise in a warm place until almost doubled (about 20 minutes). Sprinkle with remaining 1 tablespoon sugar. Bake in a 400° oven until browned (20 to 25 minutes). Serve warm. Makes 12 to 15 servings.

Per serving: 255 calories (30% calories from fat), 5 g protein, 39 g carbohydrates, 9 g total fat (5 g saturated fat), 35 mg cholesterol, 199 mg sodium

---

Chili-Cornmeal Breadsticks

Pictured on page 58

Preparation and rising time: About 1½ hours

Baking time: 20 to 25 minutes

To shape, stretch the dough into long, skinny batons.

 1 package active dry yeast
 1 teaspoon sugar
 1 cup warm water (about 110°F)
 1 teaspoon *each* grated lemon peel and salt
 2 tablespoons chili powder
 2 tablespoons plus 1 teaspoon olive oil
 2½ to 3 cups unbleached all-purpose flour
 2 tablespoons yellow cornmeal

1. Combine yeast, sugar, and water in a large bowl; let stand until softened (about 5 minutes). Add lemon peel, salt, chili powder, 2 tablespoons of the oil, and 1½ cups of the flour. Beat until stretchy and glossy (3 to 5 minutes).

2. Stir in about 1 cup more flour. To knead by hand, place on a floured surface and knead until smooth (about 10 minutes), adding more flour as needed. To knead with a dough hook, beat on low to medium speed until dough pulls away from sides of bowl (5 to 7 minutes), adding more flour, 1 tablespoon at a time, as needed.

3. Turn dough out onto a well-floured surface; pat into a 6-inch square. Brush with remaining 1 teaspoon oil, cover loosely with plastic wrap, and let rise at room temperature until puffy (about 45 minutes).

4. Grease three 12- by 15-inch baking sheets. Sprinkle both sides of dough with cornmeal. With a floured knife, cut lengthwise into quarters. Working with a quarter at a time, cut each strip lengthwise into 8 pieces. Gently stretch until about 15 inches long; arrange on baking sheets, placing at least ½ inch apart. Bake in a 350° oven until crisp (20 to 25 minutes); if using one oven, switch position of baking sheets halfway through baking (refrigerate one sheet, covered, while baking others). Transfer breadsticks to racks. Serve warm or at room temperature. Makes 32 breadsticks.

Per breadstick: 57 calories (27% calories from fat), 1 g protein, 9 g carbohydrates, 2 g total fat (0.2 g saturated fat), 0 mg cholesterol, 74 mg sodium

Cinnamon Slashed Flatbread (recipe on facing page) is a sweetly spiced adaptation of Italian focaccia. You'll hear "buon giorno" all around when you present it with foamy cappuccino or caffè latte.

143

Mega-Muffins

As the name indicates, these mighty muffins are triple the size of most. To grow them to this size, you heap the rather dry batter to the rims of custard cups. If you prefer more modestly proportioned muffins, use standard muffin cups.

Orange-Almond Mighty Muffins

Preparation time: About 20 minutes
Baking time: 35 to 40 minutes

2¼ cups unbleached all-purpose flour

½ cup granulated sugar

2½ teaspoons baking powder

½ teaspoon baking soda

¼ teaspoon salt

1 cup sliced almonds

½ cup *each* milk and orange juice

¼ cup butter or margarine, melted

1 large egg

1 teaspoon grated orange peel

Powdered sugar

1. Combine flour, granulated sugar, baking powder, baking soda, and salt in a large bowl; mix well. Stir in almonds. Form a well in center.

2. Combine milk, orange juice, butter, egg, and orange peel in a small bowl; beat well. Pour into flour mixture; mix lightly (batter should be lumpy).

3. Spoon into 4 greased 6-ounce custard cups (set cups at least 2 inches apart in a shallow baking pan) or heap filling into 6 greased or paper-lined 2½- to 2¾-inch muffin cups (use alternate cups). Sprinkle lightly with powdered sugar.

4. Bake custard cups in a 375° oven or muffin cups in a 400° oven until a wooden pick inserted in center comes out clean (35 to 40 minutes for custard cup–size muffins, 25 to 30 minutes for smaller ones). Let cool for 5 minutes. Remove from cups. Serve hot or warm. Makes 4 extra-large or 6 large muffins.

Per muffin: 668 calories (38% calories from fat), 15 g protein, 90 g carbohydrates, 29 g total fat (10 g saturated fat), 88 mg cholesterol, 749 mg sodium

Carrot-Nut Mighty Muffins

Preparation time: About 30 minutes
Baking time: 30 to 35 minutes

1½ cups unbleached all-purpose flour

¾ cup whole wheat flour

½ cup firmly packed brown sugar

2½ teaspoons baking powder

1 teaspoon ground cinnamon

½ teaspoon *each* baking soda and ground nutmeg

¼ teaspoon salt

1 cup shredded carrots

¾ cup chopped walnuts

¾ cup milk

1 large egg

¼ cup butter or margarine, melted

1. Combine all-purpose flour, whole wheat flour, sugar, baking powder, cinnamon, baking soda, nutmeg, and salt in a large bowl; mix well. Stir in carrots and nuts. Form a well in center.

2. Combine milk, egg, and butter in a small bowl; beat well. Pour into well of flour mixture; mix lightly (batter should be lumpy).

3. Fill cups, bake, and let cool as directed for Orange-Almond Mighty Muffins (at left), decreasing baking time for muffins in custard cups by 5 minutes. Makes 4 extra-large or 6 large muffins.

Per muffin: 679 calories (41% calories from fat), 15 g protein, 89 g carbohydrates, 31 g total fat (10 g saturated fat), 91 mg cholesterol, 774 mg sodium

Bran-Oat Mighty Muffins

Preparation time: About 20 minutes
Baking time: 35 to 40 minutes

1½ cups unbleached all-purpose flour

1 cup *each* bran cereal flakes and rolled oats

½ cup firmly packed brown sugar

1½ teaspoons baking soda

1¼ cups buttermilk

1 large egg

¼ cup butter or margarine, melted

1. Combine flour, bran flakes, oats, sugar, and baking soda in a large bowl; mix well. Form a well in center.

2. Combine buttermilk, egg, and butter in a small bowl; beat well. Pour into flour mixture; mix lightly (batter should be lumpy).

3. Fill cups, bake, and let cool as directed for Orange-Almond Mighty Muffins (at left). Makes 4 extra-large or 6 large muffins.

Per muffin: 554 calories (28% calories from fat), 14 g protein, 87 g carbohydrates, 18 g total fat (9 g saturated fat), 87 mg cholesterol, 786 mg sodium

Upside-Down Nut Buns

Preparation and rising time: About 3¼ hours

Baking time: 25 to 30 minutes

●

When you turn the baking pan upside-down, a syrupy mixture of brown sugar and walnuts or pecans is revealed atop these sweet wheat and oat rolls. You can also use the same dough for spicy, fruit-filled individual rolls.

> 1 cup cold water
> 1 cup quick-cooking rolled oats
> ½ cup butter or margarine
> ⅓ cup granulated sugar
> ¾ teaspoon salt
> 1 package active dry yeast
> ¼ cup warm water (about 110°F)
> 1 egg
> 1½ cups whole wheat flour
> About 2 cups unbleached all-purpose flour
> Nut Topping (recipe follows)
> 2 tablespoons butter or margarine, melted
> ½ cup firmly packed brown sugar
> 2 teaspoons ground cinnamon

1. Bring the 1 cup water to a boil in a 2-quart pan over high heat. Remove from heat and stir in oats, the ½ cup butter, granulated sugar, and salt. Stir until butter is melted and mixture cools to about 110°F. Meanwhile, combine yeast and warm water in the large bowl of an electric mixer; let stand until softened (about 5 minutes).

2. Add oat mixture to yeast and stir in egg. With a wooden spoon or heavy-duty electric mixer, gradually add 1 cup each of the whole wheat flour and all-purpose flour. Beat by hand for 10 minutes or by machine on medium speed for 5 minutes. Mix in remaining ½ cup whole wheat flour and ½ cup more all-purpose flour.

3. Turn dough out onto a floured surface and knead until smooth and springy (about 10 minutes), adding more all-purpose flour as needed.

4. Turn dough over in a greased bowl. Cover and let rise in a warm place until doubled (1 to 1½ hours). Meanwhile, prepare Nut Topping.

5. Punch dough down. Roll on a lightly floured surface into a 12- by 18-inch rectangle. Brush with melted butter; sprinkle with brown sugar and cinnamon. Starting on a long edge, roll up jelly roll style. Slice into 18 equal pieces and arrange, cut sides down, in pan over Nut Topping. Cover and let rise in a warm place until almost doubled (about 45 minutes).

6. Bake in a 375° oven until well browned (25 to 30 minutes). Remove from oven and carefully invert onto a large tray. Let stand for a minute. Lift off pan, allowing topping to drizzle over rolls. Serve warm. Makes 18 rolls.

Nut Topping. In a 9- by 13-inch metal baking pan, melt 2 tablespoons **butter** or margarine over low heat; brush some of the butter onto pan sides. Add 3 tablespoons **light corn syrup** and ⅔ cup firmly packed **brown sugar.** Stir well. Spread evenly over bottom of pan. Sprinkle with 1 cup **walnut pieces** or halves or pecan pieces or halves. Set pan aside.

Per roll: 298 calories (38% calories from fat), 5 g protein, 42 g carbohydrates, 13 g total fat (5 g saturated fat), 32 mg cholesterol, 184 mg sodium

Apple & Prune Swirls

Follow steps 1–4 for **Upside-down Nut Buns** (at left), omitting Nut Topping. Instead, in a medium-size bowl, combine 1 medium-size **Golden Delicious apple,** peeled and chopped; ½ cup finely chopped **moist-pack prunes;** ½ teaspoon grated **lemon peel;** ⅓ cup chopped **almonds** or walnuts; 1 teaspoon **ground cinnamon;** ¼ teaspoon **ground nutmeg;** and 1 tablespoon **all-purpose flour.** Mix lightly.

Follow step 5, omitting cinnamon. Instead, scatter apple mixture over sugar. Place slices in generously greased 2½-inch muffin cups. Let rise.

Follow step 6, decreasing baking time to 20 to 25 minutes. While rolls are baking, mix ½ cup **powdered sugar** and ¼ teaspoon **ground cinnamon** in a small bowl. Stir in 1 to 1½ tablespoons warm **water** to make a good brushing consistency. Invert baked rolls from pan and brush with sugar glaze while warm. Makes 18 rolls.

Per roll: 231 calories (32% calories from fat), 5 g protein, 35 g carbohydrates, 9 g total fat (4 g saturated fat), 29 mg cholesterol, 164 mg sodium

*Appease your after-dinner sweet tooth with frosty scoops of creamy raspberry-flavored
Very Berry Skinny Gelato (recipe on page 153) and irresistible Hazelnut Crescents
(recipe on page 149).*

DESSERTS

Carrot Raisin Cookies

Oatmeal Thumbprints

Hazelnut Crescents

Wheat Germ Shortbread

Fresh Apple Cake

Carrot-Zucchini Cake

Favorite Lime Cheesecake

Pumpkin Cheesecake Tart

Rhubarb-Raspberry Pie

Scottish Raisin Tart

Apricot-Blueberry Cobbler

Golden Pear Pancake Soufflé

Carrot Raisin Cookies

Preparation time: About 40 minutes

Baking time: 12 to 14 minutes

●

These tender, spicy oatmeal cookies are great for lunch boxes or to carry on a picnic.

- 1½ **cups unbleached all-purpose flour**
- 1 **teaspoon** *each* **baking soda, ground cinnamon, and ground nutmeg**
- 1½ **cups quick-cooking rolled oats**
- ½ **cup butter or margarine, at room temperature**
- 2 **large eggs**
- 1 **cup honey**
- 2 **cups grated carrots (about 2 medium-large)**
- 1 **cup raisins**
- ½ **cup chopped pecans or walnuts**

1. Combine flour, baking soda, cinnamon, nutmeg, and oats in a large bowl; mix well.

2. Combine butter, eggs, and honey in large bowl of an electric mixer; beat well. Mix in carrots. Gradually add flour mixture, beating well. Stir in raisins and pecans.

3. Spoon mixture by rounded tablespoons onto greased large baking sheets, placing about 2 inches apart.

4. Bake in a 350° oven until cookies feel firm when touched (12 to 14 minutes). Transfer to racks and let cool. Makes about 48 cookies.

Per cookie: 86 calories (33% calories from fat), 1 g protein, 14 g carbohydrates, 3 g total fat (1 g saturated fat), 14 mg cholesterol, 51 mg sodium

Oatmeal Thumbprints

Preparation time: About 45 minutes

Baking time: About 30 minutes

●

Oatmeal brings wholesome flavor to these traditional, buttery jam-filled morsels.

- 1 **cup (½ lb.) butter or margarine, at room temperature**
- ½ **cup firmly packed brown sugar**
- 1 **large egg, separated**
- 1½ **teaspoons vanilla**
- 1 **cup unbleached all-purpose flour**
- 2 **cups regular rolled oats**

  About 1½ cups finely chopped walnuts or almonds

  About ½ cup fruit jam

1. Combine butter, sugar, egg yolk, and vanilla in a food processor or large bowl of an electric mixer. Whirl or beat until smoothly blended. Whirl or stir in flour and oats.

2. Beat egg white with 2 teaspoons water in a small bowl.

3. Shape oat mixture into small balls, using about 2 teaspoons for each. Dip each ball into egg white mixture, drain briefly, and roll in nuts until coated. Arrange on ungreased large baking sheets, placing about 1 inch apart. With your thumb, press a well in center of each ball.

4. Bake in a 300° oven for 15 minutes. Remove from oven and reshape thumbprints by pressing hollow down again with rounded end of a wooden spoon. Quickly spoon about ½ teaspoon jam into each hollow (jam should not overflow rim). Return cookies to oven and continue to bake until golden brown (about 15 more minutes). Transfer to racks and let cool. Makes about 48 cookies.

Per cookie: 100 calories (57% calories from fat), 2 g protein, 10 g carbohydrates, 6 g total fat (3 g saturated fat), 15 mg cholesterol, 42 mg sodium

Hazelnut Crescents

Pictured on page 146

Preparation time: About 45 minutes

Chilling time: At least 2 hours

Baking time: 10 to 12 minutes

•

Toasted hazelnuts enrich these dainty, powdered sugar–coated crescents, a favorite holiday treat.

- ⅔ **cup hazelnuts**
- 1 **cup (½ lb.) butter or margarine, at room temperature**
- 1 **teaspoon vanilla**
- ⅓ **cup granulated sugar**
- 1⅔ **cups unbleached all-purpose flour**
- 1½ **teaspoons ground cinnamon**
- ½ **teaspoon baking powder**
- 1 **cup powdered sugar**

1. Spread hazelnuts in a shallow baking pan and toast in a 350° oven until pale golden beneath skins (about 10 minutes). Let cool slightly; then use your fingers to rub off skins. Finely grind nuts in a blender or food processor; set aside.

2. Combine butter, vanilla, and granulated sugar in a food processor or large bowl of an electric mixer; whirl or beat well. Add flour, hazelnuts, ½ teaspoon of the cinnamon, and baking powder; whirl until dough holds together (if using a mixer, stir in dry ingredients and beat until blended). Cover dough and refrigerate until firm (at least 2 hours or up to 8 hours).

3. Shape dough into ¾-inch balls. Roll each ball between your hands until about 1½ inches long and tapered at ends. Form into a crescent shape on ungreased large baking sheets, placing about 1 inch apart.

4. Bake in a 325° oven until golden (10 to 12 minutes). Meanwhile blend powdered sugar and remaining 1 teaspoon cinnamon in a small bowl.

5. Let cookies cool slightly on baking sheets on racks; transfer cookies to racks. Sift powdered sugar mixture over warm cookies. Makes about 60 cookies.

Per cookie: 60 calories (57% calories from fat), 1 g protein, 6 g carbohydrates, 4 g total fat (2 g saturated fat), 8 mg cholesterol, 35 mg sodium

Wheat Germ Shortbread

Preparation time: About 20 minutes

Baking time: 25 to 30 minutes

•

Cut into wedges, these spicy pecan shortbread cookies boast a chewy-crisp texture.

- ¼ **cup pecans**
- ½ **cup *each* plain wheat germ, unbleached all-purpose flour, and firmly packed brown sugar**
- ½ **teaspoon ground cinnamon**
- ⅓ **cup firm butter or margarine, diced**
- 1 **teaspoon vanilla**
- 1 **to 2 tablespoons powdered sugar (optional)**

1. Whirl pecans in a food processor until finely powdered or mince very finely with a knife. Mix in wheat germ, flour, brown sugar, and cinnamon.

2. Add butter and vanilla; whirl or rub with your fingers until mixture holds together.

3. Press dough evenly into a 9-inch spring-form pan or 9-inch-round cake pan with a removable bottom. Pat dough flat with lightly floured hands.

4. Bake in a 325° oven until cookie is darker brown and smells toasted (25 to 30 minutes). For a decorative rim, firmly press tines of a floured fork around edge of warm cookie. Cut into 10 to 12 wedges.

5. Let cool in pan on a rack. Remove pan rim. Sift powdered sugar over wedges, if desired. Makes 10 to 12 cookies.

Per cookie: 144 calories (47% calories from fat), 2 g protein, 17 g carbohydrates, 8 g total fat (4 g saturated fat), 15 mg cholesterol, 60 mg sodium

Fresh Apple Cake

Preparation time: About 35 minutes

Baking time: About 1 hour

●

Dense with almonds and diced fresh apples, this moist cake bakes in a tube pan.

3 cups unbleached all-purpose flour

1 cup sugar

1 teaspoon baking soda

¼ teaspoon salt

1 cup chopped almonds or walnuts

2 large eggs

¾ cup (¼ lb. plus ¼ cup) butter or margarine, melted and cooled

2 tablespoons lemon juice

1 tablespoon vanilla

3 cups diced unpeeled tart green apples (about 2 large)

1. Combine flour, sugar, baking soda, salt, and almonds in a large bowl; mix well.

2. Combine eggs, butter, lemon juice, and vanilla in another large bowl; beat until blended. Stir in apples.

3. Add apple mixture to flour mixture, stirring until evenly moistened. Spread batter in a greased, lightly floured 10- to 11-inch (about 10-cup) tube pan.

4. Bake in a 350° oven until cake begins to pull away from sides of pan and feels firm when lightly touched in center (about 1 hour). Let cool in pan on a rack until just warm to touch (10 to 15 minutes). Loosen edges and carefully invert cake onto a platter. Serve warm or at room temperature. Makes 10 to 12 servings.

Per serving: 414 calories (44% calories from fat), 7 g protein, 52 g carbohydrates, 20 g total fat (9 g saturated fat), 73 mg cholesterol, 309 mg sodium

Carrot-Zucchini Cake

Pictured on facing page

Preparation time: About 50 minutes

Baking time: About 1 hour

●

This handsome and flavorful cake is laced with shredded carrots and zucchini. Crushed pineapple adds sweetness.

2 cups unbleached all-purpose flour

1 cup whole wheat flour

2 cups sugar

1½ cups finely chopped walnuts

1½ teaspoons ground cinnamon

1 teaspoon *each* baking powder and baking soda

½ teaspoon salt

2 cans (about 8 oz. *each*) crushed pineapple

1 cup *each* coarsely shredded carrots and coarsely shredded zucchini

1 cup salad oil

4 large eggs

2 teaspoons vanilla

Pineapple Glaze (recipe follows)

1. Combine all-purpose flour, whole wheat flour, sugar, walnuts, cinnamon, baking powder, baking soda, and salt in a large bowl; mix well.

2. Drain pineapple, reserving juice for glaze. In another large bowl, combine pineapple, carrots, zucchini, oil, eggs, and vanilla; beat well.

3. Add pineapple mixture to flour mixture, stirring until evenly moistened. Spoon batter into a well-greased 10-to 11-inch (about 12-cup) tube pan.

4. Bake in a 350° oven until a wooden pick inserted in thickest part comes out clean (about 1 hour). Let cool in pan on a rack for 15 minutes.

5. Loosen edges and carefully invert cake onto a platter. Let cool completely. Meanwhile, prepare Pineapple Glaze. Drizzle over cooled cake. Makes 12 servings.

Pineapple Glaze. In a medium-size bowl, combine 1 cup **powdered sugar** and 2 tablespoons of the reserved **pineapple juice;** mix until smooth.

Per serving: 590 calories (44% calories from fat), 8 g protein, 77 g carbohydrates, 30 g total fat (4 g saturated fat), 71 mg cholesterol, 265 mg sodium

Savor wedges of wholesome Carrot-Zucchini Cake (recipe on facing page) with glasses of icy-cold milk. The luscious cake gains moistness not only from the shredded vegetables but also from a generous measure of crushed pineapple.

Favorite Lime Cheesecake

Preparation time: About 30 minutes

Baking time: 45 to 55 minutes

Chilling time: At least 4 hours

For a pretty finishing touch, garnish this tart, lime-laced cheesecake with thin lime slices.

- 1½ **cups graham cracker crumbs**
- 1 **cup sugar**
- ¼ **cup butter or margarine, at room temperature**
- 2 **large packages (about 8 oz. *each*) Neufchâtel cheese or cream cheese**
- 1 **cup light or regular sour cream**
- 3 **large eggs**
- 1 **tablespoon grated lime peel**
- ¼ **cup lime juice**
- 2 **tablespoons unbleached all-purpose flour**
  Sour Cream Topping (recipe follows)
  Thin lime slices

1. **Combine** graham cracker crumbs, 2 tablespoons of the sugar, and butter in a medium-size bowl; mix well. Press evenly over bottom and ½ inch up sides of a 9-inch spring-form pan.

2. **Bake** in a 350° oven until lightly browned (about 10 minutes). Meanwhile, in a large bowl, combine cheese, sour cream, eggs, lime peel, lime juice, flour, and remaining sugar; beat until smooth.

3. **Pour** cheese mixture into partially baked crust. Return to oven and continue to bake until center jiggles only slightly when pan is gently shaken (35 to 45 minutes). Let cool in pan on a rack. Meanwhile, prepare Sour Cream Topping.

4. **Spread** topping over cheesecake. Cover and refrigerate for at least 4 hours or up to a day. Remove pan sides. Garnish with lime slices. Makes 12 to 16 servings.

Sour Cream Topping. In a small bowl, combine 1 cup light or regular **sour cream** and 2 teaspoons *each* **sugar** and **lime juice;** mix well.

Per serving: 301 calories (52% calories from fat), 8 g protein, 29 g carbohydrates, 17 g total fat (9 g saturated fat), 90 mg cholesterol, 254 mg sodium

Pumpkin Cheesecake Tart

Preparation time: About 30 minutes

Baking time: 1 to 1¼ hours

The quick and simple crust for this luscious tart tastes just like an oatmeal cookie.

- **Oat Crust (recipe follows)**
- 1⅓ **cups (about 11 oz.) cream cheese, diced**
- 1 **can (about 1 lb.) pumpkin**
- 3 **large eggs**
- ⅔ **cup sugar**
- 1½ **teaspoons ground cinnamon**
- 1 **teaspoon *each* vanilla and ground ginger**
- 3 **tablespoons chopped candied ginger (optional)**

1. **Prepare** Oat Crust. Bake in a 300° oven until crust feels firm and is lightly browned (35 to 40 minutes). Meanwhile, in a food processor or blender, combine cream cheese, pumpkin, eggs, sugar, cinnamon, vanilla, and ground ginger; whirl until smooth.

2. **Remove** crust from oven and immediately pour in pumpkin mixture. Increase oven temperature to 350°, return pan to oven, and bake until filling is set in center when pan is gently shaken (30 to 35 minutes).

3. **Let** cool in pan on a rack. Serve at room temperature, or cover and refrigerate for at least an hour or up to a day and serve cold. Remove pan sides. Sprinkle with candied ginger, if desired. Makes 10 to 12 servings.

Oat Crust. In a food processor, combine 1 cup regular or quick-cooking **rolled oats,** 1 cup chopped **walnuts** or almonds, 1 cup **sweetened** shredded or flaked **coconut,** ⅓ cup **sugar,** and 6 tablespoons firm **butter** or margarine, diced; whirl until dough holds together. (Or, if using a blender, whirl nuts until finely ground; transfer to a bowl. Whirl coconut and oats until finely chopped; add to nuts. With your fingers, mix in sugar and butter until dough holds together.) Press evenly over bottom and 1 inch up sides of a 9-inch spring-form pan.

Per serving: 392 calories (60% calories from fat), 7 g protein, 33 g carbohydrates, 27 g total fat (13 g saturated fat), 106 mg cholesterol, 186 mg sodium

Skinny Gelato

Smooth, creamy, and intensely flavored, this frozen dessert tastes like egg-rich Italian gelato. In reality, it's a low-fat version of the Italian favorite. Fresh or frozen berries give the gelato its vibrant color and concentrated flavor.

Like traditional gelato, this version begins with a cooked base. The lean formula substitutes cornstarch for egg yolks, and low-fat milk for cream. As the cornstarch and milk mixture cooks, it forms a thickened sauce much like a pudding. Fruit purée added to the sauce provides distinctive flavor and color.

As the gelato freezes, the cooked base works like sugar to keep the texture creamy, so you can use less sweetening. Also, like Italian gelato, this version has a rather dense texture and expands very little as it freezes.

The recipe makes about a quart, just right for many frozen cylinders and other small ice cream makers. If your ice cream maker has a larger capacity, you can double the recipe if you like.

Low-Fat

Very Berry Skinny Gelato

Pictured on page 146
Preparation time: About 1 hour
Cooking time: 6 to 8 minutes
Chilling time: At least 1½ hours

Blueberry, Raspberry, Blackberry, Loganberry, Boysenberry, or Strawberry Purée (recipes follow)

½ **cup sugar**

3 **thin strips lemon peel (***each*** about ½ inch by 3 inches)**

2 **tablespoons cornstarch**

2 **cups extra-light or low-fat milk**

2 **teaspoons vanilla**

1. Prepare berry purée of your choice. Set aside.

2. Combine sugar and lemon peel in a 2- to 3-quart pan. With a wooden spoon, press peel against sugar to release oils. Mix in cornstarch. Stir in milk.

3. Cook over medium heat, stirring constantly with a whisk, until sauce comes to a boil (about 5 minutes). Boil, stirring, until starchy flavor is gone (1 to 2 minutes). Remove from heat; lift out and discard lemon peel.

4. Add berry purée and vanilla; stir well. Let cool; then cover and refrigerate until cold (at least 1½ hours or up to a day).

5. Transfer mixture to an ice cream maker and freeze according to manufacturer's directions. If made ahead, scoop into a container, cover, and freeze for up to 3 weeks. Makes 6 to 8 servings (3½ to 4 cups).

Blueberry Purée. In a food processor or blender, combine 3 cups fresh or partially thawed frozen **blueberries** and 2 tablespoons **lemon juice;** whirl until berry skins are finely ground.

Per ½-cup serving Blueberry Gelato: 133 calories (6% calories from fat), 3 g protein, 29 g carbohydrates, 1 g total fat (0.5 g saturated fat), 3 mg cholesterol, 40 mg sodium

Raspberry, Blackberry, Loganberry, or Boysenberry Purée. In a food processor or blender, combine 3 cups fresh or partially thawed frozen **raspberries,** blackberries, loganberries, or boysenberries and 1 tablespoon **lemon juice;** whirl until puréed. Pour into a fine strainer set over a bowl. With a spoon or flexible spatula, stir and press purée through strainer; discard seeds.

Per ½-cup serving Raspberry Gelato: 124 calories (7% calories from fat), 3 g protein, 26 g carbohydrates, 1 g total fat (0.5 g saturated fat), 3 mg cholesterol, 36 mg sodium

Strawberry Purée. In a food processor or blender, combine 3½ cups hulled fresh or partially thawed frozen **strawberries** and 1 tablespoon **lemon juice;** whirl until puréed.

Per ½-cup serving Strawberry Gelato: 121 calories (7% calories from fat), 3 g protein, 26 g carbohydrates, 1 g total fat (0.5 g saturated fat), 3 mg cholesterol, 36 mg sodium

The unmistakable scent of raspberries will permeate your kitchen while Rhubarb-Raspberry Pie
(recipe on facing page) bakes to juicy perfection under its lattice crust. Aromatic
raspberry vinegar flavors the pastry.

Rhubarb-Raspberry Pie

Pictured on facing page

Preparation time: About 45 minutes

Standing time: At least 15 minutes

Baking time: 40 to 50 minutes

●

Rhubarb is an all-time favorite for pie filling. In this distinctive version, it's combined with raspberries in a flaky pastry aromatic with raspberry vinegar.

- 1⅓ **cups sugar**
- ¼ **cup quick-cooking tapioca**
- 4 **cups ½-inch pieces rhubarb**
- 1 **cup fresh or frozen raspberries**
- 2 **tablespoons lemon juice**
  Raspberry Vinegar Pastry (recipe follows)

1. Combine sugar and tapioca in a large bowl; stir well. Gently stir in rhubarb, raspberries, and lemon juice. Let stand, mixing gently several times, for at least 15 minutes or up to an hour to soften tapioca. Meanwhile, prepare Raspberry Vinegar Pastry.

2. Roll half the pastry on a lightly floured board into a 12-inch circle; ease into a 9-inch pie pan. Fill with rhubarb mixture.

3. Roll remaining pastry into a 10-inch square. Using a pastry wheel or knife, cut into 8 to 10 strips. Weave strips over top of pie in a lattice pattern; trim ends. Fold bottom crust over lattice ends and flute firmly against rim.

4. Place pie in a shallow foil-lined pan. Bake on lowest rack of a 400° oven until pastry is golden brown and filling is bubbly (40 to 50 minutes); if pastry browns too rapidly, drape edge with foil. Makes 8 servings.

Raspberry Vinegar Pastry. Combine 2¼ cups **unbleached all-purpose flour** and ¼ teaspoon **salt** in a large bowl. With a pastry blender or your fingers, cut or rub in ¾ cup **solid vegetable shortening,** butter, or margarine until fine crumbs form. Sprinkle with 2 tablespoons **raspberry vinegar.** Using a fork, gradually stir in 3 to 5 tablespoons cold **water** until mixture holds together. Divide pastry in half and shape each portion into a smooth, flat round.

Per serving: 464 calories (38% calories from fat), 4 g protein, 69 g carbohydrates, 20 g total fat (5 g saturated fat), 0 mg cholesterol, 72 mg sodium

Scottish Raisin Tart

Preparation time: About 35 minutes

Baking time: 25 to 30 minutes

●

Two kinds of raisins mingle with walnuts in this handsome open-faced pie.

- **Butter Pastry (recipe follows)**
- 1 **large egg**
- ½ **cup firmly packed brown sugar**
- ¼ **cup butter or margarine, melted and cooled**
- 1 **tablespoon red wine vinegar**
- ½ **cup *each* seedless raisins, golden raisins, and chopped walnuts**

1. Prepare Butter Pastry. Press evenly over bottom and 1 inch up sides of an 8- or 9-inch spring-form pan or 8- or 9-inch tart pan with a removable bottom.

2. Combine egg, brown sugar, butter, and vinegar in a medium-size bowl; beat until blended. Add seedless and golden raisins and walnuts, stirring well. Spread mixture in pastry-lined pan.

3. Bake on lowest rack of a 375° oven until filling is firm in center when lightly touched (25 to 30 minutes). Let cool in pan on a rack. Remove pan sides. Makes 8 to 10 servings.

Butter Pastry. In a food processor or bowl, combine 1 cup **unbleached all-purpose flour** and 2 tablespoons **sugar.** Add ⅓ cup firm **butter** or margarine, diced; whirl or rub with your fingers until crumbly. Add 1 **egg yolk;** whirl or mix lightly with a fork until mixture holds together. Shape dough into a smooth ball.

Per serving: 318 calories (47% calories from fat), 4 g protein, 39 g carbohydrates, 17 g total fat (8 g saturated fat), 79 mg cholesterol, 135 mg sodium

Low-Fat
Apricot-Blueberry Cobbler

Preparation time: About 1 hour

Standing time: At least 15 minutes

Baking time: 40 to 50 minutes

●

Combine two fresh summertime fruits to make this familiar biscuit-topped dessert.

- ¼ **cup quick-cooking tapioca**
- 1 **cup plus 2 tablespoons sugar**
- 8 **cups sliced, pitted apricots (about 3 lbs. *total*)**
- 1⅓ **cups blueberries**
- 2 **tablespoons lemon juice**
  Biscuit Topping (recipe follows)
- 1 **large egg white (about 2 tablespoons)**

1. Combine tapioca and 1 cup of the sugar in a shallow 3-quart casserole; mix well. Add apricots, blueberries, and lemon juice; mix gently. Let stand, mixing gently several times, for at least 15 minutes or up to an hour to soften tapioca. Meanwhile, prepare Biscuit Topping.

2. Roll or pat biscuit dough about ½ inch thick on a lightly floured surface. Cut into circles with a 2½-inch-diameter cutter; reroll scraps and cut.

3. Place biscuits slightly apart on fruit. Beat egg white lightly; brush over biscuits. Sprinkle with remaining 2 tablespoons sugar.

4. Bake in a 400° oven until fruit is bubbly in center (40 to 50 minutes). Serve warm or at room temperature. Makes 10 to 12 servings.

Biscuit Topping. Combine 1½ cups **unbleached all-purpose flour,** 3 tablespoons **sugar,** 1½ teaspoons **baking powder,** and ½ teaspoon **salt** in a food processor or large bowl; whirl or mix well. Add ½ cup firm **butter** or margarine, diced; whirl or rub with your fingers until coarse crumbs form. Add ⅓ cup **milk;** whirl or stir with a fork just until evenly moistened. Shape dough into a ball.

Per serving: 312 calories (26% calories from fat), 4 g protein, 56 g carbohydrates, 9 g total fat (5 g saturated fat), 24 mg cholesterol, 263 mg sodium

Golden Pear Pancake Soufflé

Preparation time: About 45 minutes

Baking time: About 35 minutes

●

Spicy butter-simmered pears bake under a golden soufflé topping in this elegant dessert offering.

- 3 **tablespoons butter or margarine**
- ⅓ **cup chopped pecans**
- ¼ **cup firmly packed brown sugar**
- 1 **tablespoon lemon juice**
- 1 **teaspoon ground cinnamon**
- 3 **large firm-ripe pears (about 1½ lbs. *total*), peeled, cored, and cut lengthwise into thick slices**
  Soufflé Topping (recipe follows)

1. Melt butter in a shallow 1½-quart pan or 10-inch frying pan with an ovenproof handle over medium heat. Add pecans, brown sugar, lemon juice, and cinnamon. Cook, stirring, until bubbly. Add pears and cook, turning often with a spatula, until barely tender when pierced (5 to 10 minutes). Meanwhile, prepare Soufflé Topping (if pears are ready before topping is finished, keep pears warm over lowest heat).

2. Pour Soufflé Topping over pears. Jiggle pan to settle batter around fruit. Cook for about 30 seconds.

3. Bake in a 300° oven until top is dark golden and center appears set when pan is gently shaken (about 35 minutes). Spoon into bowls and serve immediately. Makes 6 servings.

Soufflé Topping. Combine 5 large **egg whites** and ¼ teaspoon **cream of tartar** in large bowl of an electric mixer. Beat at high speed until foamy. Continue to beat, gradually adding ½ cup **sugar,** until whites hold stiff peaks; set aside.

With same beaters, beat 5 large **egg yolks** in a small bowl at high speed until doubled in volume. Stir in ⅓ cup **unbleached all-purpose flour,** ¼ cup **half-and-half,** and 1 teaspoon **vanilla;** beat well. Stir a fourth of the egg whites into egg yolk mixture. Pour egg yolk mixture over egg whites; fold lightly until thoroughly combined. Use immediately.

Per serving: 356 calories (38% calories from fat), 7 g protein, 49 g carbohydrates, 16 g total fat (6 g saturated fat), 196 mg cholesterol, 118 mg sodium

Index

If you start with convenient frozen bread dough, making pizza is almost effortless. Colorful Yellow Bell Pizza and hearty Spinach Pizza (recipes on page 128) are just the right size for individual servings. Complete the meal with a leafy salad and a bottle of robust red wine.